"Written in the same remarkable vein as *The Oz Principle, Journey to the Emerald City* uses masterful illustrations powerful language and keen insight to continue the quest towards creating more accountable, adaptable work cultures. Read this book, apply it, and then recognize you're 'not in Kansas anymore.'"

DR. STEPHEN R. COVEY
Co-founder Franklin Covey Company
Author of #1 best-selling
The 7 Habits of Highly Effective People

"*Journey to the Emerald City* is a call to action and a significant help in setting a framework for team actions that produce more effective results. Each of us need to be reminded that the actions we take to get results are based on our experiences and beliefs and that changing those beliefs, although very hard, can greatly influence our results in business and personal life. *Journey to the Emerald City* is a 'must read' for anyone looking to create greater effectiveness in their organization."

JOHN BENT
Director, Information Systems
Amgen, Inc.

JOURNEY TO THE EMERALD CITY

ACHIEVE A COMPETITIVE EDGE
BY CREATING
A CULTURE OF ACCOUNTABILITY

ROGER CONNORS ▪ TOM SMITH

Prentice
Hall Press

Library of Congress Cataloging-in-Publication Data

Connors, Roger.
    Journey to the emerald city   / by Roger Connors & Tom Smith.
       p. cm.
    Includes index.
    ISBN 0-7352-0052-1 (case.)
      1. Corporate culture.   2. Management.   3. Organizational behavior.
    4. Success in business.   I. Smith, Tom (Thomas A.)   II. Title.
    HD58.7.C628   1999
    658.4' 063—dc21   98-49113
                                                     CIP

Acquisitions Editor: *Tom Power*
Production Editor: *Eve Mossman*
Formatting/Interior Design: *Robyn Beckerman*

© *1999 Roger Connors and Tom Smith*

Charts, diagrams, and illustrations ©1991–1998 Partners in Leadership, LLC used by permission.

All rights reserved. No part of this book may be reproduced in any form or by any means, without permission in writing from the publisher.

Printed in the United States of America

10 9 8 7 6 5 4 3

ISBN 0-7352-0052-1

Selected quotations were taken from the book The Wonderful Wizard of Oz by L. Frank Baum. The authors of Journey to the Emerald City have no affiliation with or connection to the producers or owners of the movie The Wizard of Oz.

Partners in Leadership,[SM] The Oz Principle,[SM] Creating a Culture of Accountability,[SM] Above the Line,[SM] Below the Line,[SM] The Results Pyramid,[SM] Steps to Accountability,[SM] See It,[SM] Own It,[SM] Solve It,[SM] Do It,[SM] and Culture of Accountability[SM] are servicemarks of Partners in Leadership, LLC.

PRENTICE HALL PRESS
Paramus, NJ 07652

On the World Wide Web at http://www.phdirect.com

To

Gwen and Becky
Allyse, Bryanna, Katie, Josalyn,
Michael, Brent, Seth, Stephen, Kimberly,
Mary, Audrey, Jerry

ACKNOWLEDGMENTS

The writing of this book is really the summation of years of experience and effort. Our work with clients who have engaged themselves in changing their culture has been a true laboratory of learning. To them, first, we wish to express our appreciation and acknowledgment. These clients have proven the theories and demonstrated the impact of the process we describe in *Journey to the Emerald City*.

A project of this magnitude also involves many people playing many different roles. Tom Gorman played a critical role in assisting us throughout this project. His feedback and advice proved instrumental in shaping this book. We thank Michael Snell, our literary agent, for his enthusiasm for this work and his encouragement on this project. Jeff Howlett provided important research on this project and demonstrated great ownership in interviewing our clients and providing background research. Our thanks also go to Tom Power, our editor at Prentice Hall, and to his entire team.

Our office staff, Susan Wynn, Robert Palmer, Lisa Mettler, and Terri Daines each demonstrated great accountability to achieve the result by doing whatever was necessary to meet deadlines and keep the process going. Tracy Skousen provided helpful support in the business which helped us take the time we needed to complete this book. We have used a number of illustrations throughout the book to accelerate the communication of the Cultural Transition process and to serve as device for quick review. Pete Theodore contributed in a significant way by providing effective design and quick turnaround of these diagrams and charts.

An acknowledgment of the support of our families and our wives is truly necessary, as they have endured the countless hours of travel over the last decade as our work has taken us around the world and away from them. For their sacrifices we express our gratitude.

PREFACE

In the search for increased value, improved profits, lower costs, and growing market share, corporations have demonstrated great effectiveness in picking the "low-hanging fruit" of improved performance. Reengineered processes have heightened the ability of teams to successfully capitalize on the value of the company's assets in significant ways. Yet, in the midst of almost endless performance improvement programs, we still see the single greatest asset of an organization—its people—go underutilized.

When leaders and managers begin to actively manage the cultural environment of their organization, we see an exciting, impressive, and tangible return on "human assets." Shaping culture is the process of leading people in a way that fundamentally impacts the way they think and act. We have witnessed numerous efforts to impact results by shaping culture over the past decade. Each of these efforts, when guided by leaders dedicated to the needed culture change, has been rewarded with record reductions in costs, record sales, record gains in market share, record profits, record stock prices, and record personal rewards.

In this book, *Journey to the Emerald City*, we describe a process of managing culture that accelerates the ability to achieve organizational results. In addition, we show you how to create a *Culture of Accountability*, where people think and act in the manner necessary for your organization to achieve results. And we show you how to create that culture quickly so that you can achieve competitive and organizational advantage.

Our work has as its foundation one simple idea that we described in our first book, *The Oz Principle: Getting Results Through Individual and Organizational Accountability*. An organization will perform at its highest potential if, and only if, each of its members assumes personal accountability for achieving its results. When people become personally accountable for achieving the company's results, powerful transformations occur: A goal becomes an organizing principle. A job becomes a mission. A task becomes a challenge. A company becomes a team. And a manager becomes a leader.

These may strike you as worthwhile changes, and they are. However, like most worthwhile changes, they are not easily achieved. It takes time to bring about a true cultural transformation. Therefore, managers have repeatedly asked us, "How can we *accelerate* the transition to a new, more effective culture?"

This book answers that question. Here we show you how to build an effective company culture quickly and surely. Given the pace of change today, the value of being able to quickly adjust, or even transform, company culture should be evident. Competitive, regulatory, and technological change happens so fast and frequently that the ability of a company to change rapidly and repeatedly provides a sharp competitive edge.

We pursue culture change for one reason and for one reason only: to enable companies to achieve the results they want and need to attain. Results are the product of the way people think and act. The way people think and act in an organization amounts to that organization's culture. It's as simple as that. Since management is the art and science of getting things done through others, we view managing culture—managing the way people think and act—as the essence of leadership.

We're not talking about secret methods or psychological games. Nor are we talking about social experiments or workplace engineering. Instead we offer a practical model of leadership, in which managers—openly and completely—become accountable for fulfilling the purpose of the organization. In the process, they lead others to achieve the results the organization has committed itself to achieving.

In this book, you will learn practical methods of drawing forth people's wholehearted commitment to achieving organizational results. You will discover a simple, powerful framework for understanding company culture and for changing it. In example after example, you will see what has worked for leaders in a variety of companies, specific things that you can do every day in your company to create an effective culture, quickly.

In our work with scores of organizations and thousands of individuals, we have seen the power of organizational culture, for better and worse. We've seen organizational results held hostage by a company's culture. We have also seen the transformation in performance, products and profits—and in people—that occurs when managers lead a company to a new, more effective culture. And, when they do it quickly, we have seen them gain both organizational and competitive advantage.

We want you to experience this journey as well.

CONTENTS

ABOUT THE AUTHORS

Roger Connors and Tom Smith are the authors of the best selling book, *The Oz Principle: Getting Results Through Individual and Organizational Accountability*, and the principals and founders of Partners In Leadership, LLC. Their firm is a widely respected international leadership and management consulting firm that has implemented the *Partners In Leadership*^{SM} Cultural Transition Process as well as *The Oz Principle*^{SM} Accountability Training in numerous organizations ranging from small start-ups to *Fortune* 500 companies. Their extensive client/customer list includes companies in 21 different industries. They have an international presence in several countries and have implemented their cultural transition process throughout the world, including Europe, Japan, and South America.

After receiving their MBAs from Brigham Young University, Roger Connors and Tom Smith have spent the last nine years pioneering the implementation of the principles embodied in *Journey to the Emerald City*. They have extensive experience in working with senior executive teams, as well as thousands of managers and leaders. Their work includes long- and short-term consulting engagements, speaking engagements, national sales meetings, workshops, and speeches. They have significant experience in helping management teams facilitate large-scale cultural transition. In addition, they have worked with numerous management groups to assist them in building teams and in building greater accountability throughout the organization. They are respected facilitators with extensive experience working with senior executive groups.

PART ONE
UNDERSTANDING COMPANY CULTURE

Dorothy and her friends were at first dazzled by the brilliancy of the wonderful City. The streets were lined with beautiful houses all built of green marble and studded with sparkling emeralds. They walked over a pavement of the same green marble. The window panes were of green glass; even the sky above the City had a green tint.

There were many people, men, women and children, walking about, and they were all dressed in green clothes. Everyone seemed happy and contented and prosperous.

The Guardian of the Gates led them through the streets until they came to a big building, exactly in the middle of the City, which was the Palace of Oz, the Great Wizard. There was a soldier before the door, dressed in a green uniform.

"Here are the strangers," said the Guardian of the Gates to him, and they demand to see the Great Oz.

So they passed through the Palace gates and were led into a big room with green carpet and lovely green furniture set with emeralds. When they were seated he said, politely, "Please make yourselves comfortable while I go to the door of the Throne Room and tell Oz you are here."

The Wonderful Wizard of Oz
L. Frank Baum

UNDERSTANDING COMPANY CULTURE

Before you can change something as interwoven as organizational culture, you must first understand its components and how they work together. In Part One, we introduce a practical model of organizational culture, *The Results Pyramid*. We also describe a *Culture of Accountability* and the impact that culture can have on results.

The whole issue of organizational culture may strike you as totally foreign to day-to-day business concerns. However, we would suggest that by learning to manage your organization's culture—what people think and what they do—you will also learn to exercise true leadership. Effective leaders, consciously or unconsciously, manage the beliefs and actions of their people so they will produce the results that the organization must achieve. In other words, they manage the culture of the organization because they recognize that the culture serves as the script for the organization, a script that provides the signals on how people should think and act.

Broadly, the most effective kind of culture an organization can have is what we call a *Culture of Accountability*. In such a culture, everyone assumes personal accountability for achieving the organization's results. Accountability here does not mean what it often does in business: Who fouled up? Who's to blame? Instead, it means that every individual takes personal accountability to think and act in a way that will achieve the company's results.

The Results Pyramid shows how culture works and how you can work with your culture. Part One begins the journey by setting us on the road to the Emerald City.

CHAPTER ONE

THE YELLOW BRICK ROAD
ACCELERATING THE JOURNEY

There were several roads near by, but it did not take her long to find the one paved in yellow brick.

The Wonderful Wizard of Oz
L. Frank Baum

In the story *The Wonderful Wizard of Oz,* the Yellow Brick Road is a path to change for the story's characters. As in any "road" story, to reach their destination and to get what they are traveling for, Dorothy, the Scarecrow, the Tin Woodsman, and the Cowardly Lion have to approach their problems and challenges in a different way. To reach their destination, achieve their goal, and accomplish the desired result, each of them has to think and act in ways that are different from those that were familiar and comfortable.

It isn't until the end of the story, however, that the characters realize that they have undergone a change in the way they view both themselves and the world they live in or come from. Each of them learns a new way of thinking and acting that brings him or her the results they are seeking. And it isn't until they start acting different that they reach their destination and achieve their goals: wisdom, courage, heart, and gratitude.

The journey to the Emerald City creates a new understanding of what is needed in order to achieve the goals of each person on the team. Yet, the journey not only leads to personal insight about what needs to change, but also to a collective insight about how the team needs to think and act as a whole in order to get to where they are going.

As management consultants, we believe that every organization is on this journey of understanding. Every organization must constantly discover what needs to change about the way they think and act in order to conquer the ever-changing obstacles and challenges that arise. Every year, results become more difficult to achieve. Sustaining success, capturing market share, growing profits, and increasing returns is a never-ending requirement of even the best performing organizations. All of this occurs in an environment of smarter and better competition, fewer resources, and shorter timelines.

When an organization fails to achieve its results, managers typically look outside, casting about for some resource or pat answer that will change things. Often, they resort to making repairs by utilizing the "re-" fixes of the times. They redeploy their people or ask some to resign. They reorganize their structure, reengineer their processes, rethink their plans, revisit their goals, and review their efforts. Yet most discover that the company returns to its old ways. Some ultimately decide that change is impossible and that they must resign themselves to live with the situation until "something happens."

Yet effective organizations come to understand that achieving results—consistently, repeatedly, and effectively—requires an organizational journey that channels individual and group efforts, energy, actions, and thought in a targeted and precise manner. Those who undertake the journey of cultural transition (changing the way we think about how we do business and adopting corresponding changes in actions) invariably see that it is indeed possible to more directly focus the collective cultural energy of the organization on achieving the result.

In this book, we tell you about this process of cultural transition. More to the point, we tell you how to speed up the process of cultural change. In *The Oz Principle* we presented the *Steps to Accountability*^{SM} and discussed their impact on organizational results. In *Journey to the Emerald City*, we describe how to create a *Culture of Accountability*^{SM} and show how managers can *accelerate* the transition to this culture.

FOR A CHANGE, TRY LEADERSHIP

Over the past decade, a fair amount has been written and said about organizational culture. Numerous questions have been put forward on the subject: What is culture? Is there a connection between culture and results? Can you manage or create or even change culture? And so on. We will spare you another round of this intellectualizing, as interesting as it can be, and instead take you right to the heart of our message and experience:

- An organization's leaders must create its culture.
- The organization's culture will create its results.
- A *Culture of Accountability* is the most effective culture and is defined as people being accountable to think and act in the manner necessary for their organization to achieve results.
- Accelerating the transition to a *Culture of Accountability* creates competitive and organizational advantage.

Stay with us. We think you will find the stories and examples to come in this book convincing—culture does impact results. Leaders can manage culture. A *Culture of Accountability* is the most effective culture, and companies that have created this kind of culture get results—you'll see!

A company's culture makes all the difference. So let's look more closely at the four principles at the heart of our message and experience.

LEADERS MUST CREATE THE CULTURE

We have a saying: *Either you manage your culture, or it will manage you.* In our work we meet many managers who get batted around by their company's culture. Their culture undermines the results they want to achieve. They want strong customer focus, and they can't get it. They want diversity, and they can't get it. They want regulatory compliance, and they can't get it. They want growth, quality, or productivity, and they can't get it. They want their fast-growing, entrepreneurial firm to adopt systems and controls, and it won't. Or they want their lumbering, recently deregulated company to become entrepreneurial and nimble, and it won't.

These managers must lead their companies through a journey of organizational self-discovery like that described at the beginning of this chapter and throughout this book. They must lead this effort. When they do they will create a new culture. This is not the responsibility of the organization's human resources department, although HR can certainly help create a new culture. We've found, however, that thinking of a transition to a new culture as an "HR program" promotes the wrong view of this endeavor. Creating a new culture is not an event. It is not a program. It is a leadership process. And it never stops.

Here is a comment that reveals many managers' misunderstanding of culture and how it is either created or fundamentally shifted. The November 1997 issue of *Training Magazine* reports the story of a CEO who "wanted to improve his company's performance by 'putting in a good culture." The CEO went on to explain that his company did not currently have a culture because he and his team had not yet gotten around to developing one.

We can be certain of one thing: This fellow's company did have a culture. Every group of people, from a street gang to a church choir, from a family to a nation, has a culture. If the group's leaders have not created it, perhaps some informal leaders or "influencers" have. Or perhaps the culture has developed willy-nilly, for better or worse. Every organization has a culture. The only question is whether or not that specific culture is effective in creating the results those people want.

The concept of business leadership demands that leaders take control of the company's culture and make it as effective as it can possibly be. This is, by the way, for the best of business reasons, which brings us to our next principle.

CULTURE CREATES RESULTS

An organization's culture determines the results it achieves. Therefore leaders must be careful when defining the results around which they will build the culture. They must be careful because while the culture effects results, the results affect the culture.

Here's what we mean by this. Leaders can build a company culture around any set of results they choose. Typical very broad ones might be market dominance, sales-and-profit growth, technological excellence, customer service, or stability of earnings. A company will need a certain culture to achieve any of these results. That's because the culture—how people think and act—is going to determine the results. Yet, the results an organization achieves also reinforce the culture.

For example, Ford Motor Company decided that in 1995 the Ford Taurus was going to be the sales leader, "The Best-Selling Car in America." It took a lot to do that. Ford had to cut deals on fleet sales, offer low-rate financing through Ford Credit Corporation, and run substantial rebate programs. They had, however, *decided* that the Ford Taurus—and not the Honda Accord, its chief rival—was going to be number one that year. (Did you know that the Latin root of "decide" is *decidere*, which means "to cut off"? A true decision cuts off other options.)

Achieving that result was important to Ford, and it reinforced the position of the car and of Ford's place in American car culture. This goal was not just about "bragging rights"—although they're nice to have. It was about management recommitting the company to the Taurus at a time when the car was being criticized as somewhat dated and when it was about to undergo substantial redesign. Ford reinforced not only the product's position, but also the company's position in the public mind and in their own minds by beating Honda in that key year. They created the culture that would get the result, and getting the result reinforced Ford's "number-one" culture.

This kind of "feedback loop" can work in negative ways too. A company that fails also generates a result. That result reinforces a different kind of culture. We worked with a firm that had previously elevated failing to make budget into an art. Missing its sales or expense budget had been institutionalized into the culture. Management issued budgets, and everyone, including management, knew that they were not to be taken seriously. We've also seen companies do this with deadlines. Other companies, commonly called "money losers" and firms in "dying industries," face similar cultural challenges. The more they generate negative results, the more their culture degenerates.

Because negative results have this feedback effect, leaders must develop the ability to maintain a winning culture during failures and setbacks. As you know, occasional failures are part of any effort to achieve something. How one handles them ultimately separates winners from losers.

Movie producer Samuel Goldwyn, who was a founder of Metro-Goldwyn-Mayer and saw his ups and downs, used to say, "We've been broke, but we've never been poor." He never allowed his family to develop a culture of poverty, even when they were out of money. (Coincidentally his studio, MGM, produced the most famous version of *The Wizard of Oz* in 1939. Perhaps Goldwyn, who started life in America as an immigrant glove salesman, had found *The Oz Principle*.)

Culture produces results. Results produce culture. The link between a company's culture and the results it produces represents a bedrock principle of our consulting practice and of this book. That link is the reason that creating and maintaining the right culture is one of management's most serious responsibilities. Culture is intrinsic to results.

A Culture of Accountability Is the Most Effective Culture

The most effective organizational culture can be characterized as a *Culture of Accountability*. To us, culture is the way people think *about* how they do business on a daily basis and the way they act. The word "accountability," like "culture," can have some irrelevant or inaccurate connotations in the context of leadership and business effectiveness, so let's define that term.

Webster defines "accountability" as "the state of having to report, explain or justify." This is in keeping with the command-and-control and surveillance-style management approaches that often prove ineffective in achieving results today. Unfortunately, this notion of accountability also draws forth certain behaviors from people in organizations. We call this behavior *Blamestorming*. In general, people engage in Blamestorming to avoid true accountability by generating reasons and explanations for why they are not accountable for something.

From our perspective, accountability, as we explained in *The Oz Principle*, means to proactively see the reality of a situation, personally own the circumstances, relentlessly look for ways to *Solve It*, and consistently follow through and *Do It* before it's too late. Accountability, most effectively applied, is a forward-looking concept that focuses attention on what I "can do" versus what I "did." As we see it, accountability is something people should want to take, not something they should fear.

In a *Culture of Accountability* everyone in the organization is personally committed to achieving the results the team has targeted. To maintain the focus and effort required to get this result, everyone continually asks: "What else can I do?"

This question is the mantra of those dwelling in a *Culture of Accountability*. This question is also the sure cure for Blamestorming.

There are several other characteristics of a *Culture of Accountability*, all of which we'll examine in the next chapter. However, the most fundamental characteristic is that people assume accountability in this kind of culture. They take it upon themselves. They do not have to have it foisted or forced upon them. They are not commanded to be accountable, nor are they kept under surveillance and then "called to account" for their actions. Instead, the company's leaders create this culture in a systematic manner that we have seen work effectively time after time.

ACCELERATING THE TRANSITION

In a world where being first means everything, speeding up the process of change has become essential to getting business results. While culture change takes time (and don't let anyone try to fool you—it does take time) the process of change can be accelerated, and the needed culture can be more quickly created. The ability of an organization to *accelerate* a transition to a *Culture of Accountability* will create both competitive and organizational advantage.

Take, for example, the story of Cardiac Pacemakers, Inc., formerly a subsidiary of Eli Lilly and Company, and currently a driver behind Guidant Corporation's extraordinary performance. In 1995, Guidant was split off from Eli Lilly and was considered Wall Street's most successful split-off ever. In the early 1990s, CPI was not the engine of success that it would become for Guidant. CPI President, Jay Graf, who joined the company a number of years after it was acquired by his employer, Eli Lilly, found a company that he characterized as "going 90 miles per hour on an icy road toward a cliff." This company was experiencing historic sales growth with monthly performance records. Most people were excited about the success of the organization. They were constantly celebrating their victories in the market. Indeed, the company was going 90 miles an hour, but it was also headed toward a cliff and nobody seemed to see it.

CPI's acquired technology was fueling its growth. But what people at CPI were failing to acknowledge was that Medtronic and Ventritex, formidable competitors, were on line to introduce technology that would leapfrog CPI's within just two years. Without the next new product, sales growth at CPI would indeed drop off a cliff.

What was the answer? Upcoming acquisition opportunities were not proving fruitful and likely would not be the solution. Internal new-product development was void of promise as well. CPI had not produced a major new product in years, and the common belief within the organization at the time was that they couldn't "develop their way out of a paper bag." A cultural transition was essential if they were to have any chance of creating a new, product-development environment. Accelerating this transition was imperative as time was running out.

The story of CPI's transition is told throughout this book, as are those of numerous other organizations. CPI's story is worth knowing because within a few years this company created a new, product-development culture that from 1995 to 1996 produced 14 new products in 14 months. People at CPI came to view themselves as "a product-development machine." Annual sales increased from approximately $300 million in 1993 to over $650 million in 1996. They achieved this growth with only a 20 percent increase in staff. The speed of their cultural transition gave them competitive advantage, and they have become worldwide market leaders in a number of their product lines. All of this has helped fuel their stock-price increase by ninefold since January of 1995. Speeding up cultural change means, in the end, speeding up results, providing both competitive and organizational advantage.

A CLOSER LOOK AT CULTURE

In order to most effectively shift an organization to a new culture, it's important to understand the components of culture. Figure 1-1 *The Results Pyramid*[SM] illustrates the essential components of organizational culture and how they relate to one another.

FIGURE 1-1
THE RESULTS PYRAMID[SM]

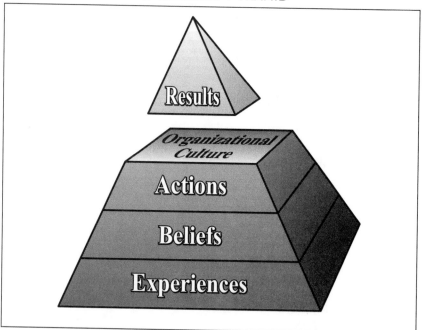

As *The Results Pyramid* shows, three components—experiences, beliefs, and actions—working together amount to culture. The culture generates results, which as we've already noted also reinforce the culture and are part of the culture. We say these components "work together" because *experiences foster beliefs, beliefs drive actions, and actions produce results.*

This model applies to virtually any culture. Experiences foster organizational beliefs. Beliefs drive actions. Actions produce results. Results become new experiences.

In this book, we examine scores of situations and examples, but here is a small one that shows you this dynamic in action. Think about what your company says about what it values most in managerial employees. Is it technical proficiency? Operational problem solving? Contributions to financial performance? Ability to support employees?

Now think about the people who have been promoted. Ask yourself this: How fully do the people we have promoted embody the qualities we value most?

When a management team promotes someone, that team creates a powerful experience. That experience is absorbed by the person promoted and by everyone else in the company. That experience of being promoted or seeing someone promoted fosters certain beliefs. Those beliefs will drive actions in the person promoted and in observers of the promotion. Their actions will produce results.

Promoting someone is an example of management creating an experience. So management creates experiences that foster beliefs that drive actions that produce results. This is a key point because it is how management creates the culture. The process is continual. It goes on all the time, not just when promotions or other big decisions are made. The president of a major pharmaceutical firm shared the following insightful guidance with his team in one of our senior management sessions: "Every one of us is creating the culture of this company every day. As a manager, everything you do, everything you say, everywhere you go in the organization leaves a footprint on the culture of this place." Clearly, your passage through your company will affect people in it for better or worse, every single day.

CHANGES DOWN THE ROAD

This book shows you how to *accelerate* the shift of your organization to a new culture. Specifically, it shows how to create a *Culture of*

Accountability and to do so as quickly as possible. Depending upon your company's current culture, this process may entail anything from a few slight shifts in the culture to a complete cultural transformation.

For now, let's assume that your current culture is not completely effective, that it is not motivating the right actions, the necessary thinking, the needed approaches, or the essential improvement. People may not be personally committed to achieving the targeted results. Or, the results themselves may be unclear. Perhaps the organization is not achieving all of its targeted results. Some people may be more focused on failure and on avoiding blame than on achieving the result. You do not have a *Culture of Accountability*.

Or, let's assume that you do have a solid, aligned, and accountable culture, but that the business environment is going to change and you doubt that your current culture will continue to produce the desired results in the coming environment. This occurs fairly often, for example, when a company faces a new regulatory environment or is purchased by a larger group or is facing new competitive threats.

Figure 1-2 depicts a cultural transition, a shift from the current culture, C^1 to a new culture, C^2. The current culture is producing results, R^1, from experiences, beliefs, and actions, E^1, B^1, and A^1, respectively. After studying the future and considering the challenges it may present, the company has defined a new culture, C^2, as essential to success in the future business environment. They have defined the C^2 culture as comprising certain experiences, beliefs, and actions, E^2, B^2, and A^2, respectively. The company expects this new culture to produce new results, R^2.

Here's an extremely important point: *You cannot take the R^2 results and superimpose them on the C^1 culture.* It doesn't work. We are not saying that there is nothing of value in your current culture. In fact, there probably is. Nor are we saying that you must always totally transform your culture to get new results. Our experience suggests that most organizations need to focus more on a transition, not on a transformation. Usually, organizations have certain attributes in their existing cultures that will serve their businesses in their pursuit of new results. But you cannot expect to get new results from the exact same culture. Remember: Insanity has been defined as continuing to do the same thing but expecting different results.

Superimposing R^2 results onto the C^1 culture doesn't work because culture is powerful and persistent. It is powerful in that it determines results. It is persistent because it transcends individuals. Again, our president of the pharmaceuticals firm said it best to his senior management

FIGURE 1-2
CULTURAL TRANSITION

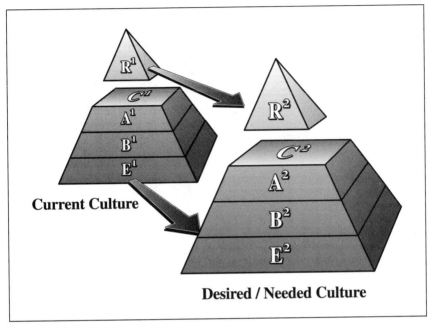

Current Culture

Desired / Needed Culture

group in one of our sessions: "Here's when I saw that culture was real. Early in my career I spent some time in the Italian affiliate. Then I left for a new assignment and lost touch with them. I came back five years later, and I didn't see one familiar face. They'd had one-hundred-percent turnover. Yet the culture was exactly the same in that company. Nothing in the culture had changed, even though all the people were different!" *You can change all of the people and still have the same culture.*

That is why the traditional management fix of injecting "new blood" by moving a new person into a culture won't work, at least not by itself. This tactic works only when other aspects of the culture are shifted as well.

A division of a major business-information firm learned this when its Boston sales office stopped getting results. The staff in that office had gone sour over a change in the commission structure. A fit of Blamestoming cited the change in the compensation plan as the cause of diminished performance. But senior management was committed to the new plan, which was weighted to encourage sales of new products. The division CEO terminated the head of the sales office for poor performance. Then he sent in Danny Borges, one of his star sales managers, to head the office. Two months later, however, the CEO was heard complaining that Danny was "going native" up there in Boston. (The expression comes from the practice of some early European missionaries joining native cultures instead of converting the natives to European ways.)

In the Boston office Danny had enough experiences—including conversations with salespeople about "those unfair bozos at headquarters" and difficulties in selling new products in that conservative market—to change his beliefs. Eventually and inevitably, his actions and results also changed, for the worse. Danny could not overcome the culture. In truth, he had been sent on something of a fool's errand, because management had to do more than change the sales manager to improve results in Boston. They had to effect a cultural transition in that office, which they eventually did.

A BIT ABOUT ALIGNMENT

We place results at the top of *The Results Pyramid*. The other three elements of the organization's culture—actions, beliefs, and experiences—are the pieces upon which results are based. For a company to achieve the desired result, its culture—what people think and do—must be aligned with the result.

The organization is out of alignment when the actions, beliefs, and experiences of its people are not aligned with targeted results, as shown in Figure 1-3. Conversely, the company is in alignment when people's actions, beliefs, and experiences are aligned with results. Moreover, everyone's actions, beliefs, and experiences must be aligned from person to person and across functions for the company to enjoy the benefits of complete alignment (which we explore more thoroughly in Chapter Eight).

This figure suggests that the more powerfully aligned the culture, the more intense the focus on results will be. The more intense the focus on targeted results, the more likely people will be to achieve them.

Effective leaders manage in ways that get a culture aligned with results, and then they keep it aligned. They say and do things, that is, they create experiences to generate or reinforce beliefs that motivate actions that produce the result. They avoid saying and doing things that put the culture out of alignment. For example, in the case of who gets promoted in your company, if you promote people who have not

FIGURE 1-3
ALIGNMENT BETWEEN CULTURE AND RESULTS

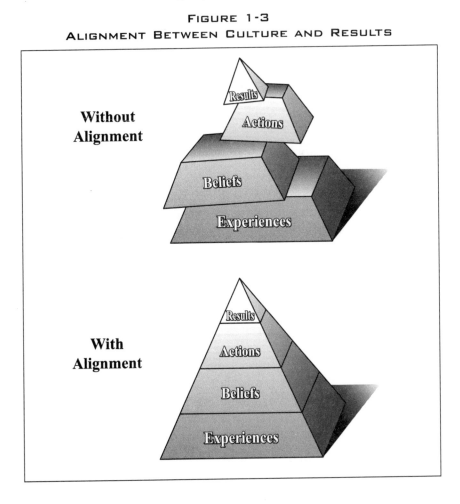

produced the desired results, you are probably putting your culture out of alignment by sending the message that something else is more important. We have found it interesting to have employees in a company list the criteria they believe are used for advancing people. It is not uncommon for results to be entirely absent from their list in favor of other more subjective, ambiguous, and sometimes political, criteria.

Promotions create experiences that foster beliefs that motivate actions. Therefore your company must promote people who produce the results you want (and in the way you want them produced). Doing otherwise puts your culture out of alignment. It's akin to driving your car over a foot-deep pothole and expecting the front end to stay in alignment. It won't. In fact, if you do it often enough, the car will ulti-mately be undriveable.

The need to stay "in alignment" despite contrary forces is the main reason that culture is not something you can "install" and then forget about. Managing a culture is a process, not an event. It is a process that begins with defining new results.

WORKING WITH THE WHOLE PYRAMID

The power and persistence of culture explains why the usual fixes that managers use to improve results often don't work. Most of the usual fixes—new people, new marching orders, new technology, new strate-gies, or new structures—work only at the level of actions, when they work at all. Too often, leaders attempt to change the way people act without changing the way they think, that is, their beliefs. Figure 1-4 shows the imaginary line commonly drawn by managers who focus their attention only on actions and results when working to improve performance. By working with just the top of the pyramid, leaders leave unchanged the things that can be the hardest to change but make the greatest impact on performance.

FIGURE 1-4
A COMMON MISTAKE:
WORKING WITH ONLY THE TOP OF THE PYRAMID

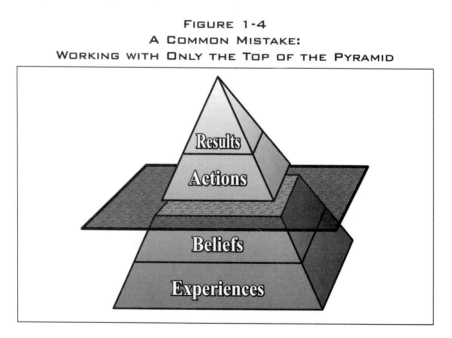

We believe, on the basis of our experience, that managers will more significantly and permanently improve results by working at the level of employees' beliefs. And to impact beliefs, managers must focus on creating new experiences for people. You will see how to do this in Part Two. Without that change in beliefs, you certainly cannot shift the culture. Without a cultural shift, any improvement in actions or results will be at best both temporary and partial. To *accelerate* culture change, leaders must work with both the top and the bottom of the pyramid.

A THREE-PART PROCESS FOR CULTURE CHANGE

Many managers find it useful to think of change in three phases as shown in Figure 1-5: deconstructing, reconstructing, and sustaining the culture.

- In *deconstructing* the culture, the management team becomes fully aware of the current culture. Senior management and other key people examine the experiences, beliefs, and actions that constitute the culture and honestly consider their effectiveness in achieving results. They decide what is working and what isn't.

- In *reconstructing* the culture, management considers the coming business environment and defines the results the company must achieve in that environment. Then they go on to define and create the experiences, beliefs, and actions to constitute the culture that will enable people to achieve those results. In this phase, management creates the new culture according to its designs.

- In *sustaining* the culture, management continues to provide experiences that foster and reinforce the desired beliefs. In this phase, leaders monitor the culture to maintain a focus on results and the actions and beliefs required to attain these results.

Depending upon the size and structure of the company, most middle managers and other key people should be involved at some point in this process. This incorporates shop-floor reality into the analysis and facilitates broad-based buy-in, without which there can be no new culture.

FIGURE 1-5
BUILDING THE PYRAMID

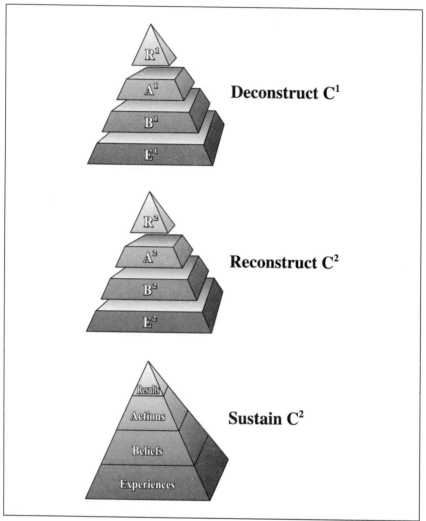

Please keep this process in mind as we move through the material to come, particularly Part Two. Culture can become overwhelmingly complex, and shifting culture can be a long-term, time-consuming process, without a step-by-step method of separately considering the components of the culture and their effects on one another, and then putting them back together.

But We're Just a Small Company

Some managers of small companies, say, those under $10 million in sales or with fewer than 50 people, believe that culture isn't an issue for their companies. However, even munchkin-sized companies have a culture. Remember, any group of people develops a culture. The only question is whether or not that culture will achieve the targeted results. So, yes, managers in small companies must definitely manage their culture. In fact, small companies face special issues that can make creating a *Culture of Accountability* extremely important.

First, even more so than in large companies, the leader—and it is often just one leader—dictates the culture, either consciously or unconsciously. Given that culture determines results, that culture had better be positive and had better be consciously created as opposed to unconsciously dictated.

Second, small companies generally don't spawn subcultures. In large companies people can work in a subculture, find professional satisfaction, and make a solid contribution to the entire company. In large companies a strong marketing culture, as exists in Procter & Gamble, or financial culture, as in AT&T, or product development culture, as in 3M, can come to distinguish the entire company. A small company usually lacks the critical mass to offer subcultures, so the company culture is "it." So "it" had better be effective.

Third, by the same token, small companies have little margin for error. If the culture doesn't work, the organization may well be doomed, particularly when a crisis arises. Typical crises that can capsize a small company with a weak, negative, or ineffective culture include the departure or death of one or more key people, loss of several major customers, acquiring venture-capital financing, going public, or acquisition by or alliance with a larger company. Weathering any of these crises would demand the ability to shift to a new, effective culture.

Finally, there is our view of true accountability, which as you will see calls for everyone throughout the entire organization to take accountability for the results of the company. That is another characteristic of a *Culture of Accountability*. Leaders need to seek and be open to the perspectives of others. Many an autocratic founder has sabotaged his or her company by failing to listen to reason or "let go" at the right time. An effective culture demands an openness on the part of management. This openness can be particularly beneficial—and eye-opening—in a small company.

ANALYSIS OF HOW WELL YOU MANAGE YOUR CULTURE

As a thought-starter and diagnostic tool, Figure 1-6 is a checklist that you can use to analyze how well you manage the culture of your organization.

Directions: Using the ten statements on the following page, carefully consider how you currently operate. Circle your assessment of your culture-management practices on the ten-point scale provided. (This can be particularly powerful when done in a group, especially if participants first rate the company privately and then share their assessments.)

Now, add up the numbers you circled for each dimension. The total is your score. If you scored above 80, your management team has an above-average understanding of organizational culture and puts that understanding into practice much of the time. Keep up the good work, and keep improving.

If you scored between 60 and 80 you are about average, which means that your company would benefit greatly from management's learning more about organizational culture. One outcome will be improved results.

If you scored below 60 get your management team on the next jet for the Emerald City. Please know, however, that your organization has lots of company.

MILESTONES ON THE YELLOW BRICK ROAD

In this chapter we've seen that creating and maintaining the right culture represents the key challenge before an organization's leaders. That is because the company's culture generates its results. Culture is the way people think and the way they act, and those two things generate results. This renders the issue of culture a day-to-day, practical concern rather than one that is long term and theoretical.

In our world, accountability means making a personal commitment to achieving the organization's results. A *Culture of Accountability* has proven itself the most effective organizational culture. In this kind of culture people feel accountable to think and act in the manner necessary to achieve results. In this kind of culture, everyone continually asks: What else can I do? This question keeps people's efforts focused

FIGURE 1-6
DIAGNOSTIC TOOL TO ASSESS HOW WELL
YOU MANAGE YOUR CULTURE

Culture Management Self Test

DISAGREE   AGREE

1 People at all levels in the organization would say that desired company results are clearly defined.
1 2 3 4 5 6 7 8 9 10

2 We understand the culture we currently have -- what it is and how it came into being.
1 2 3 4 5 6 7 8 9 10

3 We see managing our culture as a daily activity, not as an occasional event.
1 2 3 4 5 6 7 8 9 10

4 There is a clearly defined set of cultural beliefs that are well understood throughout the company.
1 2 3 4 5 6 7 8 9 10

5 We consciously adjust our culture when we experience significant changes in the business environment.
1 2 3 4 5 6 7 8 9 10

6 Leaders consistently manage the experiences they create to ensure they promote specific cultural beliefs.
1 2 3 4 5 6 7 8 9 10

7 The majority of managers in the company consistently practice managing the culture along with other business processes.
1 2 3 4 5 6 7 8 9 10

8 The experiences, beliefs, and actions in our culture are aligned to produce the results we've targeted.
1 2 3 4 5 6 7 8 9 10

9 We have made at least one major cultural transition effectively, we know how we did it, and we could do it again.
1 2 3 4 5 6 7 8 9 10

10 We have created and maintained a Culture of Accountability in our company.
1 2 3 4 5 6 7 8 9 10

and directed toward achieving results rather than escaping responsibility. Managers must foster this kind of commitment, and this question helps people maintain top-of-mind awareness of that commitment.

Culture is made up of experiences, beliefs, actions, and results. Experiences foster beliefs. Beliefs drive actions. Actions produce results. Results become new experiences. Every organization, every group of people, has a culture. The only question is whether or not that culture is effective today and can produce the results that you need now and in the future.

Creating the culture you want and need is no longer an option. It is a business necessity. Creating that culture at all levels in the organization and doing it quickly and effectively creates organizational and competitive advantage. Unlike the characters in *The Wonderful Wizard of Oz*, you don't have to walk to the Emerald City. There are things you can do and a process you can use to speed you on your journey to a new culture. That is what this book is about. As we take the next step to the next chapter, we look more closely at the behaviors that add up to a *Culture of Accountability* and at why this culture is so effective.

THE EMERALD CITY

BUILDING A CULTURE OF ACCOUNTABILITY

In front of them, at the end of the road of yellow brick, was a big gate, all studded with emeralds that glittered in the sun.

The Wonderful Wizard of Oz
L. Frank Baum

In *The Wonderful Wizard of Oz*, Dorothy and her companions have great hope that the Emerald City will be a place of answers, solutions, assistance, and success. They have every expectation that all their troubles will be over once they arrive in this wondrous place.

Not unlike the characters in *The Wonderful Wizard of Oz*, everyone with experience in the quest for results, no matter how successful, can testify that troubles, obstacles, and challenges will undoubtedly present themselves—that is a part of the journey. And usually that's a part of the journey we cannot control. However, as in the Emerald City, an organization can function as a place where these troubles, challenges, and obstacles can be solved—a place where solutions can be uncovered and answers obtained.

The Emerald City *is a Culture of Accountability.*

It is a place where, on a daily basis, people think and act in the manner necessary to successfully develop solutions, find answers, overcome obstacles, and triumph over any trouble that might come along. A *Culture of Accountability* is a place where everyone continually asks, "What else can I do to achieve results, attain objectives, and accomplish goals?" It is a culture that is based on certain experiences, beliefs, and actions, all geared to generating desired results. In this chapter we examine what goes on in a *Culture of Accountability*. And since organizational culture is the sum total of how people think and act, we will examine how people think and act in this kind of culture.

CREATING ACCOUNTABILITY

In *The Oz Principle: Getting Results Through Individual and Organizational Accountability*, we identified four *Steps to Accountability* that produce results. These four steps describe what we see in the presence of true accountability. Consistently taking these four steps will create individual and organizational ownership for achieving results and attaining objectives.

The four *Steps to Accountability* are *See It, Own It, Solve It,* and *Do It*. We have found that consistent performance of these steps characterizes those who think and act in an accountable manner. People who do not take the accountable approach are typically somewhere *Below the Line^SM*, either passing through or stuck in the Blame Game, feeling victimized by circumstances that are seen as outside their control.

As you can see in Figure 2-1, we draw a clear line to separate the *Steps to Accountability* from the Blame Game. The *Steps to Accountability* represent *Above the Line* actions and thinking. The Blame Game represents *Below the Line* habits of thought and behavior. As you might imagine, when individuals consistently engage in these two very different modes of thinking and acting they, in turn, create very different organizational cultures as well.

Before we examine in detail the actions associated with the *Steps to Accountability*, let's first briefly examine what it means to be *Below the Line*.

WHAT GOES ON BELOW THE LINE

We'll start with *Below the Line* habits of thought and action because that is where people and organizations often go when results aren't forthcoming and performance is lacking. These habits of mind and behavior can become so accepted as part of an organization's culture that people become unaware of their pervasiveness. Though ineffective, these behaviors do serve a very definite purpose. They help people to avoid or deflect accountability for something that has happened or something that should have happened but did not.

Let's take a brief excursion *Below the Line* and play the Blame Game. As we Blamestorm excuses and describe *Below the Line* think-

FIGURE 2-1
THE STEPS TO ACCOUNTABILITY CHART

ing and acting, please understand that these behaviors occur on both the individual and the collective levels. An individual or an entire organization can be functioning *Below the Line* relative to a specific result (or results) they are trying to achieve.

1. Ignore/Deny: At this stage of the Blame Game, people fail even to see that a problem exists. Here, people are often heard making such statements as:

- "What number did *you* think we were trying to achieve?"
- "From where *we* sit, we don't see a problem."
- "That's not what *my reports* are telling me."

As we engage in this round of Blamestorming, consider your own organization and what you hear people saying at each of these stages. What do you hear people in your organization typically say when they are in the ignore/deny stage? Write it down in the space provided:

Ignore/Deny: _____

2. It's Not My Job: This is where people narrowly define their job as performing specific, and sometimes ambiguous tasks as opposed to defining their job as getting the result. Here people find safety under the cover of "I did my part," rather than "I did what was necessary to achieve the result." When people are at this stage of the Blame Game they are often heard saying such things as:

- "It's not my responsibility."
- "That's not in my job description."
- "That's not what I'm paid to do."

What would this stage sound like in your own organization?

It's Not My Job: _____

3. Finger-Pointing: Blamestorming intensifies with finger-pointing as people blame other people as well as things for their failure to achieve results. They make statements such as:

- "The people in sales just don't know how to sell sophisticated products."

- "Marketing gave us bad forecasts."
- "If R&D would get its act together and develop something the customers will buy, then we could hit the targets."

What would you add from your own experience?

Finger-pointing: _____

4. Confusion and Tell-Me-What-to-Do: This is where people use confusion as an excuse to mask their accountability for results. Confusion is claimed in the face of unclear priorities, changing objectives, and competing requirements. When people are at this stage of the Blame Game they might say:

- "Which did you want us to focus on, quality or quantity?"
- "I thought you said customer satisfaction is how we would be measured."
- "You actually expected us to deliver against those numbers?"

What does confusion sound like in your organization?

Confusion: _____

When confusion is used, people further abdicate their accountability as they throw up their hands in resignation and exclaim: "Just tell me exactly what you want me to do, and I'll go do it." Then, if things go wrong, the persons providing the direction remain accountable for the outcome—because it was their idea, their direction, and their responsibility.

5. Cover Your Tail: At this stage, people establish why they are not at fault by documenting their potential excuses throughout the year just in case they are asked to account for missed results. They say such things as:

- "We hired the best in the business and they recommended that we do this. Look it's right here in the report I sent you May 15."

- "I as much as warned you that this would happen—here's a copy of the e-mail I sent you."

What have you heard in your organization? Write it down in the space provided:

Cover Your Tail: _____

6. Wait and See: This is where people put off taking action, relying instead on wishful thinking and the passage of time. When people are at this stage of the Blame Game they are heard saying:

- "We are in transition. Once we get through it things will quickly improve."
- "Things will get better as the year progresses, you'll see."
- "We're in the early innings here."

What do you hear from your organization?

Wait and See: _____

And the game continues, perpetuating continued excuses, repeated explanations, and performance that falls short of achieving the result.

In the Blame Game people get stuck *Below the Line*—unable to move forward in their quest for results. It's not wrong to go *Below the Line*. We all do it from time to time. In fact, there is often a therapeutic effect that comes in venting our frustrations about things that we feel are holding us back and that seem to be out of our control.

If people remain stuck *Below the Line*, however, they become more focused on what they can't do than on what they can do. They set their sights on the obstacles before them, rather than on the results they need to achieve.

People are frustrated *Below the Line*. They are stalled in their progress. They can't move their organizations or their careers forward. Often because their achievements are lacking and fall short of their potential, they don't find fulfillment in what they have done.

ABOVE THE LINE^{SM} BEHAVIOR

People who are *Above the Line* recognize that they are, and must be, part of the solution in order to achieve results. They focus on what they can do, rather than on what they cannot do. They look for creative ways to deal with obstacles, rather than being stopped by them. *Above the Line* people move forward. They get results. They feel satisfied. They progress in their careers and in their quest for improved performance. The more time we spend *Above the Line*, the greater will be our results. The more time an organization spends *Above the Line*, the greater will be its results.

When people operate *Above the Line*, they assume full accountability. We define accountability in a highly proactive and empowering manner. Think about the times you have typically heard someone ask the question, "Who's accountable for that?" Almost unanimously, people tell us it's when something has gone wrong. Seldom is the question asked, "Who's accountable?" when things are working well. As a result, the notion of accountability for many employees has taken on a hard critical edge that is often negative. Yet almost all would agree that it is a foundation principle central to the effective functioning of any organization.

We prefer to ask the question, "Who's accountable?" before it is too late, prior to deadline, in advance of the problems, and way ahead of the competition. By establishing accountability up front as shown in Figure 2-2, you are enlisting people and empowering the work force to do all they can to ensure the result. As you look at Figure 2-2, ask yourself the question, Which orientation will have the greater effect on fostering and improving, your organization's ability to achieve results: the before-the-fact approach to creating accountability or the after-the-fact way to establishing blame? Which will lead to greater motivation, greater commitment, and greater fulfillment?

To us, accountability is defined as "to relentlessly pursue results by operating *Above the Line*, anticipating and overcoming obstacles, and consistently asking, What else can I do?" This view leads one *Above the Line* to the *Steps to Accountability*.

When you take the *Steps to Accountability* to *See It, Own It, Solve It,* and *Do It,* you are taking steps toward achieving the desired result. Each of these steps represents a process that must be undertaken, in sequence, in order to move or stay *Above the Line.* Each step builds on the previous one.

FIGURE 2-2
TWO VIEWS OF ACCOUNTABILITY

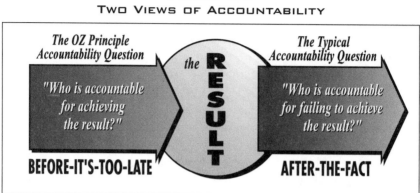

See It^SM is the vital first step in moving *Above the Line* or in staying there when a new challenge arises. *See It* means that you must first acknowledge the reality of your situation: A problem exists, an issue must be resolved, an obstacle must be overcome, or a circumstance must be conquered. This, of course, short-circuits both denial of the problem and any wait-and-see notions that you may be entertaining. To *See It* takes courage, that same quality the cowardly Lion on the Yellow Brick Road had to muster.

Own It^SM is the second step in moving or staying *Above the Line* because it is all too easy to see a problem and then to say that it isn't yours. It takes heart to *Own It*—to take ownership of the problem—and heart is what the Tin Woodsman needed in order to reach full functionality. The *Own It* step lies at the heart of accountability. Ownership is the ability to tie where you are with what you have done, and where you want to be with what you are going to do. You must *Own It* in order to move forward.

Solve It,^SM the third step, requires persistent effort as you encounter obstacles that stand in the way of achieving the result. This step often requires a new way of thinking and always demands a high level of personal engagement, things the poor Scarecrow sought in his journey to the Emerald City for a brain. You *Solve It* by continually asking the essential *Solve-It* question: What else can I do to move forward, overcome obstacles, and achieve the result?

Do It,^SM the final step in the process, represents the natural culmination of the first three steps: Once you *See It*, *Own It*, and *Solve It*, you must take this final step to *Do It*. You must take action. You must implement the solution that grew out of applying yourself after seeing and owning the problem. In the Land of Oz the stakes were highest for Dorothy; she had to get back to Kansas and she was determined to keep trying until she got there. This involved putting all four steps together to get the result she sought. You can take all three previous steps, but to stay *Above the Line* and achieve the result, you must take the fourth and final step to *Do It*.

As you can see, taking the steps to greater accountability moves the entire issue of "who's accountable?" from the commonly understood meaning of "getting caught failing" to a more proactive view of "starring in the solution." Moving and staying *Above the Line* is about impacting the situation before it's too late—mustering the ability to *See It*, having the heart to *Own It*, applying the thinking to *Solve It*, and making the commitment to *Do It*.

DEFINING THE STEPS TO ACCOUNTABILITY^{SM}

The *Steps to Accountability* work. They work for groups, teams, and organizations. But, perhaps more important, they work for us as individuals.

Each of these steps represents a set of behaviors, things that you can do that will enable you to practice accountability and teach others how to do the same. This is not theory but practice, and practice makes perfect. When the *Steps to Accountability* are applied to the way of thinking and acting that will produce results for your organization, then you are creating a *Culture of Accountability*.

After years of assisting organizations in *accelerating* their transition to a *Culture of Accountability*, we have defined the most significant actions and beliefs that comprise the four *Steps to Accountability*. These definitions are based upon our observations of numerous companies that were performing at extremely high levels as well as of some that were struggling to achieve results. After each of these companies defined the shifts that they needed to create in their cultures to achieve future results, we distilled them. On the basis of this analysis, we have identified 16 key behaviors and beliefs that go into the four steps. Organizations and individuals that do these things produce results—great results—consistently, over time. We will describe each of the definitions and break them down for you into the four key attributes for each definition. As we do, you will see how these four steps can help you *accelerate* your transition to a *Culture of Accountability*.

As we go through each of these definitions, we'll give you the opportunity to measure how well you and your organization are doing on each of the four attributes of each definition. Please do this by assigning a letter grade for each attribute in the definition on the scorecard we provide after each of the next four major sections. Use the following system for grading: A = Excellent, B = Good, C = Average, D = Poor, F = Failing. For greater precision, you can also use plus or minus grades.

As we describe each definition, carefully consider how it applies to you as a manager and to your organization. Again, *after each* of the next four major sections, you'll have an opportunity to rate both yourself and your organization on each attribute.

THE SEE IT^{SM} DEFINITION

> I am accountable to *See It* by (1) obtaining the perspectives of others; (2) being open and candid in my communications; (3) asking for and offering feedback; and (4) hearing the hard things.

The *See It* definition embodies those actions and beliefs that help an organization and individuals see things as they really are. The clearer the picture of how things really are, the better one can move forward. Let's take each of the four key attributes of this definition and explore them in turn.

ATTRIBUTE NUMBER 1: OBTAINING THE PERSPECTIVES OF OTHERS

We have found that in order to *See It*, you have to become good at obtaining the perspectives of others, finding out what people really think and why they think it. Understanding others' perspectives in today's complex business environment is not a luxury or a nice-to-have, but a necessity. Asking questions such as: Who else might be able to contribute to our thinking? Who might be seeing something that we are not? Who will need to implement the decisions we make, and how might their views change our approach? What functions are not represented in our thinking? Who's new to the team and might offer a different view? Often, these perspectives can help us see the whole picture, something more complete than any one of us might see on our own.

Obtaining perspectives requires that we seek them, ask for them, and go out and get them. The only way to get the perspectives of others is to communicate openly, ask for those views, and then listen. We can't *See It* until we fully perceive it, and that's what obtaining the perspectives of others is all about.

ATTRIBUTE NUMBER 2: BEING OPEN AND CANDID IN MY COMMUNICATIONS

We have found that within organizations there are many beliefs around what you can say, when you can say it, and to whom you can say it. Often, we hear people describe the "career-limiting remarks" for their organization, you know, the particular "unmentionables" that if said could cause one to feel that they have stepped over the line and dashed their hopes for advancement. Acting on these beliefs, people consciously gauge what they can say and often fail to be open and candid. In some organizational cultures, people have learned that avoiding conflict is "how things work around here." In a sense they enter an informal, mutually beneficial contract stating that "I won't tell you what I think if you won't tell me what you think." Actually, saying what we think enables others to see the reality of their situation.

ATTRIBUTE NUMBER 3: ASKING FOR AND OFFERING FEEDBACK

In almost every organization in which we have worked over the past decade feedback has been perceived as "something we really need but just don't get enough of." Many CEOs, division presidents, middle managers, and line supervisors have told us that they don't get the feedback they need. Clearly, if you're not getting feedback on a regular basis then you are missing perspectives and information that would be useful to seeing situations as they really are.

Our view is that people in organizations are accountable to both ask for and offer feedback. Organizations that create environments where feedback is freely shared tend to do so by getting more of their people asking for feedback rather than waiting for someone to offer it.

ATTRIBUTE NUMBER 4: HEARING THE HARD THINGS

Many of us have had the experience of sitting with someone who simply refuses to *See It*. Often this refusal is expressed in an unwillingness to hear the hard things. But without the commitment to hear the message as it is, and not how you may want it to be, you will frequently miss the information that could enable you to achieve the result. Organizationally, the price paid for not hearing the hard things can be very high.

THE SEE IT SCORECARD

Employing the A-through-F grading system (and plus or minus grades if you wish), use the following scorecard in Figure 2-3 to assess yourself and your organization on how well you demonstrate each of the four attributes of the definition of *See It*. On this and on the three scorecards to follow, be as objective and honest as possible so you can *see* the reality of your situation. You might even ask for input from others on your team before completing the scorecards.

FIGURE 2-3 SEE IT SCORECARD

SEE IT ^{SM}	Grade yourself on how well you do these things	Grade your organization on how well these things are done
Obtaining the perspectives of others		
Communicating openly and candidly		
Asking for and offering feedback		
Hearing the hard things		
OVERALL GRADE FOR *SEE IT*		

THE OWN IT^{SM} DEFINITION

I am accountable to *Own It* by (1) being personally invested; (2) acknowledging my involvement; (3) creating and maintaining a sense of alignment; and (4) owning both my personal and my team's objectives.

Personal ownership is the linchpin in the framework for achieving results. Everyone counts! That's the message—results cannot be obtained in today's ever-changing environment without enlisting the hearts and minds of all the people at all levels of the organization.

ATTRIBUTE NUMBER 5:
BEING PERSONALLY INVESTED

Personal investment may be hard to describe, but it is easy to see in the actions of others. We heard of one military official who used to measure how far the members of his platoon could run after he pulled the pin of a practice grenade. He had all of the distances recorded for each of the men. After practicing for a week he told the men that this drill would be done with live ammunition. He told the men to get ready to run after he pulled the pin. He was not the least bit surprised to find record distances for every single member of the platoon with a number of the men nearly doubling their past personal best. When people in organizations are invested in the work they are doing they put more of themselves into their individual efforts to achieve results.

One manager described the people in her organization as "punching the clock and checking their brains at the door." Her frustration stemmed from seeing people simply doing what they were told, but not really striving for results. Employees struck her as more effective in their off-duty activities, where they demonstrated great creativity and innovative thinking. This same manager observed that her people were personally invested at home and in their off-duty lives, but not in their jobs. High personal investment on the job characterizes workers in a *Culture of Accountability*.

ATTRIBUTE NUMBER 6:
ACKNOWLEDGING MY INVOLVEMENT

We define ownership as the ability to tie where I am with what I have done and where I want to be with what I am going to do. In our view, if you cannot "make the tie" then you don't *Own It*. Recently, one of our clients was discussing the issue of diversity and the lack of ownership for making real headway on creating greater diversity throughout the organization. They determined that as long as diversity was an "organizational" issue, rather than a "personal" issue, one in which each individual "made the tie" to him- or herself every day, people would continue to let the organization wrestle with the problem and allow actual progress to go unrealized.

ATTRIBUTE NUMBER 7
CREATING AND MAINTAINING A SENSE OF ALIGNMENT

Getting everyone moving in the same direction often represents the greatest challenge to getting results. Ultimately, alignment is a personal choice that reflects a sense of ownership for where things are headed. Since personal ownership is at the heart of alignment, everyone in the organization must be accountable both to work toward creating alignment and toward maintaining it. Alignment does not mean agreement with a decision. Rather it means agreeing to move in the same direction once a decision has been made, whether or not we agreed with that decision.

ATTRIBUTE NUMBER 8:
OWNING BOTH MY PERSONAL AND MY TEAM'S OBJECTIVES

Sometimes significant conflict exists between achieving one's personal objectives and contributing to the organizational and team results. While ownership for personal objectives is important, a shared commitment to achieving team results is imperative. Thinking solely of our own career, function, team, department, division, product line, or territory will cause organizations to fall far short of achieving results. Making the tie between individual and team objectives on a daily basis speeds action toward results.

THE OWN IT SCORECARD

Again, score yourself by giving yourself and your organization a letter grade for each attribute for the *Own It* Definition in Figure 2-4.

FIGURE 2–4
OWN IT SCORECARD

OWN IT^{SM}	Grade yourself on how well you do these things	Grade your organization on how well these things are done
Being personally invested		
Acknowledging my involvement		
Creating and maintaining a sense of alignment		
Committing to both my personal and my team's objectives		
OVERALL GRADE FOR *OWN IT*		

THE SOLVE IT^{SM} DEFINITION

I am accountable to *Solve It* by (1) constantly asking, "What else can I do?"; (2) actively redefining boundaries; (3) creatively dealing with obstacles; and (4) staying focused on results.

This third definition, *Solve It*, boils down to not taking "no" for an answer and not accepting failure as an option. This definition embodies the key attributes and actions that are necessary to breaking through and achieving the result.

ATTRIBUTE NUMBER 9:
CONSTANTLY ASKING, WHAT ELSE CAN I DO?

Many problem-solving techniques tout themselves as organized approaches to discovering root causes and sure solutions. But in the *Solve It* definition, we see the key elements of a *Culture of Accountability*. Developing the ability to *Solve It* is more about attitude than technique. When people continually ask what else they can do to achieve results, they tend to consistently achieve their objectives—making deadlines, staying on budget, and hitting sales quotas. Any target that is established is made more achievable when people focus intently on that target. Constantly asking, "What else can I do?" ultimately brings progress toward achieving the result.

ATTRIBUTE NUMBER 10:
ACTIVELY REDEFINING BOUNDARIES

Boundaries may be functional, financial, geographic, or industry-specific. Or they may be internally imposed in the form of assumptions that may or may not be justified. Remember Captain Kirk of Star Trek fame in the Kobiashi-Maroo scenario? He passed a test that no one had ever succeeded in passing before by changing the boundaries and reprogramming the simulation. Testing boundaries, checking assumptions, and redefining the challenge can significantly impact our eventual success. Hewlett Packard got into the ink-jet paper business because they sell ink-jet printers. They didn't sit there and say, "We're in high-technology, not the paper business." It worked. McDonald's started serving breakfast, igniting a new fast-food category. Nike and Reebok and Adidas went into clothing. American Can Company got out of making cans and reorganized itself into Primerica, a financial-services giant. Successful mail-order houses such as Eddie Bauer and The Sharper Image opened retail stores. Boundaries, even when they are real, may be movable.

ATTRIBUTE NUMBER 11:
CREATIVELY DEALING WITH OBSTACLES

Obstacles, on the other hand, are generally not self-imposed. The tricky thing about obstacles is that they are usually seen as outside of one's control, which can send an individual or organization *Below the Line*. Creatively dealing with obstacles helps you stay focused on the results. While some obstacles can be ignored, most require us to deal with them creatively in an *Above the Line* manner.

ATTRIBUTE NUMBER 12:
STAYING FOCUSED ON RESULTS

Solving problems, reshaping boundaries, and dealing with obstacles all require a commitment to not get lost in the problem but rather to stay focused on achieving results. Reaching the destination of desired results, not overcoming obstacles, must be the focus. Maintaining a focus on results is critical as organizations move from one set of challenges and obstacles to the next. We have seen teams actually overcome the most significant obstacle they faced and still fail to achieve the result. Yet we have also seen teams who dealt with obstacles in an *Above the Line* manner, but never overcame them, and still achieved the targeted result.

THE SOLVE IT SCORECARD

In Figure 2-5, score yourself by giving yourself and your organization a letter grade for each attribute for the *Solve It* definition.

FIGURE 2-5
SOLVE IT SCORECARD

SOLVE IT ᔆᴹ	Grade yourself on how well you do these things	Grade your organization on how well these things are done
Constantly asking, "What else can I do?"		
Actively redefining boundaries		
Creatively dealing with obstacles		
Staying focused on results		
OVERALL GRADE FOR SOLVE IT		

THE DO IT ᔆᴹ DEFINITION

I am accountable to *Do It* by (1) reporting proactively; (2) relentlessly following up; (3) doing the things I say I'll do; and (4) measuring my progress toward achieving the intended result.

The *Do It* definition describes the essence of full accountability—the will and commitment to follow through and achieve the result.

Implementing the plan while staying *Above the Line* is the fourth and final step in the *Steps to Accountability*. It is this final step that validates the effort spent on the first three.

ATTRIBUTE NUMBER 13:
REPORTING PROACTIVELY

Proactive reporting demonstrates personal accountability as the people responsible take the initiative to keep everyone abreast of the current issues and obstacles they face. This allows a larger group of people to be engaged in asking, "What else can I do?" Someone who is proactively reporting doesn't let out a sigh of relief when the agenda for the management meeting doesn't allow for a report on her item. Instead she seeks to bring everyone up to speed on where they are concerning the result. What would you rather have—ten people who proactively report on their progress or ten people you must constantly pursue for progress reports?

ATTRIBUTE NUMBER 14:
RELENTLESSLY FOLLOWING UP

Relentless follow-up begins the moment future actions are decided. Everyone who shares any portion of accountability for the result will see that what needs to be done, gets done. Relentlessly following up means looking for ways to support others to ensure success, rather than looking for what people are doing wrong. While constructive input is important, fault-finding is so prevalent that we have become desensitized to its negative impact on the human will. If leaders relentlessly follow up to ensure the success of their people, and if people constantly seek ways to ensure the team's success, their energy will not only be focused but amplified.

ATTRIBUTE NUMBER 15:
DOING THE THINGS I SAY I'LL DO

At some stage in the process of cultural change, a personal "contract" takes shape that essentially describes what everyone has agreed to do. Success or failure depends on people having the integrity to say, "I will do what I said I will do." Only when people do the things they say they'll do will results be forthcoming. Keeping commitments, holding to agreements, and delivering on promises are key parts of the *Do It* step.

ATTRIBUTE NUMBER 16: MEASURING MY PROGRESS TOWARD ACHIEVING THE INTENDED RESULT

Without measurements of progress accountability is only an idea. By monitoring progress along the way we communicate that the back door is closed, that the ships in the harbor have been burned, and that there is no turning back. In a *Culture of Accountability* people do not wait until they are asked for a report on their progress, nor do they wait to be told to follow up. Rather, they report proactively and follow up constantly. They also measure their own progress toward achieving the result. That's because they have taken the critical step in assuming accountability: They have *internalized* their commitment to achieving the result. They are vitally interested in their progress toward the result. Waiting to be asked for a progress report or to be told to follow up is antithetical to a *Culture of Accountability*. In fact, requests for information and follow up usually elicit *Below the Line* behavior. That entire mind set has to shift.

THE DO IT SCORECARD

Once again in Figure 2-6, score yourself by giving yourself and your organization a letter grade for each attribute for the *Do It* definition.

FIGURE 2-6
DO IT SCORECARD

DO IT SM	Grade yourself on how well you do these things	Grade your organization on how well these things are done
Reporting proactively		
Relentlessly following up		
Doing the things I say I'll do		
Measuring my progress toward achieving the intended result		
OVERALL GRADE FOR *DO IT*		

COMPARING YOUR SCORES

These 16 attributes we have reviewed in the preceding pages are the key things that we see people and organizations do to create accountability for results. These are the things that people do when they feel accountable. These are also the things that people do to become accountable. Doing them well *accelerates* the process of getting results.

After you have objectively and candidly completed your score-cards for each of the four *Steps to Accountability*, please examine the following scores we've compiled for three representative clients of ours. (To respect client confidentiality we cannot, of course, reveal the names of these companies. However, they are well-known, well-respected organizations. We have found that the companies that most want to improve their cultures and that expect the most of themselves are often the toughest in their self-assessment.) For convenience, you can transfer your company's scores to the column provided in Figure 2-7.

These three companies are fairly representative of the companies in our database. It may be helpful to know that each of these organizations is successful in its own right within its given industry. We offer these companies' scores so you can see how others score themselves and so you can informally compare your scores to theirs. We also offer the following observations of these three companies' scores.

As you can see, if you scored yourself as average or below in a number of these categories, you are not alone. Notice first, across the board, that there are very few As among the scores for these companies. On the 16 individual attributes within the four steps, Company X gave itself two As, Company Y gave itself none, and Company Z, one. This is representative of our broader experience, and while it may partially reflect modesty, it is also a realistic assessment. Very few companies are doing a truly superior job in more than one or two of these areas. In fact, a review of our database of companies demonstrates that these 16 attributes reflect skills, practices, and approaches that are not necessarily done well by most organizations. They are also the things that come up in our assessments time after time as those employees and managers feel their organization needs to do better in order to make their plans, produce their products, and achieve their results.

Within *See It* among the three companies, we see the highest scores on "Obtaining the perspectives of others," one B+ and two B- grades. Yet all three companies score themselves relatively poorly—D, C, and D, respectively—on "Communicating openly and candidly."

FIGURE 2-7
COMPARATIVE SCORECARD FOR
THE STEPS TO ACCOUNTABILITY

		Company X GRADE*	Company Y GRADE*	Company Z GRADE*	My Company GRADE
SEE IT	Obtaining the perspectives of others	B+	B-	B-	
	Communicating openly and candidly	D	C	D	
	Asking for and offering feedback	D	C-	C	
	Hearing the hard things	B+	B	D to F	
	OVERALL GRADE FOR *SEE IT*	C	B-	C-	
OWN IT	Being personally invested	B	C+	D	
	Acknowledging my involvement	B-	B	D	
	Creating and maintaining a sense of alignment	C	C	C	
	Committing to both my personal and my team's objectives	B-	C+	C	
	OVERALL GRADE FOR *OWN IT*	B-	C+	C-	
SOLVE IT	Constantly asking, "What else can I do?"	D	C	B	
	Actively redefining boundaries	C	C	D	
	Creatively dealing with obstacles	A	C+	C	
	Staying focused on results	A	B+	A	
	OVERALL GRADE FOR *SOLVE IT*	B	C+	B-	
DO IT	Reporting proactively	C	C+	D	
	Relentlessly following up	D	B	C	
	Doing the things I say I'll do	C+	B	D	
	Measuring my progress toward achieving the intended result	B	B	C	
	OVERALL GRADE FOR *DO IT*	C	B-	D	

*Company "X" is a division of a major consumer packaged goods firm, "Y" is a major company in the health care industry, and "Z" is a computer services company.

This points to the unsettling possibility that although they are obtaining the perspectives of others, they are not getting open and candid perspectives. As is the case with most companies, these three do not rate themselves very high on "Asking for and offering feedback." This is why we spend a fair amount of time with clients, as well as in Chapter Seven of this book, dealing with how to use feedback effectively.

The preceding analysis raises a key point: As you examine your own scores, check them for internal consistency. For example, how can people in an organization be good at obtaining the perspectives of others, yet not be good at asking for feedback? Sometimes our assessments of ourselves and our organizations become skewed by what we want to see or by our failure to consider our strengths and weaknesses consistently along various dimensions. When you see these inconsistencies you can perhaps diagnose problems in perception as well as in performance.

Among the four attributes of *Own It*, Company X and Y each scored themselves the lowest on "Creating and maintaining alignment." The scores here reflect a general trend we see regarding alignment, and it is why we work closely with clients on the issue of alignment and devote Chapter Eight to it.

The *Solve It* step usually draws forth the highest scores from clients. This is true both for the individual attributes of this step and for the overall score on it. We think this is because *Solve It* focuses on getting results, and most companies value and try to develop a strong focus on results. Despite this, companies often fail to achieve their results. We believe that a relative lack of focus on other attributes in the *Steps to Accountability* explains much of this failure. In addition, an equally large issue looms over most companies: Are the results people are focused on really those that the organization is trying to achieve? In other words, people can feel that they're focused on results, but if they aren't communicating openly and candidly or aren't aligned with one another, are they really shooting for the *organization's* results? In a *Culture of Accountability* people are not only focused on results, they're focused on the organization's results.

The *Do It* step is about following through. Most companies score themselves relatively high on measuring progress. This probably reflects a fairly widespread focus on measurement, or at least on financial measures such as sales and earnings, in most companies. However, as the discussion around measurement develops, people quickly raise the question of whether the right things are being measured.

As you can see, two of the three companies had the lowest over-all scores for this step. The third company had only one B and the rest were Cs and Ds. Overall, organizations struggle with the *Do It* step, not because they are not busy taking action, but because people often struggle with taking action in the proactive and accountable manner outlined in the *Do It* definition.

You might ask yourself, "So which of these three companies is the best?"

On the face of it, Company Y appears to have the best overall scorecard on the four steps (B-, C+, C+, B-), while Company Z appears to be the worst (C-, C-, B-, D), and Company X falls between them (C, B-, B, C). Of course, these grades are all relative. An organization with a history of years of dominance and control may rate itself rather high given slight improvements in communication, whereas an organization with a practice of open and honest dialogue that is well entrenched within the culture may be quite hard on itself as it seeks to perfect an aspect of its environment that it feels has helped to produce results. The real value of any of these self-assessments comes from understanding where you are today, really, and where you feel you need to be. Even more important is what a company does with the resulting insights. Getting a diagnosis is one thing. Finding and implementing a cure is another.

So in terms of your own scorecard, we suggest that you use it to locate problem areas as revealed by low scores or inconsistencies. Also, try to be objective about differences between your personal scores and those you gave your organization. If you are actually doing a superior job in an area, the question is how can you assist others in your company to do the same? If you are doing poorly in an area, what can you do to improve? And if you and your organization both need improvement somewhere, what steps can you take? Throughout this book you will find answers to all three of these questions.

USING THE STEPS TO CREATE A CULTURE OF ACCOUNTABILITY^{SM}

We use the other-worldly example of the Land of Oz as our metaphor in books on accountability for a reason: To create a *Culture of Accountability* you must leave behind many of the standard management tools and practices you have been using. You must forget what you knew back in Kansas and begin to think and act differently.

Culture changes one person at a time. Since culture is what people think and what they do, each individual in the organization must think differently and act differently in order for the culture to change.

As you will see, these steps are essential to creating a *Culture of Accountability*. By applying each of them to the way you need people to think and act, you will accelerate the cultural transition you need and the attainment of the results you want. Remember, the process starts with management. Managers move a company to a *Culture of Accountability* by creating experiences that foster beliefs that drive actions that produce the desired results. Conversely, managers must stop creating experiences that foster beliefs that drive actions that produce unwanted results.

This is the essence of true culture change in organizations. As we said earlier, your company has a culture—one way or another. You, as a manager and leader, are promulgating an organizational culture whether or not you are thinking about it. By taking conscious control of your culture, you can make it a *Culture of Accountability*.

We believe that most people want to operate *Above the Line* and that these steps enable them to do so. The consciousness and effort entailed in the *Steps to Accountability* counteracts the forces working to pull people *Below the Line*. These forces include remembered negative experiences, persistent useless beliefs, and ineffective habitual actions as well as external obstacles, inexperience, and human nature, with all its territorialism and self-protection. All of these are forces that you and your company can address. We have seen other organizations do it, including some that were extremely far *Below the Line*. We also fight the good fight every day in our own rapidly growing company.

We repeat, managers move a company to a *Culture of Accountability* by creating experiences that foster beliefs that drive actions that produce results as shown in Figure 2-8.

Part Two will show you as a manager how to do exactly these things. We begin in Chapter Three by defining results that people can and will deeply commit themselves to achieving.

MILESTONES IN THE COURSE OF THE JOURNEY

In this chapter we've examined *Above the Line* and *Below the Line* behaviors. *Below the Line* behaviors include the Blame Game and a range of Blamestorming tactics. These are the things people do to

FIGURE 2-8
THE PROCESS OF MANAGING CULTURE

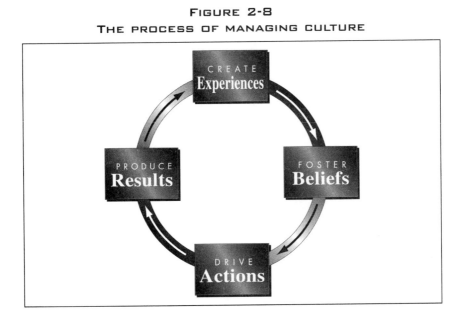

avoid personal accountability for a situation. Watch for these behaviors: ignoring or denying the problem, "it's-not-my-job" posturing, finger pointing, confusion and "tell-me-what-to-do" statements, cover-your-tail moves, and "wait-and-see" proclamations. These are sure signs that the organization is not achieving its results and that it may be incapable of doing so.

The thing to do in such a situation is to become accountable. The *Steps to Accountability* are *See It*, *Own It*, *Solve It*, and *Do It*, and they are essential to moving *Above the Line* and staying there. These steps are defined by specific behaviors and attitudes that, when applied to specific beliefs and actions, create a *Culture of Accountability*.

Managers are responsible for moving their companies *Above the Line* and keeping them there. Managers must commit themselves to sharpening the ability of people to *See It*, deepening their willingness to *Own It*, empowering them to *Solve It* and supporting them in their efforts to *Do It*. There is one proven way for managers to do this: create experiences that foster beliefs that drive actions that produce results.

Having examined the nature and role of organizational culture in Part One, we turn in Part Two to ways of working with each distinct segment of the culture in order to generate rapid organizational change.

PART TWO
SHIFTING TO A NEW CULTURE

The north and south wind met where the house stood and made it the exact center of the cyclone. The house whirled around two or three times and rose slowly through the air. Dorothy felt as if she were going up in a balloon.

In the middle of a cyclone the air is generally still, but the great pressure on every side of the house raised it up higher and higher, until it was at the very top of the cyclone; and there it remained and was carried miles and miles away.

Hour after hour passed away, and slowly Dorothy got over her fright. At first she had wondered if she would be dashed to pieces when the house fell again; but as the hours passed and nothing terrible happened, she stopped worrying and resolved to wait calmly and see what the future would bring. At last she crawled over the swaying floor to her bed, and lay down upon it. Toto followed and lay down beside her.

In spite of the swaying of the house and the wailing of the wind, Dorothy soon closed her eyes and fell fast asleep.

The Wonderful Wizard of Oz
L. Frank Baum

SHIFTING TO A NEW CULTURE

When managers effectively lead an organization to a new culture, they actually lead people through a series of significant shifts. In the next four chapters we examine each of these shifts.

Management must first identify the results that the organization must achieve. Since we undertake a cultural transition in order to produce new and better results, this represents the logical beginning of the process. The results you must start producing will in part shape the other elements of your culture, people's beliefs, behaviors, and actions. Therefore, you must carefully and thoughtfully define the results that the organization will pursue.

Most organizations have certain actions that they must continue to do on the journey to achieve new results. But to achieve the new results, people in the organization must stop doing certain things and start doing other things. These changes in the way people act will amount to the behavioral shift people must make in order for the cultural transition to occur.

A key insight is that true behavior change will not occur, nor last, without an accompanying change in belief. As you will see, effective leaders manage at the level of people's beliefs. They do so because beliefs dictate actions that produce results. Extinguishing old, negative, worn-out beliefs, that cannot produce positive action, and, equally important, shifting people to new, positive, useful beliefs, stands as the central task of managing culture change.

Experiences determine beliefs and beliefs motivate actions, so ultimately, leaders must create experiences that foster beliefs in people that will work for them in the new culture. We will show you how to change people's beliefs in the organizational context by describing how to shift the experiences people have on the job.

In sum, Part Two reveals the practical steps you can take to, first, identify the shifts that must occur in your organization and, second, to make those shifts happen. To shift people to the new culture, you must shift the four components of the culture—results, actions, beliefs, and experiences. The next four chapters show you how to do this.

CHAPTER THREE

DEFINING RESULTS THAT LEAD TO SUCCESS

There is now but one Wicked Witch left in all this land, and when you can tell me she is dead I will send you back to Kansas.

The Wonderful Wizard of Oz
L. Frank Baum

In *The Wonderful Wizard of Oz* all four characters clearly describe the results that they personally yearn to achieve. Dorothy wants to go home to Kansas. The Tin Woodman wants a brain. The Scarecrow wants a heart. And the cowardly Lion wants courage. The clarity of their individual objectives drives them to work together to get to the Emerald City. But when they arrive at the Emerald City and meet the Wizard of Oz, they find yet another goal to achieve. The Wizard demands that they bring him the broomstick of the Wicked Witch of the West, a feat that he deems impossible. Getting the broom is beyond the ability of any one of the characters, so the absolute need to achieve this result binds them more closely together. Having the result *the group* must achieve clearly defined drives the story forward, generates action, and heightens the interest of readers.

Many companies don't do as good a job of clearly defining results for their employees as L. Frank Baum does for his characters in *The Wonderful Wizard of Oz*. In fact, most successful storytellers give their characters clearer, more motivating targets than most managers give to their living, breathing employees. Storytellers have to give their characters clear, defined, meaningful results because it's the only way to drive the story forward. Clear, defined, meaningful results are also the only way to drive real people forward.

Organizations do not work on their culture for the sake of having a better culture. We've never seen leaders expend effort and resources just because "our culture could be better." A shift to a new culture, particularly to a *Culture of Accountability*, is generally motivated by a changing business environment that makes continued high performance harder to achieve. In addition, in most organizations results achieved in one year become more difficult to attain the next year as the bar is raised and the goals are stretched. Today's business environment demands growth, increased profits, and continual improvement from every company that wants to stay competitive. Frequently, we hear management teams discuss last year's results in terms of this year's requirements with a hint of skepticism.

It *is* harder and it *is* tougher to get results. That's why culture is important.

RESULTS AND THE BUSINESS ENVIRONMENT

A thorough discussion about results calls for examining the context within which those results will be attained. That context is the business environment. Many organizations have found that simply maintaining the same level of achievement becomes harder due to a rapidly changing business environment. It would be the unusual organization, indeed, that could not describe significant shifts in its business environment that have translated into new challenges, and opportunities.

Figure 3-1 provides a listing of some of the changes in the business environment that we have compiled from clients as they have described the shifts they see. This is an aggregate listing from a number of industries.

These changes potentially represent significant shifts that can undermine an organization's ability to achieve results.

To make this applicable to your own organization, check the shifts that apply to your situation. In addition, add the specific shifts you are facing that are not mentioned on the list.

An important question to ask at this point is: Will the current C^1 culture (consisting of A^1, B^1, E^1) produce the right thinking and motivate the needed actions to produce success in this changing environment? If it will not, then you need to define and create C^2. Usually, the more rapidly you can create C^2, the more effective you will be in achieving your desired results in the face of significant environmental shifts.

FIGURE 3–1
OFTEN CITED CHANGES IN BUSINESS ENVIRONMENT

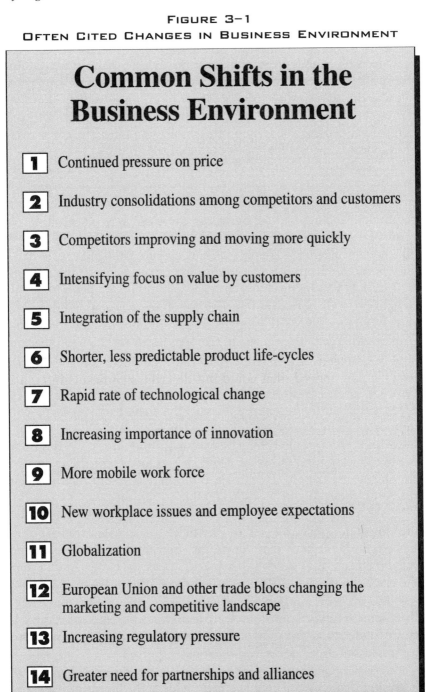

FIGURE 3–1
OFTEN CITED CHANGES IN BUSINESS ENVIRONMENT

Common Shifts in the Business Environment

1 Continued pressure on price

2 Industry consolidations among competitors and customers

3 Competitors improving and moving more quickly

4 Intensifying focus on value by customers

5 Integration of the supply chain

6 Shorter, less predictable product life-cycles

7 Rapid rate of technological change

8 Increasing importance of innovation

9 More mobile work force

10 New workplace issues and employee expectations

11 Globalization

12 European Union and other trade blocs changing the marketing and competitive landscape

13 Increasing regulatory pressure

14 Greater need for partnerships and alliances

START WITH RESULTS

The decision to shift a company to a new culture starts by considering the results you want the company to achieve. You start with results because the organization exists in order to produce results. Therefore, the targeted results should drive the activity, energy, and effort of the company. Focusing squarely on the results you must achieve provides an important context for the needed cultural change.

The Results Pyramid in Figure 1–1 back in Chapter One implies that you cannot superimpose the results you want to achieve, the R^2 results, onto your current, C^1, culture. That is to say, you can't get new results by thinking and acting in the same old way. To produce new results people must shift their thinking and behavior. If you accept the notion that culture is what people think and do, then you realize that to change the results people are producing you must change their culture.

Would you be surprised to learn that although clients engage us to help them get better results, they are often unclear about the results they want to achieve? It happens frequently. For instance, one company we worked with, a growing regional fast-food chain in the southwest United States, had a performance measure they were trying to hit. They needed to achieve a return on total investment of 5.5 percent. Or was it 7.5 percent? Actually it may have been 3 percent. The point is that the divisional president of the chain had not clearly communicated to his senior staff exactly what number they were trying to hit. Mixed messages led to confusion about the target. Confusion led to a lack of focus on the result. And lack of focus sent the team *Below the Line* where they would remain until the leadership clearly defined the result the company was accountable to achieve.

We met with the president of the chain during a break at an off-site meeting and asked him to tell us why there was so much confusion over this target. He told us that the parent company had clearly communicated the result they needed to achieve. In fact, he had been told that if the chain did not achieve the specified target, that they were, indeed, at risk of being sold. Corporate had stated that similar restaurant chains in the parent company's portfolio were achieving the expected return. He clearly understood that if his chain failed to match this return then there was no justification for keeping them in the portfolio.

That seemed pretty clear to us. However, the president had not been sure that his team could actually achieve the number he had been given. He wasn't sure that the team would align themselves around it. He knew that several key players felt corporate expectations were unrealistic. We asked him what he wanted from the team, and he told us that he needed greater accountability and ownership for achieving their numbers, from the restaurant manager down to the busboy. With that in mind, we told him that without clearly defining the results for which the team would be held accountable, the ownership he sought could not occur.

In the course of this conversation, this leader became determined to clearly communicate the results the chain was expected to deliver. Upon returning from the break, he laid things out on the table. Over the next several hours the team got aligned around the result and determined what shifts in their thinking and behavior would be needed if they were to deliver on their commitment. We watched with great interest as this team set out to create this sense of accountability and ownership.

Today, we are told that the chain has progressed at a rate that amazes even themselves. They have improved their return to the corporation by over 200 percent and are now seen as a valuable contributor to the overall success of the corporate portfolio, delivering on the commitment of 7.5 percent. Within the chain itself the "December Meeting" has become an important cultural reference. When someone refers to the "December Meeting" they do so to emphasize the importance of clearly defining results and creating alignment and ownership for the cultural shifts required to achieve results.

In this part of the book, we will explore the mechanisms by which this kind of change takes place. A fundamental dynamic in this process is the sense of alignment that clear results create once they are communicated throughout the organization. The president of this restaurant chain had not clearly communicated the result because he hadn't decided whether the team was up to hearing what it really needed to achieve. This is a common reason for lack of clarity and communication around results. Yet the alignment created by clearly defined results represents a powerful force in organizations.

DEFINING RESULTS THAT GET RESULTS

Keep in mind that the goal of culture change is to shift the way people think and act in order to achieve a new result. Once you define results, you can then identify the actions that will produce those results, the beliefs that will motivate those actions, and the experiences that will foster those beliefs. ("Actions" are the subject of the next chapter, "beliefs" the subject of Chapter Five, and "experiences" the subject of Chapter Six).

Before going further, one point warrants elaboration. We usually use the term "results" rather than "goals" or "objectives" because the word "results" is broader and more inclusive. Most companies define results in terms of sales growth, greater profits, market-share gains, new-product launches, increases in units produced, or other performance measures such as those associated with quality or cost. In addition to quantitative measures, however, results can also include qualitative achievements such as solving a problem, implementing an initiative, or realizing a corporate value, for instance total customer satisfaction.

The word results is also inclusive in the sense that whether your organization achieves a certain goal or not, it is always producing results. Thinking about the results your company produces will broaden your thinking about organizational culture. Just as your company has a culture (whether or not someone thinks it does), that culture is also producing results (whether or not someone thinks it is). The word "goal" often sets up a yes-no, win-lose frame of mind: We either achieved it or we didn't. Results are always being produced, one way or another. The question then becomes: Is your organization producing the results it should be producing?

WHEN DOES A NEW RESULT REQUIRE A SIGNIFICANT SHIFT IN CULTURE?

Our experience suggests that most management teams are working to achieve some set of R^2 results. By definition, a result is considered an R^2 result when the current culture will not produce the thinking and acting necessary to achieve R^2. If it is considered R^2, then a culture change is necessary to achieve it.

The significance of the needed change in culture depends on the degree to which the R^2 result meets the following four criteria:

- Difficulty
- Direction
- Deployment
- Development

1. Difficulty: If the R^2 result is significantly more difficult to achieve than past results, then you more than likely will need significant shifts in at least some aspects of your culture. This increased difficulty may be the result of tougher objectives or similar objectives in a tougher business environment—or tougher objectives in a tougher environment.

2. Direction: If R^2 signals a change in direction for the organization, then this may also require significant cultural change. A change in direction may involve developing new core competencies or applying current ones in new ways to take advantage of a market opportunity. Even an effort to refocus on a reentrenchment in a core competency can require significant change, particularly if that effort involves stopping certain things that may be deeply ingrained in the culture. On the whole, the more different the new direction, the greater the needed change in culture.

3. Deployment: Will the R^2 result require large-scale redeployment of people or other resources? If so, a significant change in at least part of the culture may be necessary. A redeployment of resources from one part of the organization to another, or from one area of focus to another often requires a new way of thinking both for those losing resources and for those gaining them. A significant deployment of resources in the form of an investment may also signal a needed change in culture of some significance.

4. Development: If R^2 demands that the organization develop a new capability, then you are likely to face a significant culture shift. Here, the term organizational capability includes processes, systems, skills, and structure. If any of these require significant development then a cultural shift of some magnitude is likely to be unavoidable.

Of course, a single R^2 result may fit into each of these categories and often will fall into more than one. It may be helpful now for you to examine some of the shifts from R^1 to R^2 that your organization is experiencing. In Figure 3-2 list the key R^1 to R^2 shifts that your group, team, or organization must achieve. Then measure the significance of that shift by considering the four criteria listed above.

FIGURE 3-2
IDENTIFYING YOUR R¹ TO R² SHIFT

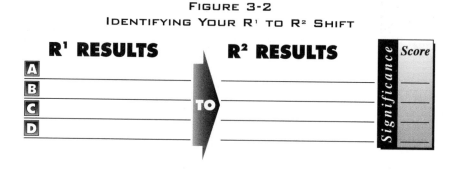

FIGURE 3-2
IDENTIFYING YOUR R¹ TO R² SHIFT

Use the following scale in Figure 3-3 to evaluate the significance of the shift by rating R^2 against the four criteria. Place the letter A, B, C, or D representing the result on each of the four scales that depict the relative significance of the shifts that will be necessary:

FIGURE 3-3
SCORING YOUR SHIFT IN RESULTS

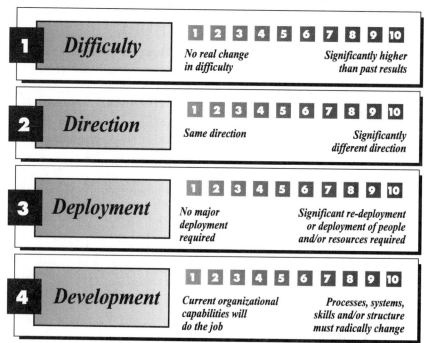

Now, total your points for each result and place the number in the significance score box next to the R^2 result you listed earlier.

A score of 28–40 represents a very significant shift from R^1 to R^2—your culture may need to shift dramatically to achieve R^2.

A score of 16–27 means the shift may be somewhat moderate, but significant enough to suggest the need for a serious effort to bring about cultural change.

A score of 4–15 signals that the needed shift in culture will likely be more isolated and tactical, as opposed to an overarching change for the organization.

You may find it particularly useful to do this analysis with feedback from your group or team. You may discover that you share a common view on how significant the shift from R^1 to R^2 may be. On the other hand, you may learn that there are diverging views as to the organizational challenge R^2 may really pose. In either case, an open discussion leading to alignment on this point is well worth the time invested.

We offer these four criteria—difficulty, direction, deployment, and development—as subjective guidelines to assist you in exploring the significance of the culture change that may be required as you shift to R^2.

RESULTS THAT CREATE ALIGNMENT

Essentially, there are three steps to creating (or keeping) a culture aligned around results:

- Clearly define the targeted result.
- Drive the result throughout the organization.
- Hold people accountable for achieving results, rather than for doing their jobs.

Let's examine each of these steps.

STEP 1: DEFINE RESULTS CLEARLY

"Swing for the fences," the coach instructs the batter. "We expect straight A's from you," Mom tells her daughter. "Take that hill," yells the lieutenant to the platoon. Clear goals create focus. People know what they're working for, and they know whether or not they succeed.

They also develop a sense of what they need to do and a willingness to do what it takes to achieve a clearly defined result.

This holds true regardless of the venture or the venue. Consider a story from the battle of Gettysburg in the Civil War. As the Confederate forces rushed to take the heights behind the town of Gettysburg on the second day of battle, the Union troops moved into position on a strategic hill known as Little Round Top. From this summit, the Confederate forces would have the advantage of a clear field of artillery fire upon the entire Union line. Protecting this key defensive position, and the flank of the Union Army, was Colonel Joshua Lawrence Chamberlain of the 20th Maine.

Having been placed in this position with orders to "hold this position at *all* costs," Colonel Chamberlain and his men repelled numerous attacks as the Confederate troops sought to weaken the flank and capture the summit. After waves of intense fire and aggressive attempts to break the Union line, and facing the seemingly impossible task of holding his position with only half the strength of his initial force and no ammunition, Colonel Chamberlain—a former college professor from Emory University—called for a bayonet charge. He and his men charged in a desperate counterattack that broke the Confederate line.

Chamberlain had the result clearly defined for him: "Hold this position at all costs." And he made it clear to his troops that he was committed to achieving this result. Clear results led to clear action. Everyone in an organization needs to know that "the back door" has been closed for everyone, including management, and that retreat is not an option.

At another well-known international restaurant chain we provided training to create greater accountability in the organization. Upon arriving on the morning of the training, we met with the divisional vice president, who said, "I hope you guys are entertaining because my team was out late last night and they're pretty tired." We chose to not respond directly. Instead we asked him about the result that his team was accountable to deliver by the end of the year. He stated their target rather flippantly and began to explain why they would not achieve it.

As we began the meeting, it was clear that the team was looking to see if their leader was going to let them "off the hook." However, in the course of the meeting the vice president seemed to see that this team, if properly focused, actually could achieve the result. Following the meeting the team, with the leadership of the vice president, became incredibly resourceful in asking what else they could do to achieve the result.

The result that everyone thought to be out of their reach became the target that each of them committed to, beginning with the vice president. They went the extra mile, to the point of canceling landscape contracts and mowing lawns themselves, taking personal accountability for finding every possible way to save money without diminishing customer satisfaction. Not only did they achieve the targeted result, they were the only division in the company to exceed their annual budgeted plan.

In another client company the vice president of sales told us that he didn't believe in targeting numerical results. We found this posture unusual, to say the least, in a sales manager. He told us, "We believe in everyone just doing their best. We just do the very best we can." This may be a laudable sentiment, but in no way does it provide clarity around a targeted result. Nor did it produce results that would have enabled him to keep his job.

Some managers avoid clear results because they believe that murky objectives conceal failure. Actually, murky results create failure. They create failure due to lack of organizational alignment. People know when their organization lacks focus, and without a clear organizational result to strive for, people are forced to pursue their own individual goals. This typically drives them to define success in their own terms, which may be professional ("As long as I hit my quota, I'll be fine.") or personal ("As long as I'm out of here by five o'clock, I'll be fine."). Teamwork evaporates.

Unclear goals also promote cynicism. People are not fooled by managers who avoid setting clear, meaningful goals due to incompetence or a desire to dodge accountability. The tone in an organization is set by those at the top, and if senior management will not commit to producing a certain result then middle management and the rank and file certainly won't. This leadership vacuum contributes to everyone guarding his or her own turf and seeking his or her own rewards, which is antithetical to an effective culture. Companies with effective cultures always target clear results.

STEP 2: DRIVE THE RESULT THROUGHOUT THE COMPANY

At times, management has a clear result in mind but fails to communicate it effectively or completely to everyone in the organization. For an organization to be aligned around a result, everyone must be aware of it and understand it. This may seem unnecessary because, after all, many employees may play only indirect roles in achieving the broader results of the company. Many will have their own targets to achieve, which in turn feed into the broader performance of the organization. However, everyone in the company must know what the company is shooting for, what the CEO is responsible for achieving. If results are going to drive the thinking and behavior of everyone in the organization, everyone must understand the result the organization is attempting to produce.

Many companies fail to communicate results down far enough to affect people's day-to-day thinking and behavior. For instance, a client of ours, a retail food chain on the West Coast, had to achieve certain budgeted annual sales and profit goals. But accountability for those financial results were kept at the store manager level. In no way did they drive that result down below that level, to the supervisors, shift leaders, and employees.

As we worked with the chain's senior and middle management we asked, "If you have accountability for that result only at the store-manager level and above, will you be able to achieve this objective?" The answer was a resounding, "no." To achieve it they knew they needed every employee in the company to be accountable for it. They needed to do something they had never done before. They needed to drive accountability for the result to every level of the organization. Not incidentally, doing this would significantly impact the company's culture.

We are not suggesting a command-and-control approach to driving the result throughout the company. Two-way communication is the best tool for defining results so as to create true alignment. To the extent possible, when you are defining results, take time to gather the views of as many people as you can. This is not just about getting buy-in regarding the result, which is important in and of itself, but is also about getting information from those who will be responsible for getting the result. What's possible? How did we really do last year? What are the barriers to improving our results?

We've all seen organizations fail in their efforts to implement new policies intended to improve performance. We witnessed one company that, in order to reduce costs, enacted a policy of not flying business class to Europe any longer. Sound familiar? The policy stated that coach was adequate for such trips. The policy was perceived to be arbitrary, and people looked for any way to get around it, and get around it they did.

Failure to clearly communicate *why* changes in policy are needed and the expected impact on results almost always ends in weakened or failed implementation. Interestingly, the same company that failed to change the travel policy overwhelming succeeded in another policy change.

Midway through the year this *Fortune* 500 company found themselves behind their targeted pace of financial performance. Being entirely aligned around these financial results, management agreed that a rigorous freeze on all costs should occur and that it needed to occur quickly. Immediately, independent contractors were let go, overseas trips delayed, and magazine subscriptions canceled. They also discontinued using outside consultants throughout the organization. To our surprise, we received calls from people around the world stating that they needed to postpone all scheduled engagements. Though we were on the receiving end of these cost cuts, it was impressive to see the immediate response of the organization at all levels. It was solid. It was fast. And it was done! This disciplined cost reduction at all levels enabled the organization to achieve their year-end result and maintain their growth for the thirty-fifth consecutive year.

What was different about this policy? We were curious, so we asked. In this case, the senior policy committee had stated that there was a dire financial need to reduce costs for the rest of the year in order to achieve their projections. They also explained that they had sought options that would be easiest on the business, including discontinuing all outside training and consulting engagements. In a meeting, senior management had shared the different options and asked for input. It was clear to all attendees that eliminating outside consulting engagements represented one of the highest impact measures in terms of dollars, yet was among the easiest and fastest for the organization to implement. Everyone believed this change made sense. They could understand it, and they could communicate it so that others could understand it.

Unlike the travel policy, which seemed arbitrary, this policy was clearly connected to organizational results. It was well thought out, and key organizational leaders were involved in establishing the policy. These factors enabled this organization to implement this policy with precision and speed. Within a week, the gain was already being realized.

Moreover, various groups within the organization took this as a signal to explore ways to manage the cost of all outside vendors more effectively. As a result, the company has achieved huge reductions in its number of suppliers. For example, they eliminated over 50 engineering companies. They went from 110 suppliers of pipe valves and fittings down to just one. They reduced the number of maintenance contractors from 20 to just three. In manufacturing alone they cut $230 million out of the cost of acquiring goods and services.

This example shows the value of driving the result throughout the company. However, it must be done correctly. Employees sometimes fail to take results seriously and become embittered because managers dictate the achievement of unattainable results. Statements from managers such as, "We are going to achieve this even if it kills you," and "Stop whining," have created legions of cynical workers in the downsized business world of today. To pretend otherwise is unrealistic. To leave the matter unaddressed is poor leadership.

If your employees disagree with the targeted result—particularly if they have been repeatedly asked to produce better results with decreasing resources—their input may help you create more achievable goals. Failing that, at least you can take the opportunity to explain the importance of the result you are targeting, defuse objections, lower barriers, and potentially win them over. Open communication requires no dollar outlay, yet it is the best investment you can make when trying to align your company around results. And honest, two-way communication includes a heavy proportion of listening.

Here's one last example of the importance of creating alignment around the result throughout all levels of the organization. Mike Eagle and the Global Manufacturing group of Eli Lilly and Company proactively established a targeted result to reduce the unit cost by 25 percent over four years while improving their already high level of quality. They communicated the result to everyone within the organization. They discussed the shifts in thinking and acting that needed to take place in order to achieve these results. In the course of these discussions, they identified two major shifts that were necessary: First, they needed to generate widespread accountability for achieving the result, where people constantly asked themselves what else they could do to achieve it. Second, they needed to create and maintain alignment around the stated objectives and timelines.

This global manufacturing organization did create this shift to widespread accountability and alignment throughout their entire organization. During interviews, people told us that a major contributor to their breakthrough performance was the clarity around the result, which people displayed on a daily basis. It's not been quite four years since the organization established these clearly stated results. Here's a snapshot of their scorecard:

1. They achieved a 25 percent reduction in unit costs after just three years and are close to achieving 40 percent today.
2. Their customer service measure has increased from 90 to 97 percent.
3. The proportion of lots manufactured right the first time have gone from 80 to 95 percent.
4. Regulatory compliance rose dramatically and the number of recalls dropped.
5. They have no manufacturing sites anywhere in the world with any significant compliance issue in the eyes of regulatory agencies.
6. Factory losses of material discarded have dropped precipitously.
7. Head count is down by 16 percent, with some 650 people having been redeployed into growth areas of the company.
8. The on-the-job accident rate was cut in half.
9. They have taken 100 days of stock out of inventory.

This is a scorecard worth celebrating. This same manufacturing organization used to be happy limiting cost increases to the rate of inflation. Today they're beating that rate significantly while improving quality. Driving the top-level result—in this case the 25 percent reduction in unit costs—throughout the company brought about this massive change.

Step 3: Get People to Be Accountable for Achieving Results, Not Doing Jobs

Organization charts and job descriptions push people into boxes. They give people the idea that they are getting paid and using their skills to perform a defined function or set of tasks. This can lead people to believe that if they perform their functions they've done what they're supposed to do, whether or not the result was achieved.

Effective leaders operate on the premise that their people *must* focus on achieving the result. Rather than treating the circles shown in Figure 3-4 as mutually exclusive, they manage their people so that their "job" is to achieve the results. The daily activities that comprise people's jobs must then be consistently in alignment with the targeted results.

FIGURE 3-4
A COMMON VIEW: DOING THE JOB
VS. ACHIEVING THE RESULT

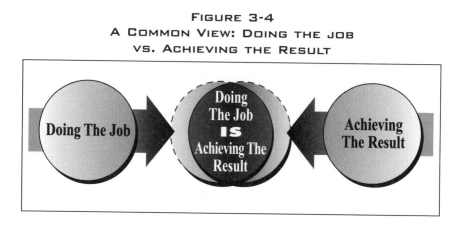

How many times have you heard a leader in real-life or fiction demand: "I don't care how you get it done. Just get it done"? Leaders lead people beyond the boundaries of their jobs and inspire them to relentlessly pursue results by creating an environment that motivates them to ask, "What else can I do?" over and over until the results are achieved. This mind-set can become part of the culture only if people understand the results they are supposed to achieve in the job they are to perform.

Management must also generate joint accountability for results. Joint accountability occurs when everyone in the company assumes accountability for the result. In an environment of joint accountability, it is impossible for anyone even to think, let alone say, that he has done his job if the team has not achieved its targeted result. It is also impossible for anyone to think or say that he or she has achieved his or her individual result if the company has not achieved its result. Joint accountability demands that everyone become accountable for producing the results the company must achieve.

How can leaders use results to create joint accountability? If you have targeted a clear result, if you drive the result though the company, if you hold everyone accountable for achieving the result and not just doing his or her job, won't it just happen? The answer is maybe, maybe not.

WHAT'S MINE—AND YOURS—IS OURS

Often companies define results in a way that drives people into their individual boxes and undermines joint accountability. For instance, a global Fortune 500 company had set revenue and operating income goals for its European operations, and the president of European operations was accountable for those results. In addition, each national affiliate, that is, the French affiliate, the German affiliate, and each of the others, had its own goals for revenue and operating income. The president of each affiliate was accountable only for his or her respective affiliate's results. They were not responsible for one another's revenue or operating income, nor were they accountable for the results of the overall European operation.

The lack of joint accountability on this team surfaced when year-end currency transactions resulted in an operating-income shortfall of some $30 million for European operations. The president of European operations met with the heads of the affiliates and informed them that they were "projecting a revenue shortfall for European operations of about $30 million." He stated that this was due to unforeseen losses on foreign-exchange transactions and asked each of them to go back and find every franc, mark, lira, pound, and so on, that they could contribute so that the European operation would meet its revenue goal.

The response from the affiliate heads was lukewarm. Their entire focus was and always had been on meeting their respective country's individual goals; that was their job. The country managers had never felt accountable for the revenue goals of the European region as a whole. Therefore, no one stepped up. The European president asked them to go back again and see what they could do to enable the region to hit its expected corporate target.

Now these affiliates had long engaged in a practice known within the company as "sandbagging" or "the old-gray-fox syndrome." This occurred when an affiliate would, after meeting the revenue and operating income goal for the period, begin to stow away known sales for the next period just in case the numbers were more difficult to achieve in the coming year.

At a second meeting with the affiliates they discussed barriers to finding the additional sales to make up for the regional shortfall. To a person, everyone believed that if they sacrificed self-interest for the good of the team no one in senior management would remember what they did. This was a particular concern if a country were to fail to meet its goal the following year. It took some discussion, but ultimately they agreed to create a "team memory" of contributions made toward achieving the regional number. The European president stated that if they managed to come up with a contribution against the $30-million shortfall he would personally remember it in the coming year. He also told them that from the next year forward, their compensation would reflect their ability to achieve their country's number *and* the number the European region was accountable to deliver.

One of the affiliate heads had been quite reluctant to come up with additional income. To everyone's surprise, however, by the end of this meeting she "found" $5 million to contribute to making up the shortfall. Once she came up with money, other affiliates rapidly followed. Going forward, joint accountability for European results generated unprecedented teamwork across the affiliates and an aligned commitment throughout the team to assume accountability for achieving the European results.

We have seen too many managers try to rely on the goodwill of their subordinates, rather than work to create joint accountability. It's tempting to think that when the chips are down people will step up for the team. In fact, goodwill is a wonderful thing, and many people bear tremendous amounts of it toward their bosses and fellow managers and employees. However, to rely upon it as a business tactic or to let it take the place of accountability is at best optimistic and at worst irresponsible. Superior leaders focus their people on results, reward them for that focus, and ensure that the work done by individuals and teams is, indeed, the work that will produce the targeted results.

RESULTS AND THE FOUR STEPS TO ACCOUNTABILITY℠

After you define the results you must then create accountability for achieving them. This is where the four *Steps to Accountability—See It, Own It, Solve It,* and *Do It*—come to the fore.

The first two steps are particularly important with regard to results. People must understand and own the current R^1 results of the organization. They must develop a sense of personal ownership for those results, either good or bad. Their ability to tie the results they've produced to what they have or have not done is the single greatest reflection of their level of ownership. They must also understand and own the future, desired R^2 results that the organization needs to achieve. This process begins with the organization's leaders. The leaders must step up and send unmistakable messages to everyone in the company that the current, unsatisfactory R^1 results are indeed the company's current results. They must lead people to see and own these results and hold themselves accountable for them. As you will see in Chapter Six the simple (but not necessarily easy) act of senior management claiming accountability for current and past results creates a powerful, positive experience for a company.

Then the leaders must enable everyone to see and own the future R^2 results. Ideally, the middle and lower levels of management should play a role in defining these future results. In very small companies, so should the employees. As noted, having as many levels as possible involved in defining the results builds buy-in and enables senior management to gather valuable information about what is possible and what is not and about where the culture really stands.

The *Solve It* and *Do It* steps work themselves out more in the realm of actions, which we take up in the next chapter. For now, please recall that *Solve It* and *Do It* demand that each person does whatever it takes (within legal, moral, and ethical boundaries) to achieve the results. The key part of the definition of *Solve It* states that this step involves constantly asking, "What else can I do?" If you have clear results and you have driven those results down and through the organization to create individual and joint accountability for them, you are well on your way to shifting your company to a new, far more effective and productive culture.

THIS PIECE OF THE PYRAMID

Each chapter in Part Two will use this section, titled "This Piece of the Pyramid," to clarify and illustrate the process of cultural transition. This section will focus on the evolution of a cultural transformation that occurred in a company called Cardiac Pacemakers, Inc. (CPI), which we spoke of briefly in Chapter One.

In the late 1980s when Jay Graf became president of CPI, he found a company with a product-development process that was slipping behind schedule by three weeks a month. This is, according to Jay, "another way of saying we got about 12 real weeks of work done every year. We took four steps forward and three steps back."

Jay decided it was most important to shift results in R&D, Manufacturing, QA, and Marketing, the functions he viewed as having shared responsibility for product development. In fact, he saw it as essential. However, there were initially other views among CPI senior management, the most prevalent being that the firm should again obtain new technologies through acquisition or license. To Jay this reflected the prevailing belief that "everything was external as opposed to fixing the engine." Jay believed, "We weren't going to learn how to be competitive if we didn't go through this baptism of fire, this difficult period, and struggle through it ourselves." He believed that going through the work of building a first-rate, on-time product-development effort would turn the company around.

The R^1 results were clear enough: no new products and a new product development function that, based on years of dismal performance, lacked confidence. The future was worse than bleak, particularly given the industry's relentless pace of technological change.

The company culture that Jay found was characterized by meaningless development schedules, with no one agonizing over the slippage. Functional responsibilities for product development, for everything actually, were so widely distributed that it was hard to hold anybody accountable. There were no consequences for failure to achieve results. Despite the company's performance, people were never demoted or fired. Managers rarely did performance appraisals, nor did they confront performance problems.

To get any of this to shift, Jay had to get results, the R^1 and R^2 results, on the table. For starters, he had to disabuse people of the notion that CPI would succeed in the long run by acquiring and licensing technology. Acquiring technology has its place, but when you are losing money, missing the market, and watching your product development efforts fall apart, *and* you're relying on what Jay called "the heroin fix of the next acquisition," then the tactic is not working. So the major R^2 result required was a product-development effort that could make and keep the company competitive. Getting aligned around this result involved a focus on other results as well, including sales and earnings targets and market leadership.

We will explore the details of the cultural changes—changes in actions, beliefs, and experiences—that this entailed in the next three chapters. For now, please note that at the outset the culture was marked by "functions kind of holding camp against one another," according to Jay. This undermined the cross-functional effort and communication that product development demands. There was also an underdeveloped work ethic, a lack of energy, no commitment to meeting deadlines, and no consequences for poor performance or, more important, recognition of good performance. All of this had to change if CPI were to succeed in the future. The major goal was to build a product-development effort, but because of the cross-functional nature of product development and the pervasiveness of the ineffective culture, the entire company had to shift to a new culture in order to get that result.

The table in Figure 3–5 lists the major R^1 and R^2 results that CPI had to shift from and to in order to succeed:

FIGURE 3-5
THE SHIFT IN RESULTS AT CARDIAC PACEMAKERS, INC.

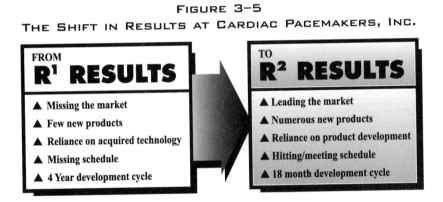

FROM **R^1 RESULTS**	TO **R^2 RESULTS**
▲ Missing the market	▲ Leading the market
▲ Few new products	▲ Numerous new products
▲ Reliance on acquired technology	▲ Reliance on product development
▲ Missing schedule	▲ Hitting/meeting schedule
▲ 4 Year development cycle	▲ 18 month development cycle

Our clients have found that charting the shifts that their companies must undergo in this manner, even if those changes are not as radical or encompassing as those needed at CPI, can be extremely useful. Charting the necessary shift in results always reveals the need to shift the way people think and act in order to achieve those R^2 results.

MILESTONES ALONG THE YELLOW BRICK ROAD

In this opening chapter of Part Two we begin at the logical starting point for a culture change: the result that you want your company to achieve. The future R^2 results that you define will shape the organization, particularly when the organization becomes aligned around those results. This does not happen automatically, however. You must work to get your people aligned around the company's targeted results. This represents an essential leadership skill, because the more strongly aligned people are around a result, the more likely they are to achieve it. (Again, we devote Chapter Eight to the task of creating alignment.)

Determining when a new R^2 result will require a significant shift in culture is largely a function of the degree of Difficulty the new result presents, the change in Direction it defines, the extent of resource Deployment it necessitates, and the amount of Development of organizational capabilities it demands. Understanding the significance of the culture change required to achieve R^2 is an important early step in the transition.

When beginning the shift from your current, C^1, culture to your future, C^2, culture you must:

- Clearly define the targeted result
- Drive the result throughout the organization
- Hold people accountable for achieving results, not for doing their jobs

If you do these three things and actively foster joint accountability, you will have taken the first step toward creating a *Culture of Accountability*. Remember that in an environment of joint accountability no one can say or think that they have achieved their result unless all the participants have achieved their result. Nobody wins unless everyone wins. In a *Culture of Accountability*, everyone holds everyone accountable for all results.

CHAPTER FOUR

GENERATING ACTION THAT GETS RESULTS

*We must journey on until we find the road of yellow brick again,
and then we can keep on to the Emerald City.*

The Wonderful Wizard of Oz
L. Frank Baum

Until Dorothy comes along, her new friends find their actions and efforts unproductive in helping them to achieve the wish of their hearts. The Scarecrow was literally stuck, unable to move forward and progress, wishing he had a brain. The Tin Woodman was frozen in place, unable to act until a bit of machine oil helped him get moving again. The Lion spent his time trying to do something that he really didn't believe in—jumping out from behind trees to scare passers-by. What a waste. Once Dorothy gets this group focused and helps each of them see what he needs to do differently they are able to create action that produces results.

The single greatest management task is, and probably always will be, getting people to take the right action on the job. That's because management is, by definition, the art and science of getting things done through others. To get things done through others, you must get them to take action, specifically, action that will produce the desired results for the organization. This cannot, particularly in today's environment and with today's workers, be done by command and control—issuing orders and edicts that "tell people what to do" rather than engaging their hearts and minds in fulfilling the purpose of the organization. Business has become too complex and workers have become too independent for that to work. Yet the definition of management remains the same: getting things done through others.

Effective managers recognize that the organization's culture sends signals to its people on how to act. They understand that action, focused action, doing-the-right-things-at-the-right-time kind of action, produces results. They also understand that the culture (the whole pyramid) drives actions. You can't pay attention to the culture without paying attention to actions.

YOU WANT TO GENERATE ACTION, NOT MOTION

Ernest Hemingway said never to mistake motion for action. Motion is movement, and in this context movement for its own sake. Think of some of the more ineffective programs, efforts, initiatives, and meetings that you have been part of in your career. That's what we mean by motion. Although we are defining it as ineffective, motion can be soothing. It can even give the appearance that something is being accomplished when nothing really is. Motion produces activity. Action produces results. An important question faced by every organization seeking to accelerate cultural transition is, Where and to what extent does our culture drive motion rather than action?

The distinction between motion and action underscores the need to have people assume accountability for producing results rather than for performing their function. Performing a function or "doing a job" all too often amounts to nothing more than motion when what is needed is action. Action is focused on results—the desired results—not on activities.

Here's an example of motion as opposed to action: We worked with a U.S. grocery chain whose management was committed to a strategy of total customer satisfaction. Reasoning that satisfied customers would keep returning to the store and that the chain's reputation would spread by positive word of mouth, their growth strategy hinged on becoming known as *the* store for customer service and wide selection. Notwithstanding an all-out focus by management on customer service, growth was not materializing. Management suspected that the reason lay somewhere in the stores.

When we interviewed the store managers and department heads, we found them to be extremely dedicated, hard-working individuals. And yet they were utterly frustrated by management's so-called focus on customer satisfaction. During our interviews we learned that the store and department managers were receiving mixed messages on a daily basis. One department head told us that he had been visited by three different company managers—the district meat manager, the district manager, and the regional manager—all in one day. He told us that he didn't have a problem with the number of visits. What troubled him was that each of these company managers had delivered completely different messages about how to arrange products for display. After each of the respective managers left the store, the department head would obediently rearrange the display of his products to conform to the instructions he had just received. After his third and last visit of the day, the department head threw up his hands and decided that the only way to win was to forget about satisfying the customer and instead focus on pleasing the "last manager from headquarters who came through the door."

Actually, he and other store managers got really smart about this: They started to focus on pleasing the *next* manager to come through the door. Immediately after a store got a visit from someone from headquarters, they would call the next store in the area to alert them about who was coming and what the orders of the day would be. The manager at the next store would then scurry around to arrange things in a way that would get the best possible reviews from that manager who was on her way to visit.

All of this energy in the stores was directed toward pleasing management rather than pleasing the customer. Motion rather than action. There's something else about motion: In addition to being useless, it is far more exhausting than action. Flailing about misdirects energy, wastes time, and—since it fails to get results—breeds frustration. In our example, the store managers felt powerless to use their ideas and observations regarding customer responses to their displays. Instead, they thought more about doing what they were told than about ways of generating sales and satisfying customers. They were particularly frustrated that they were held accountable for sales from their displays but were not given freedom to try their methods for generating those sales. When asked why their sales were not growing at the targeted pace, several of them told us, "I just did what I was told to do."

Senior management did not, of course, set out to create all this "motion." Actually, they had thought they were communicating the importance of pleasing customers with their "all-hands-on-deck" approach that put company managers out in the stores to help create satisfaction and sales. Yet their uncoordinated, overly involved approach sent the wrong message and motivated the wrong action at the expense of taking personal ownership for driving sales.

This example highlights the importance of directing people toward the right actions when you want to shift the culture. It is not enough to announce the new result, "We want satisfied customers, customers who return repeatedly and enjoy shopping here so much that they tell their friends and neighbors." Nor is it enough for management to be on board, even for them to be out in the trenches trying to get everyone to take action. Granted, over time motion will often produce results. But action, not motion, accelerates transition and purposefully impacts performance.

Knowing Is Not Necessarily Doing

Every company we have worked with over the past decade has had within it a resource of knowledge residing in its people regarding what is "working" and "not working" in the organization. We have spent countless hours interviewing and surveying thousands of people in these organizations who typically have no trouble telling us what is effective and ineffective about the way people operate, what they do that gets in the way of getting results and what they do that fosters achievement.

From time to time we are asked by leaders, "If my people know how to act differently in order to be more effective, then why don't they do it?" One answer is culture, and culture is more easily seen in the actions of others than in oneself. While people may be able to describe the actions that need to change in order for the company to be more effective, they are personally restrained from shifting their own actions by "cultural handcuffs" placed upon them by their environment. Getting people to change the way they act and to become more effective is most quickly achieved when a leader begins to manage culture by working with the whole team using the entire pyramid.

For example, one of our clients was implementing SAP (a systems integration process) on a global scale within their manufacturing organization. Installing a fully integrated operating system that serves several parts of the organization is no small task. Everyone knew that an integrated system would carry with it both pluses and minuses. They also knew that implementing a system of this magnitude would require a commitment of local resources at manufacturing sites around the world. Concerned about an already heavy load of initiatives, cost objectives, and new-product launches, many of the local plant-management teams resisted and resented the decision to implement SAP, as well as the schedule for implementation. They were used to fulfilling the needs of their plant. Now they were being asked to share greater accountability for the corporate good and to give up resources that might affect their ability to perform in exchange for a system that might not be of much greater benefit to their particular situation.

Of course, as they pointed out to their management when asked, nothing about their culture reinforced a shift in the required thinking or acting. Their "scorecard" and bonuses focused solely on their plant's performance, and none of their counterparts was visibly willing to support the new direction—and no one wanted to be the one to "go first." While the plant managers could describe how they would need to act differently in order for the organization to *really* shift to a new way of doing business, the C^1 culture constrained the new actions needed to make it all work. Clearly, in this case, *knowing* was not *doing* for the plant managers, and SAP was doomed to failure unless people quickly began to act differently.

Going back to our Cultural Transition model, which we introduced in Chapter One, if you are not producing the right results, or if the new results will prove significantly more difficult to achieve, then you have to shift from the current C^1 "way we do things around here" to a new C^2 way of doing things. To move the culture from C^1 to C^2, you must shift people from A^1 to A^2 actions. While some of the A^1 actions will continue to be important in the C^2 culture, some will need to disappear. In addition, the new culture will require some entirely new actions.

An important step in achieving the shift from C^1 to C^2 is identifying what new, A^2, actions people will need to adopt. In essence, you must analyze and evaluate the actions taken at every level of the organization, with particular emphasis on actions currently taken by the management. Note that "the organization" may be a department, a division, a product team, or a company. Whatever the size of the organization, the senior management team must, in a collaborative way, decide which actions must stop, which should start, and which should continue.

STOP, START, AND CONTINUE

Accelerating a shift in the way people act requires a clear understanding of what you need to stop doing, what you need to start doing, and what you need to keep doing. The following exercise will show you how to go about this.

Directions:

1. Start with your top two targeted results clearly in mind. These results will be the R^2 results that you need to achieve—the new results that require a new way of thinking. You can use the following table in Figure 4-1 as you complete this particular exercise.

2. List the actions you see people taking that get in the way of getting the result. These are things people should stop doing.

3. Think of the actions people aren't taking now, but that would lead to achieving the result if they were to take them. You may want to consider the actions defining each *Step to Accountability* listed in Chapter 2 as you think about this. Record these as actions people should start doing.

4. Determine key actions that people now take that are central to success and must be continued. List these as actions that people should continue doing. Don't limit yourself by how hard it may be to start or stop something. If the action is needed or if it is undesired, then go ahead and list it.

This brief exercise will help you to begin to identify the actions and behaviors that you need in C^2. Consider what would happen if you were able to generate the actions you described in the following table. How would they affect your ability to achieve the two R^2 results you listed? Now consider how your ability to achieve R^2 results will be impacted if you cannot generate the listed actions in your organization. If people continue to operate the way they do now, how will it affect your ability to achieve the needed results? One additional question worthy of consideration is the extent to which you will create a competitive and organizational advantage if you can get people living

FIGURE 4-1
YOUR STOP/START/CONTINUE ANALYSIS

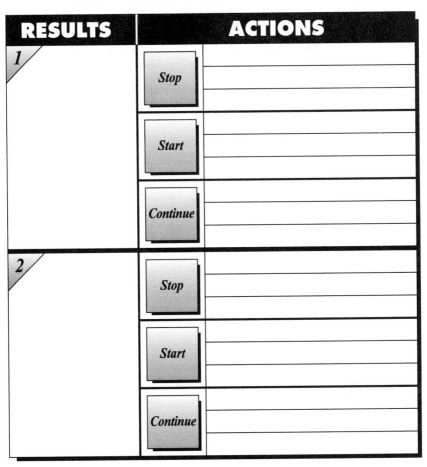

the A² actions right away. *Accelerating* the shift to these desired *behaviors* and *actions* is the aim of the journey to the Emerald City.

WHAT ARE WE DOING?

Let's examine some cases in which clients of ours went through the process of identifying the actions that they should stop, start, and continue. Figures 4-2 and 4-3 provide examples of two companies' major findings regarding actions after this assessment, plus thoughts about new actions needed to produce the targeted results.

FIGURE 4-2
ONE COMPANY'S STOP/START/CONTINUE ANALYSIS

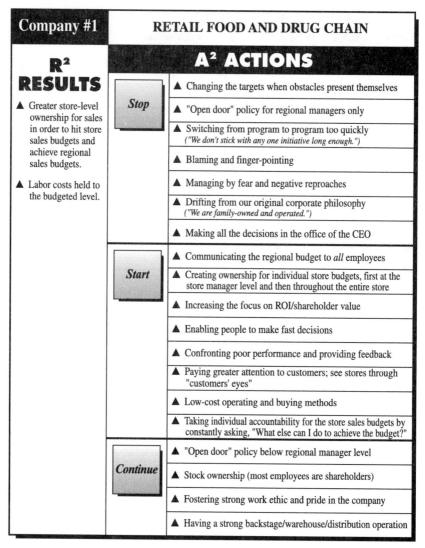

Company #1	RETAIL FOOD AND DRUG CHAIN

R² RESULTS	A² ACTIONS
▲ Greater store-level ownership for sales in order to hit store sales budgets and achieve regional sales budgets. ▲ Labor costs held to the budgeted level.	**Stop** ▲ Changing the targets when obstacles present themselves ▲ "Open door" policy for regional managers only ▲ Switching from program to program too quickly *("We don't stick with any one initiative long enough.")* ▲ Blaming and finger-pointing ▲ Managing by fear and negative reproaches ▲ Drifting from our original corporate philosophy *("We are family-owned and operated.")* ▲ Making all the decisions in the office of the CEO
	Start ▲ Communicating the regional budget to *all* employees ▲ Creating ownership for individual store budgets, first at the store manager level and then throughout the entire store ▲ Increasing the focus on ROI/shareholder value ▲ Enabling people to make fast decisions ▲ Confronting poor performance and providing feedback ▲ Paying greater attention to customers; see stores through "customers' eyes" ▲ Low-cost operating and buying methods ▲ Taking individual accountability for the store sales budgets by constantly asking, "What else can I do to achieve the budget?"
	Continue ▲ "Open door" policy below regional manager level ▲ Stock ownership (most employees are shareholders) ▲ Fostering strong work ethic and pride in the company ▲ Having a strong backstage/warehouse/distribution operation

In creating this listing, three levels of management were involved in an open, candid dialogue regarding the needed shift to a C^2 culture. Their start/stop/continue analysis began to describe the shift from C^1 to C^2 in the context of desired results. It is this context that makes *these* particular actions so relevant: They are specific to a particular result or set of results.

Here's a second example:

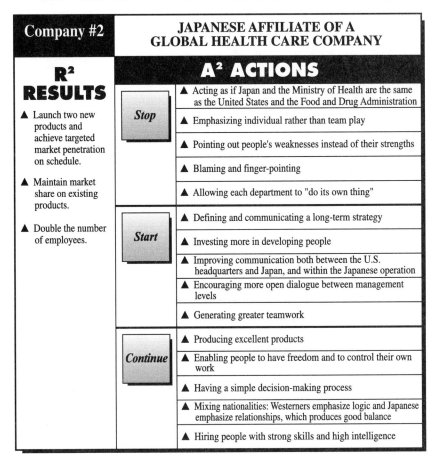

FIGURE 4-3
ONE COMPANY'S STOP/START/CONTINUE ANALYSIS

Company #2	JAPANESE AFFILIATE OF A GLOBAL HEALTH CARE COMPANY	
R² RESULTS	**A² ACTIONS**	
▲ Launch two new products and achieve targeted market penetration on schedule.	*Stop*	▲ Acting as if Japan and the Ministry of Health are the same as the United States and the Food and Drug Administration
		▲ Emphasizing individual rather than team play
		▲ Pointing out people's weaknesses instead of their strengths
▲ Maintain market share on existing products.		▲ Blaming and finger-pointing
		▲ Allowing each department to "do its own thing"
▲ Double the number of employees.	*Start*	▲ Defining and communicating a long-term strategy
		▲ Investing more in developing people
		▲ Improving communication both between the U.S. headquarters and Japan, and within the Japanese operation
		▲ Encouraging more open dialogue between management levels
		▲ Generating greater teamwork
	Continue	▲ Producing excellent products
		▲ Enabling people to have freedom and to control their own work
		▲ Having a simple decision-making process
		▲ Mixing nationalities: Westerners emphasize logic and Japanese emphasize relationships, which produces good balance
		▲ Hiring people with strong skills and high intelligence

This second example underscores something we have noticed in our work in Europe and Asia. Although distance and a mix of nationalities can exacerbate communication problems, organizations' cultural problems tend to be remarkably similar across national borders. Blaming and finger-pointing come up repeatedly, as does the need to improve teamwork, communication, accountability, and cross-functional interactions. The problems of organizational culture are largely rooted in human nature rather than in the business practices or national character of any given country. While there are obviously cultural differences among countries and societies that affect the work environment to an extent, people are people. We hear managers in Ireland, Brazil, Japan, France, England, Spain, Germany, Italy, and Puerto Rico commonly describe similar behavioral changes that would increase effectiveness. This is particularly true when the organization is part of a multinational company.

A WORD OF CAUTION

It is tempting for a management team to think that they can list what people should stop doing, start doing, and continue doing and feel that they have achieved a level of definition necessary to enact a culture change. Clearly, the listing that management derives is a good start. But while that initial effort provides an overall context, the goal is for management to create an environment in which people at all levels ask themselves, "What should *I* stop, start, and continue doing given the results we are seeking?" The culture that management creates will signal their correct answers.

By involving people in the process, you create ownership for the necessary actions. You also get a better list of actions. Who could better answer the question about what behaviors should be different than those who do them every day? By involving people in defining actions, you also create organizational capability: You teach others how to analyze what they are doing in light of the results that you are working to achieve.

The initial efforts of the management team to define A^2 are essential to making the change. This is, however, the starting point, not the end point. Engaging everyone else in this process at all levels of the organization is equally important to the *acceleration* process.

MAKING THE CONNECTION: ACTIONS AND RESULTS

The whole point of shifting culture is getting people to act in a new desired way. When people in organizations act differently in the context of C^2, they will achieve R^2 results. We are talking about true behavior change—real change in the way people do things, not a cosmetic shift but actual, permanent adjustments in the way people do things. This is why it is so important to talk about culture when you talk about behaviors and actions. Institutionalizing a new way of doing things *is* shifting culture. The cultural change makes the behavior change lasting and consistent over time. It's the culture that motivates, reminds, signals, suggests, dictates, and reinforces "the way we do things around here" today as opposed to times past. It is the new actions taken in the context of the new culture that produce new results.

Thus after announcing new results that are to be achieved, management must clearly, although broadly, describe the kinds of actions that will achieve the results. Earlier we noted that knowing is not necessarily doing, that people can know what to do and yet be hampered from doing it by the organizational culture. In some cases, however, they may not even know which actions will achieve the result, even when opportunities to take the right action abound.

Here's an example in which people failed to shift their actions although they clearly knew the result they had to achieve:

A plant manufacturing bulk materials had targeted a maximum of five OSHA (Occupational Safety and Health Administration) recordable accidents a year. This result was one of the bonus criteria affecting supervisor levels and above, and everyone had committed themselves to achieving it. The goal was reviewed in most meetings, posted on signs throughout the plant, and even printed on the reverse side of the employee badge that hung around the neck of everyone on the site.

Within the plant were two large tanks that were separated by only ten feet or so. Between these tanks ran a pipe that carried water to each of the tanks. The pipe crossed over the pathway between the tanks, which were situated so that the pathway was a primary access point to one portion of the plant site, and people regularly would walk through this area. For some time, this pipe had been leaking a small dribble of water. In fact, during the time that the leak existed, there may have been some 30,000 passes—100 people-passes a day for 300 days during the year.

However, people would walk through the pathway and do nothing about the leak. There were people with wrenches, people with the ability to have someone "do something about it," but no one did anything. As a result, spring turned to summer, summer to fall, and fall to winter, and the leak was still there. With the onset of winter, this little leak formed a pool of water that turned to ice. And this pool of ice, sitting in the midst of the pathway, became a safety hazard that eventually led to an injury, thus becoming an OSHA-recordable accident.

Here, people's actions were not consistent with the desired result. Everyone knew what the targeted result was. Everyone bought into the result as being a good idea, or so they said until it affected their own actions. But the organizational culture was such that the actions necessary to achieve the result were not performed. They failed to make the connection between actions and results.

In this example, management's role is to create a dialogue that helps people describe for themselves what actions are needed. This also includes the leadership specifying, broadly but with specific examples, the actions that people should take that would create the desired result. Once this process begins, people catch the "spirit" of the effort and find ways to remind one another about what they are trying to accomplish. For instance, signs such as "If It's Broken, Report It Now!" or "Stop Leaks at First Sight" might have been posted as people became focused on making sure they *got* the result.

The entire issue of creating and managing diversity in organizations represents another instance in which people need to consciously develop the specific actions they must take in order to produce the desired results. One large organization we know of worked hard to create a diverse organization, but they failed. The problem was that people in the company saw the issue of diversity as an organizational problem, not as a personal problem. Although they believed in the benefits and fairness of diversity and felt something should be done about it, they never assumed deep personal ownership for creating diversity in the company.

Had management ensured that people were engaged in the process of describing the kinds of actions they could take to help create diversity, they might have fostered the necessary sense of ownership. People had to assume accountability for *doing* the things that create diversity, such as recruiting in new channels, placing employment advertising in media that reach groups that would make the workplace more diverse, becoming comfortable with new kinds of people, and coaching minority applicants and employees on how to maneuver within the organization. These actions, and not just a conceptual commitment to the organizational goal of diversity, are necessary to create a diverse corporate culture.

When people know *what* actions to take to create a result, they see a clear link between their actions and that result. Many employees, particularly rank-and-file employees, see themselves as unable to move the company toward the results it's pursuing. For instance, the company may target a certain level of sales growth or profitability. The employees may even believe that achieving this result would be a good thing. But how can the actions of one employee contribute to the achievement of that result?

Retailing giant Sears Roebuck and Company explicitly addressed this problem. As reported in the October, 13, 1997, issue of *Fortune* magazine, in 1994 the company began training employees to understand two levels of information: First, according to chief learning officer Anthony Rucci, workers were trained in "economic literacy" so that they would understand the goals of the business. Second, management helped every employee understand what he or she could do to help achieve those results.

Initially, management was surprised at employees' misunderstanding of the company's business and goals. Rucci points out that in meetings with workers, "I would ask, 'How much profit do you suppose Sears keeps on every dollar of revenue?' The median response was 45 cents after tax." At the time, Sears' profit was 1.7 percent. Rucci concluded, "We have an economic literacy problem here. That's management's fault."

The necessary training in economic literacy was not a full-scale program in finance, but short presentations focused at the operational level. For instance, management told workers about trends in retailing and in customers' lives and shopping patterns. They also focused on Sears' internally tracked customer-satisfaction ratings, which had been poor. This first part of the training culminated in what employees could do to impact the results: increase customer satisfaction.

The second part of the training focused on the actions that employees could take every day to increase customer satisfaction. This behavioral component of the training covered providing service, being friendly, exhibiting courtesy, displaying product knowledge, and resolving problems. These were things employees could do to increase customer satisfaction, which in turn would help the company reach its newly articulated goal of becoming a "compelling place to shop, work, and invest" and increasing profits.

Sears' management went to considerable effort and expense to help people understand both the result and the actions that would create the result to connect the two. Has it paid off? Rucci points out that net margin increased from 1.7 to 3.3 percent, which, although short of where the company wants to be, represents the right trend in that it nearly doubled. As to customer service, internally tracked ratings improved and, moreover, *Fortune*'s survey of customer service earlier that year revealed that Sears showed the fifth highest improvement among 206 companies.

ACTIONS THAT WORK

It is not necessary to create an exhaustive list of A^2 actions for people. Once engaged, they will determine these on their own. Instead, provide several specific actions as examples of the needed shift. Aside from being specific without being exhaustive, we suggest you consider the following criteria when defining A^2 actions for both yourself and for the organization:

- Results-oriented
- Realistic
- Recognizable
- Real-time

Results-oriented actions are those that are connected with the result in a meaningful, cause-and-effect manner. When testing for this criterion, apply an "if . . . then" logic. If we take this action, then this will be the result—and that is the result we are trying to achieve. This test will enable you to quickly see whether the action in question is results-oriented. If employees take this action and get a different result (or no result), it is not results-oriented. In other words, they were wrong about this action and need a different one in order to get the result.

Realistic actions are those that are connected to the level, skills, and ability of the leader, manager, or employee. When we talk about changing behaviors we are not usually dealing with anything monumental. When monumental change occurs in an organization, it typically occurs because people have made numerous small changes in their behavior—they may begin to say what they think, to listen more carefully to feedback, or to proactively seek the perspectives of others.

Recognizable actions are those that are observably different from what people were doing before. Change means doing things differently. Therefore, the new actions and behaviors should be recognizable as different and should be readily distinguishable from what people had been doing. In fact, to shift to a new organizational culture, there must clearly be a new version of "the way we *do* things around here."

Real-time specifies the action as something people can do today, rather than something they may hope to do at some time in the future. No one will ever have "change company's culture" on his or her "To Do" list. People need things on their lists that they can do that day, that week, or that month that will contribute to the results the company is committed achieve. Culture change must find its way into the meetings and tasks that already exist on people's "To Do" lists. That is why it is so important to enroll everyone in understanding and describing what A^2 looks like for them. A "tell-me-what-to-do" environment or a "command-and-control" approach to culture change will fail to inspire the commitment and energy needed to bring about *real* change.

Here are some quick examples of useful actions from the extremely competitive world of sales. A *Fortune* 500 client of ours has created a *Culture of Accountability*, particularly in their sales function and, as a result, their salespeople took the following actions (among others) to produce results:

- After getting new territory assigned to him, sales representative Scott Olsen approached a physician who was using Diatrol on only 5 percent of his diabetic patients. (The names of the salesperson and medication have been changed to preserve client confidentiality.) As a new rep to the area, Scott had little rapport with this physician, who believed that Diatrol causes significant weight gain and therefore rarely prescribed it. Scott had to take action to alter this impression. He did this by learning that, although this physician was, at 70 years of age, among the oldest he called upon, he was aggressive in his treatment strategies, closely followed new developments in medicine, and loved to read. Every time he called on this physician, Scott either left a copy of a study that showed the benefits of Diatrol or discussed the previous study he had left. By meeting this physician's needs, answering his questions, and showing a genuine interest in his practice rather than just "pushing pills," Scott won him over. This physician's use of Diatrol has grown to 25 percent, at the expense of competitors' shares.

- Sales rep Mary McKeon faced a situation at a large medical group in which sales representatives were not given face-to-face time with physicians except at a once-a-year lunch. This wasn't enough time. She needed to convince this group that regular meetings would be valuable for the physicians. Through the medical group's office manager, Mary coordinated a meeting with a sister company (owned by the same parent) in which an expert on a medical topic would speak to the physicians at a scheduled lunch-time meeting. Given this, the physicians made time for the meeting. The reps from the two companies had an opportunity to distribute information and answer questions about medications relating to the subject of the presentation. Similar meetings are planned for the future. Mary points out, "We've set an innovative, popular precedent in a previously no-see account."

- Ingrid Selleman, another sales rep, usually does not call on oncologists but received a call from one from The City of Hope, a premiere cancer-research institute in Los Angeles. This oncologist had gotten Ingrid's name from the hospital pharmacy and called her to try to get a particular antidepressant for a patient who had lost her job and health insurance and could no longer afford to pay for her medication. Ingrid wanted that physician to know that her company was patient-oriented and willing to go the extra mile, so she put together a care package for the patient that included a month's supply of the antidepressant and a patient diary and delivered it to the very pleased physician the next day. Ingrid points out, however, that the success did not stop there: "I received a message on my answering machine from that patient that brought tears to my eyes [because it meant so much to the patient to have her depression lifted]. This reminded me of the true meaning of the work I do."

None of these actions are sweeping, revolutionary or "Big Picture." But they are the sum and substance of true cultural transition in which changes in action find their way into the meetings and tasks that define the work day. They are things that people do, not because they are told to do them, or because someone is checking up on them, or even because they are going to be rewarded directly and immediately for doing them. These sales reps did these things because they believed that taking these actions was the right thing to do for the company and its customers.

USING THE STEPS TO ACCOUNTABILITY℠ WITH ACTIONS

To identify the actions that your organization is currently engaged in, to discover what's working and what isn't, you must *See It* and *Own It*. In order to learn what actions your organization should start and continue in order to make the shift to a *Culture of Accountability* and to produce the desired results, you must *Solve It* and *Do It*.

Some organizations "groove" certain behaviors into their culture to the point that they believe they cannot really change them. In fact, many may not even see these actions for what they are—simple behavior patterns. They may believe that they are intrinsic to the business: "We can't change that. That's the way we've always done it." Long-standing reasons or excuses can also be seen as barriers to changing a set of actions. "We don't have money for training, and in any case the only way to learn this business is by doing it." In such situations—in any situation involving changes in organizational behavior—all four *Steps to Accountability* are important.

Managers and employees must *See It* by getting the perspectives of others on what's working and what isn't. They must communicate openly and candidly and ask for and accept feedback and hear the things that are hard to hear about which actions must stop, start, and continue. And they must be able to see the change they personally must make.

They must *Own It* by being personally invested in their actions and in those of the organization and by acknowledging their involvement. It is tempting when a useless or negative behavior is identified to try to avoid any association with it. If it is happening in the organization, however, everyone is accountable to some degree.

Ownership of actions extends to creating alignment between actions, results, beliefs, and experiences and, ultimately, to each person committing to undertake the actions that the organization commits to and not holding back. Unless people own the shifts personally, change will not happen.

Remember the key part of the definition of *Solve It?* It is to ask continually, "What else can I do?" That question is key in defining the actions necessary to produce the result before you begin the shift to a new culture. And it is key to actually achieving the result as you move into and then function in the new culture. To ask, and then answer, that question is the essence of taking positive action and avoiding useless motion. You also *Solve It* as you consider the actions necessary to actively redefine boundaries, deal creatively with obstacles, and stay focused on results.

Finally, *Do It* means taking action. It means that all your people must do the things they say they will do. It means reporting proactively, following up relentlessly, and measuring progress toward the result as you act.

The scorecard for the *Steps to Accountability* we introduced in Chapter Two can be a valuable tool for people in any organization shifting from a current, A^1, set of actions to new, A^2, actions. Those four steps and the 16 attributes that make up their four-part definitions provide a constant guide and ready measure of how people are doing individually and as a group in making this shift.

What About Backsliding?

Behaviors do not change overnight. Some people will be able to comprehend the new set of behaviors and execute the necessary actions more quickly than others. Yet even those who fully embrace the need to act differently will backslide from time to time.

Backsliding can often be traced to vestiges of the old C^1 culture that persist in the new culture. This persistence will be strongest when a true culture change is not attempted, yet some features of the C^1 culture will hang on even when you are trying to shift a culture completely. These vestiges of old behavior represent a barrier to culture change. Leaders work hard to deal with C^1 actions effectively, using feedback (which we will examine in Chapter 7) as a key means of eradicating old behaviors. For now, please know that the more you use the right tools, and the more effectively you use them, the farther and more surely you will be able to shift your company's culture.

We contend that the single most effective way to get people to change the way they act is to change the way they think. As we said in Chapter 1, when leaders work only with the top of the pyramid—results and actions—they are limiting their ability to achieve the fundamental change in "the way things are done" necessary to achieve results.

How many times have you seen the program-of-the-month come along and have no lasting impact on what people do? Accelerating culture change demands that you work with all levels of the pyramid simultaneously, and in sequence (which we discuss in Chapter 10). Attempts to work at *only* the action level usually fall far short of the intended impact. It's just not enough to work only on *what* people do, you also have to work on *why* they do it.

Culture is what people think and do, their beliefs and behavior, and our years as management and leadership consultants have continually reinforced the following idea. If you change the way people think, you will change the way they act. If you change someone's beliefs, you will change their behavior. We examine beliefs and how to change them in the next chapter.

THIS PIECE OF THE PYRAMID: THE CONTINUING CASE OF CPI

At the end of Chapter Three, we left Jay Graf of Cardiac Pacemakers, Inc., with a new set of R^2 results that CPI needed to achieve and a new set of C^2 cultural characteristics that the company needed to adopt if it were to become the worldwide market leader in cardiac-rhythm management. Next, CPI needed to define the actions that it should stop, start, and continue in order to get those results. The company needed to define the shift in actions that needed to occur if CPI were to produce different results.

They needed to ask, what actions were going to get CPI back on track?

Most fundamentally, Jay had to make product development the top priority and get people to see product-development activities as the ones that would enable CPI to move forward. He got the rest of management's agreement that "there aren't going to be any more acquisitions; we are going to dig out of this hole on our own." Looking toward the next acquisition had seemingly enabled people to avoid accountability for the state of product development at the company.

To improve alignment and communication, Jay and others in management realized that they would need to act differently as a management team and to hold regular meetings in which the targeted results, assigned tasks, schedule status, and progress toward results were openly discussed. They also had to share financial information, which had been held close to the vest, much more openly. Jay knew that people needed to be rewarded for good performance and suffer consequences for poor performance. Of course, blaming and finger-pointing had to stop. Figure 4-4 summarizes the key actions that had to stop, start, and continue at CPI in order to shift the culture.

FIGURE 4-4
STOP/START/CONTINUE ANALYSIS AT CPI

Stop	▲ Relying on acquisitions for technology and growth
	▲ Ignoring performance problems
	▲ Ignoring commitments to deadlines and schedules
	▲ Blaming, finger-pointing and "holding camp against one another"
Start	▲ Holding regular meetings to openly and candidly discuss goals, schedules and progress
	▲ Providing rewards and consequences for good and poor performance
	▲ Providing timely feedback and coaching regarding performance
	▲ Sharing financial information much more openly
Continue	▲ Supporting the sales of the primary product line
	▲ Producing top quality products
	▲ Focusing on existing product lines

We will examine the underlying beliefs—seven core beliefs CPI developed to guide their actions—in the next chapter, and we'll look at the experiences that CPI managers created in order to foster those beliefs in Chapter Six. For now, let's just look at a sample of some of the actions that individuals took after the culture change was underway. Each of these individuals, and scores of others, earned the President's Award at CPI for demonstrating actions consistent with driving product development in the organization:

- Gordon Barr, advanced manufacturing engineer at CPI, had always been an excellent engineer. He's so passionate about technology and dedicated to inventing that he has a machinist's shop set up in his garage. In 1994, knowing that "speed to market" was paramount and that any time shaved from the schedule would help the cause, he put in extraordinary effort and hours and developed a means of building prototypes using stereolithography, a technology for modeling components with quick-curing plastic. Unfortunately, parts produced by stereolithography were not usually representative of the real thing. However, Gordon had followed developments in this technology, and even though he was not working directly on the prototype being developed, he worked closely with a vendor who had pushed stereolithography forward. As a result, a ten-week process was compressed into nine weeks, and the parts delivered were so similar to actual parts that a design engineer thought the real parts had arrived early.

- Craig Bloom, a member of CPI's finance staff, understood that any costs saved would support the product-development effort, which was sucking up the organization's cash. He challenged a state tax assessment, a project demanding enormous time, dedication, and research. From November 1994 through March 1995, he devoted 290 hours to the state audit and saved the company $150,000. This was in addition to his already heavy schedule and at a time when other tax resources were stretched thin and the tax department was short one person.

- A three-person team working on development of CPI's new Mini II pulse generator for pacemakers managed to squeeze *five months* out of a 16-month development schedule. The goal was to get the most compact product ever to market on an aggressive deadline, while most of the firm's engineering resources were dedicated to the first-generation Mini I ramp-up. They did it by rapidly becoming proficient in new spot-welding technology, by learning techniques for shortening equipment-validation time, and by going directly to supplier development or manufacturing when engineers were tied up. This was, of course, a marked contrast to the way product development had been functioning at CPI.

Note again that these were not things that people were told to do by management. These were actions that people undertook as a result of the shift in the culture initiated by management. These are the kinds of actions that people will take to get the result, once they have a clear, meaningful result to shoot for and they understand that management is totally committed to supporting them by acting differently to get there. These actions stemmed from a shift to certain Cultural Beliefs at CPI. At the close of the next chapter we will learn what those beliefs were.

MILESTONES ALONG THE YELLOW BRICK ROAD

This chapter examined the process of defining the actions that an organization must shift to in order to get new results. A distinction worth making is the one between action, which produces results, and motion, which can look like action but does not produce results. The process of making this distinction can begin when you examine your current, A^1, actions. Ask yourself: Which of these behaviors are producing the results we want and which are not?

In defining actions you must honestly assess what your organization is doing. What's working? What isn't? Which actions are those that you should stop, start, and continue in moving to the new culture. Those that you will stop and continue are now part of your current, C^1, culture. Those that you will continue and start will become part of your new, C^2, culture.

A successful culture change hinges on changing the way people think and act. Knowing that people need to act differently and their actually acting differently are two different things. Regarding actions, an organization must engage people at all levels in defining for themselves the A^2 behaviors that should be part of the new culture. These actions must be ones that most everyone sees as those that will produce the desired results. These actions will best serve the company if they are specifically, but not exhaustively, defined and are results-oriented, realistic, recognizable, and real-time.

The *Steps to Accountability* play a crucial role both when a company is identifying the A^1 and A^2 behaviors and when it is implementing the new actions. Individually and collectively, the people in the organization must be able to *See It, Own It, Solve It* and *Do It* with regard to the actions that the organization needs to shift from and to.

The behavioral shifts themselves will be motivated mainly by beliefs, that is, by new beliefs that are aligned with the actions needed to produce the new, R^2 results. In the next chapter we describe how you can accelerate the shift to a new culture by identifying and creating beliefs that motivate the right kind of actions and the desired results.

IDENTIFYING BELIEFS THAT PRODUCE ACTION

Well Oz can do anything:
so I suppose he will find Kansas for you.

The Wonderful Wizard of Oz
L. Frank Baum

As we know, the Wizard of Oz possesses no real magical powers. However, he is able to get others to believe that he does. Throughout the Emerald City and the entire land of Oz, the Wizard has a reputation as someone who can do anything. He got that reputation by helping others believe that they could do whatever they needed to do, such as building the Emerald City itself or killing the Wicked Witch of the West.

Throughout their journey, the Scarecrow believes he has no brain, the Tin Woodman believes he has no heart, and the Lion believes he has no courage. Yet, by the end of the story the Wizard has each of them believing quite the opposite about themselves. Once their beliefs change, they find that a fresher view of life awaits them, a view that will enable them to achieve greater success and happiness.

The Results Pyramid shows that people's beliefs—how they think—determine their actions—what they do. By moving down to this deeper, more fundamental level, leaders work with the more hidden, and more influential, aspects of the organizational culture—people's beliefs. Leaders find that they're most effective when they work at the level of people's beliefs.

It's the beliefs people hold that will either move forward or shut down an organizational initiative, effort, or program. It's the beliefs people continue to hold that keep the restructuring of an organization from having the impact on behavior that management intended. One of the most effective illustrations of the role of beliefs on behavior and actions is a job promotion. How often have you seen someone, perhaps yourself, get a promotion to a new job and in a matter of days come to view the workplace entirely differently? Where they may have shown no interest in a corporate program before, they are now advocates. Remember the guy who worked in the plant and was always cavalier about safety? Now he is responsible for safety, and you wonder what inspires his zealotry.

Changing jobs can change beliefs quickly. Beliefs about what is important, what should and should not be done; beliefs about how my performance will now be judged and rewarded. More important, changing beliefs changes actions, and then results. Remember our new devout convert to safety? Before the promotion, his belief was "it's not my job." After the promotion, his belief became "this is my crusade." Imagine the change: His actions will now impact safety in a way that will produce results.

Unfortunately, few managers work at that level. Instead, when an organization is not getting the result they want, many managers try to solve the problem by—well, yes—changing the result. How many times have you seen "the number" change through the course of the year as circumstances change? Redefining targets is common, but it is not a solution. Alternatively, management may create action plans that define what people should do differently to get the result. Or they may unveil new policies and procedures intended to bring about a new result. These plans, policies, and procedures clearly have their place, as we discussed in the previous chapter, but they usually fail to bring about lasting change.

In many companies, managers have told us that one of their organization's strengths is that they are good in a crisis. They say that if they could just take the "crisis mode" and apply it to the normal workday, they could achieve far more than they can now. They are describing the propensity of people to suspend their beliefs and operate by an altogether different belief that is motivated by survival—"All that other stuff doesn't matter right now; if we don't solve this, there may be no tomorrow."

An interesting example of this phenomenon comes from World War II and the Normandy invasion. To secure the liberation of western Europe, the Allied invasion required the creation of two harbors, a feat never before attempted. Until the capture of existing harbors along the French coast, the Allies needed two artificial harbors capable of accommodating 7,000 tons of stores and 1,250 vehicles per day. Without these harbors, the allied forces could not support the planned invasion.

The synthetic harbors would have to act as breakwaters against the swell, as wharves for unloading men, equipment, and other supplies, and as piers to connect the wharves to the land. Eisenhower spoke of this feat when he said:

> We knew that even after we captured Cherbourg its port capacity and the lines of communication leading out of it would not meet all of our needs. To solve this apparently unsolvable problem we undertook a project so unique as to be classed by many scoffers as completely fantastic. It was a plan to construct artificial harbors on the coast of Normandy.
>
> The first time I heard this idea tentatively advanced was by Admiral Mountbatten, in the spring of 1942. At a conference attended by a number of service chiefs he remarked, "If ports are not available, we may have to construct them in pieces and tow them in." Hoots and jeers greeted his suggestion but two years later it was to become a reality.

Once there developed a belief that it could and would be done, then people set about to find a way to accomplish it, and they did. Massive breakwaters, 70 yards long and 30 feet high, were constructed of metal. They were filled with 2,000 tons of water each and strung together with only a 15-foot gap between them. Three and a half miles of these breakwaters were floated across the English channel the day after D-day. In addition, some 60 ships, which if placed end to end would make an additional breakwater two miles long, were situated to create the shape of a bay around these metal structures. Ten miles of flexible roadway was placed afloat in the harbors to create the piers. All of this contributed to the success of the landing and the invasion of France. Without it, the invasion could not have been sustained.

The leaders of the allied forces created the belief that it could be done. Each played a role in helping groups from different countries and different branches of the service develop the belief that it would work. They moved forward and acted as if it could be done and were inspired by admonitions such as Churchill's: "Let me have the best solution worked out. Don't argue the matter. The difficulties will argue for themselves." The mobilization of millions of troops and the commitment of those troops on foreign soil demonstrated the extent of that belief.

THE POWER OF BELIEFS

Every organization has a set of beliefs that are commonly shared by people about how the organization functions, what they should and should not do, and how they should and should not do it. An informal inventory of your own beliefs about how your organization works may reveal interesting insights into your own actions and behavior. Here are some beliefs that people have shared with us about their organizations regarding what is *not* working, beliefs that negatively affect the ability of employees to perform and of an organization to deliver:

- Accountability is sometimes used as a cross between a hammer and an excuse. It goes too long before we hold people accountable; and when it finally comes down, it comes down hard. We have excellent hindsight.

- The primary issue is that people are not empowered to make decisions. We come to an agreement on central issues, but we don't follow through. In our group, we run it up the flagpole and someone else will make the decision.

- We need to get people to believe that the way things get solved starts with them, rather than waiting for the boss to tell them what to do.

- I find that people won't take power. They just don't grab it and run with it. There is safety in committees and passing it up, rather than going out and making it happen on their own.

- Too much negative feedback from above. I haven't been thanked for anything in years except from store management, and yet I would think that with the law of averages, I must have done something right, sometime. We need job security.

While these negative beliefs are balanced with positive perspectives about their company or team, they do represent a powerful, day-to-day force that blocks the behavior that will produce results. Beliefs such as these inspire action, or inaction, that negatively impacts results.

These beliefs do not just float in upon an organization and temporarily land there. They are part of the culture, imbedded in the fabric of the group. They are often unstated, but are nonetheless apparent. The more widely negative beliefs are shared in an organization, the more significantly they hinder actions that produce results.

Think of a key result you are now working to achieve in your organization. Pick a result where you may not be making much progress or one that you are concerned about achieving and record it in Figure 5-1. Now identify one belief that is at least somewhat commonly shared in the organization today that, *if changed*, would measurably improve the chances of achieving the result.

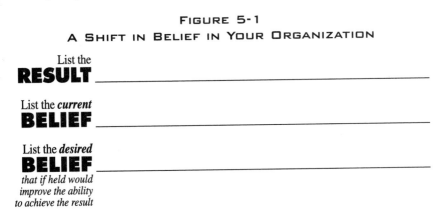

FIGURE 5-1
A SHIFT IN BELIEF IN YOUR ORGANIZATION

List the
RESULT _____

List the *current*
BELIEF _____

List the *desired*
BELIEF _____
that if held would
improve the ability
to achieve the result

To what degree would you see people acting differently if they subscribed to, embraced, and were led by this belief? To what extent would that belief lead to an improvement in results? What stands in the way of getting people to believe this?

BELIEFS DRIVE ACTIONS

Attempts to shift people directly from A^1 to A^2 actions in order to move from R^1 to R^2 results, without working on a shift from B^1 to B^2 beliefs, are misguided. Just telling people to start performing A^2 actions might work for a while, but not for long. Worse, you will potentially have to tell people every move to make, and that's just impossible. Even if you could do it, they would resent it and become frustrated. Instead, you need a set of beliefs that will guide people's actions. When people hold the right beliefs, then in any given situation they will select the right action from the whole range of actions that those beliefs would suggest to them.

Nothing changes behavior more quickly than the adoption of a new belief. Almost instantly people start doing things differently because they are thinking about the situation differently. In addition, people figure out for themselves what they should do because they see their circumstances framed by their new belief, which tells them to behave differently.

Recall the Sears story from *Fortune* magazine in Chapter Four, where action was taken to create "economic literacy" at the store level throughout the company. During his first 90 days with the company, chief learning officer Anthony Rucci met with employees in about 50 Sears stores and asked, "What do you think is the primary thing you get paid to do here?" He states that over half the people answered, "to protect the assets of the company." Employees held the belief that "protecting" the company was their number-one priority. With that belief came the corresponding actions and results—some of the lowest customer-satisfaction scores in the retail industry.

Rucci was amazed at how the focus on financials led to Sears's losing sight of the importance of employees and customers. Rucci shares a widely held view that "what gets measured, gets done." He says, "We knew that unless we produced credible, auditable measurements in all three areas—shop, work, and invest—all the attention would gravitate to the financials, and we wouldn't get the traction we need on shop and work." To make the "soft" concepts more concrete, they analyzed 13 financial measures for 820 full-line department stores, millions of data points on customer satisfaction, and hundreds of thousands of employee-satisfaction data points. Their analysis told them "that employees' attitudes about the job and about the company are the two factors that predict their behavior in front of the customer, which in turn predicts the likelihood of customer retention and customers' recommending us to others, the two factors that, in turn, predict financial performance."

Using empirical data, Rucci demonstrated the connection—beliefs drive actions and results. Employee attitudes reflect the beliefs that employees hold. Sears learned that a shift in employee satisfaction ratings (employees' beliefs about the store and the company) by five measuring units (on Sears' internal scale) in one quarter would translate to a two-unit increase in customer satisfaction scores the next quarter (the result of employees' actions based upon their new beliefs) and to revenue growth the following quarter that beat their stores' national average by 0.5 percent. They believed so strongly in this relationship that the top 200 executives had 30 to 70 percent of their incentive compensation linked to nonfinancial performance measures.

Sears worked to shift their culture. They wanted to shift the way sales associates think in the stores and they wanted to drive some key beliefs through the organization. One of those shifts was toward economic literacy. They began by educating the employees on the changes in the business environment that had occurred since the 1950s, for example, in the ten years preceding 1995 consumers reduced their trips to shopping malls by over 66 percent. One forklift operator in Detroit considered this shift and said, "Wait a minute—if people are going to the mall one third as often, and all our stores are in malls, why are we spending so much money remodeling those stores?" Rucci commented, "I'm sitting in the back of the room going hallelujah! You want people to know enough about the business to ask those kinds of questions."

The management team adopted many new beliefs about how to bring about positive change in the organization such as, "Access to information is what motivates change and improvement," "People in the stores have to participate in whatever goal-setting process you've set up; that's how you promote ownership," "When people get a chance to accomplish something themselves, they build self-esteem; they just come to life." Rucci and his team recognized that changing beliefs would lead to a change in action and results; they even proved it to themselves statistically. *Fortune*'s latest survey showed that Sears Roebuck delivered the fifth-highest improvement among 206 companies in customer satisfaction. This extraordinary change in performance clearly depicts the power of working with beliefs.

LEVELS OF BELIEF

Not all beliefs are equal. People hold varying levels of belief. Some beliefs are held with great conviction, while others are less deeply entrenched. Understanding how deeply or strongly a belief is held, and how easily it may be abandoned and another view adopted, is important to shifting a culture rapidly. Figure 5-2 shows three distinct levels of beliefs that individuals may hold within organization.

A Level-One Belief does not inspire a high level of personal investment in positions that belief would dictate. For example, a sales representative may feel that the most effective way to make a presentation to a customer is to use only a portion of the marketing materials provided. On a joint call with a supervisor, however, the rep may see how the materials can be used to more effectively motivate a customer to make

FIGURE 5-2
LEVELS OF BELIEF

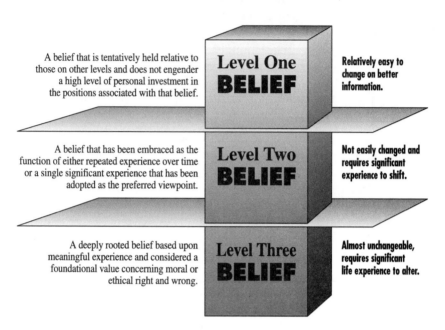

A belief that is tentatively held relative to those on other levels and does not engender a high level of personal investment in the positions associated with that belief.

Level One BELIEF

Relatively easy to change on better information.

A belief that has been embraced as the function of either repeated experience over time or a single significant experience that has been adopted as the preferred viewpoint.

Level Two BELIEF

Not easily changed and requires significant experience to shift.

A deeply rooted belief based upon meaningful experience and considered a foundational value concerning moral or ethical right and wrong.

Level Three BELIEF

Almost unchangeable, requires significant life experience to alter.

a decision now. As a result, the rep quickly abandons the old belief and adopts the new belief relatively easily, given the better information.

A Level-Two Belief, steeped in experience, is one that is strongly held, fully embraced, and not easily abandoned. For instance, when people in an organization believe that "you can't say what you really think to management—they don't want to hear it," you are hearing a Level-Two Belief. This belief is developed over time, reflecting a strong opinion based upon powerful personal experiences. Shifting this belief is difficult because people see this view as accurate and associate a downside with abandoning it.

A Level-Three Belief is a foundational value concerning perceptions of moral or ethical right and wrong. These beliefs are deeply held and are extremely difficult to change. An example of a Level-Three Belief would be someone believing that intentionally falsifying information on a production report would be unethical, immoral, and against his or her values. Trying to get a person to believe any differently would probably be futile and a waste of time.

A real-life example of conflict between maintaining a production schedule and ensuring the safety of others provides an example of a Level-Three Belief in action. A nuclear-power plant sought to minimize downtime during a planned outage to make repairs and complete a maintenance inspection. Each day the plant was down cost the company one million dollars in lost revenue. Management, with a keen interest in minimizing the downtime, continually required shorter and shorter outages.

These shortened time frames led to more "Band-Aid" fixes in order to keep things going. Many of the workers in the plant felt the Band-Aids were not enough and that some parts ought to be replaced outright, which would require more time and expense for the repair. Plant employees felt that management was asking them to change what we would call a Level-Three Belief. To management it appeared to be a Level-One or Level-Two Belief. Worried about their safety and that of their families, who lived nearby, the plant workers saw an issue of right and wrong—and believed management was wrong. Because no one would listen, the workers took the matter into their own hands and sabotaged the valve that had been bandaged one too many times. This forced the plant to shut down an additional three or four days.

When we talk about shifting beliefs in order to change the culture, we are talking about working with Level-One and Level-Two Beliefs that speak to "how things are done around here." Shifting a Level-One Belief can generally be accomplished relatively easily. However, shifting a Level-Two Belief requires greater skill and thought, particularly if you need to do it quickly. Significant culture change can involve, at least from the perspective of some employees, a Level-Three Belief. This is particularly the case if the shift involves changing the "social contract" that people perceived to be in effect before the change. Such shifts may involve, for example, reducing the work force, changing the working hours, changing the rate of pay, or requiring training in new skills. Certain employees feel that such changes violate rights to which they believe they are entitled. A Level-Three Belief may also be involved if you must stop some unethical or immoral practice that has become institutionalized. We've all read about companies that have closed their doors because they couldn't eliminate such practices. It is useful for leaders to understand how deeply or strongly held a belief may be so that you can anticipate the amount of effort, energy, and attention it will take to make that shift happen.

Discovering Which Beliefs Need to Shift

People change as they form new beliefs. We see it all the time. Think about your most recent new hire. During the first few weeks, he will probably visit with longer-term employees and ask, "So how do things *really* work around here? What do I need to watch out for? What do I need to make sure I do? How do people get promoted? How do they get in trouble?" The answer to these questions perpetuate the culture.

The answers to these questions represent employees' *beliefs* about "how things work around here." Along with their answer comes a story backing up their assessment, something that happened to them or someone else that illustrates their point, usually quite vividly. This is one of the powerful ways in which culture is transmitted. When you think about the beliefs that you need to shift—the ones you want to create and those you need to discard—consider the things you hope people will say when they're asked "how things *really* work around here."

Of course, there are shared beliefs in the organization that you want to keep because they motivate actions that produce results. In the course of identifying the beliefs that need to shift, these "keepers" will become apparent. Becoming conscious of those beliefs is essential. You must to pay attention to these beliefs in order to maintain them as a part of your culture as you move forward.

In examining ways to accelerate the shift in culture from C^1 to C^2, we will focus on two kinds of beliefs: those that are going to help people achieve the R^2 results and those that won't. We want to develop the former and extinguish the latter. The company's leaders, with the help of anyone else who can lend a hand, must identify these two sets of beliefs by answering two questions:

What are the current beliefs that *will hold us back* from achieving the desired results?

What are the needed beliefs that *will help us* achieve the desired results?

The first question identifies beliefs that stand in the way of achieving results. They either fail to motivate action, or they motivate the wrong actions. The second question identifies beliefs that are missing but that would help people achieve results. These beliefs motivate people to take actions that will produce the desired results. In other words, if you could script what someone would say to that new employee, what would be their answer to his question "How do things really work around here?"

Figure 5-3 lists some examples of the B¹ beliefs that need to be discarded and extinguished and the B² beliefs that need to be created and adopted for the same two companies whose actions we examined in Chapter Four. Both of these companies were very successful in shifting their beliefs.

FIGURE 5-3
SHIFTING FROM B1 TO B2 BELIEFS

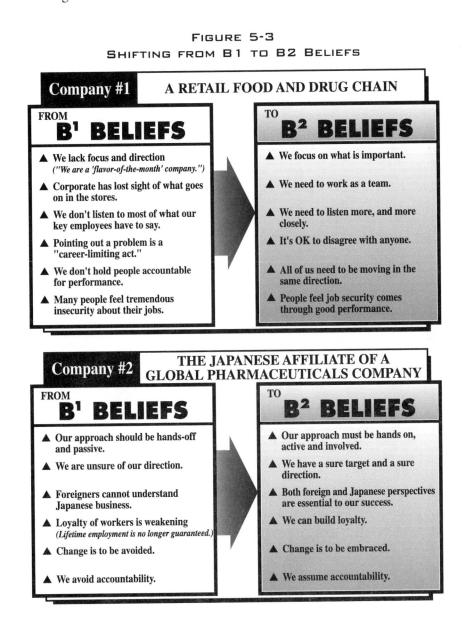

Company #1 — **A RETAIL FOOD AND DRUG CHAIN**

FROM
B¹ BELIEFS

▲ We lack focus and direction
("We are a 'flavor-of-the-month' company.")

▲ Corporate has lost sight of what goes on in the stores.

▲ We don't listen to most of what our key employees have to say.

▲ Pointing out a problem is a "career-limiting act."

▲ We don't hold people accountable for performance.

▲ Many people feel tremendous insecurity about their jobs.

TO
B² BELIEFS

▲ We focus on what is important.

▲ We need to work as a team.

▲ We need to listen more, and more closely.

▲ It's OK to disagree with anyone.

▲ All of us need to be moving in the same direction.

▲ People feel job security comes through good performance.

Company #2 — **THE JAPANESE AFFILIATE OF A GLOBAL PHARMACEUTICALS COMPANY**

FROM
B¹ BELIEFS

▲ Our approach should be hands-off and passive.

▲ We are unsure of our direction.

▲ Foreigners cannot understand Japanese business.

▲ Loyalty of workers is weakening
(Lifetime employment is no longer guaranteed.)

▲ Change is to be avoided.

▲ We avoid accountability.

TO
B² BELIEFS

▲ Our approach must be hands on, active and involved.

▲ We have a sure target and a sure direction.

▲ Both foreign and Japanese perspectives are essential to our success.

▲ We can build loyalty.

▲ Change is to be embraced.

▲ We assume accountability.

A different set of actions will follow from each of these beliefs, both in B[1] and in B[2]. For example, the food-and-drug chain identified that a current unwanted B[1] belief included "pointing out a problem is a career-limiting act." As the management team discussed this belief, each member of the team acknowledged that this belief was widely shared in the organization. They did not like it. It's not the belief they wanted people to have. But they knew it was the prevailing belief. Some members of the management team even acknowledged that they, too, felt this way.

The A[1] actions that resulted from this belief are listed in Figure 5-4 and include the following:

FIGURE 5-4

A[1] ACTIONS FROM THE B[1] BELIEF
OF THE FOOD-AND-DRUG COMPANY

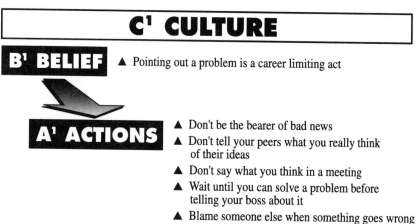

As the team analyzed what people were doing in their culture because of this belief, they realized that their culture stood in the way of the results they were pursuing. Each of them acknowledged that it would not be possible to create success in their regions without changing this belief as well as others. They worked as a team in answering the questions:

> What are the current beliefs that *will hold us back* from achieving the desired results?

> What are the needed beliefs that *will help us* achieve the desired results?

In answering these questions, they obtained the perspectives of employees in the stores. After all, the beliefs of store-level people most affected store performance. We conducted interviews throughout all levels in the stores and found out what people (who answered anonymously) really thought, what they really believed about "how things were." This is key in the process of developing useful beliefs. You have to know what people really think. Using outside people in the assessment phase can help because people are more apt tell someone from the outside what they really think about the company. They do it all the time. They are always telling their friends, their family, and their peers in other jobs "how things are" where they work.

With the management team, we reviewed the beliefs from the interviews. In most cases, the management team was not surprised. In others, they understood what they heard but felt there was no basis for people to believe what they were believing. That's when the role of a facilitator is useful in helping the team understand the "current state." A management team must be able to "see things as they really are" from the perspective of the employees, because those beliefs are driving actions that matter. Whether those beliefs are right or wrong, accurate or inaccurate, true or false, they drive what people do. That's why leaders *must* understand what people think—what's driving their current actions. If the management team doesn't come to understand this, they miss an opportunity to truly improve their organization, and their results.

After understanding the current state and describing the attributes of the necessary cultural shift, the team then identified the B^2 beliefs needed to motivate the actions necessary to achieve the R^2 results. Figure 5-5 is a sample of what they came up with:

As you compare the list of B^1/A^1 beliefs and actions with B^2/A^2 beliefs and actions, the impact on results is apparent. The C^1 culture stands in the way of results, while the C^2 culture facilitates, enhances, fosters, promotes, and drives key actions that are essential to achieving results. The management team clearly saw that creating the C^2 environment would be to their advantage. Creating it as quickly as possible would bring all the more advantage.

Now consider some of the beliefs that you need to shift in your own organization, group, or team. What are the B^1 beliefs that are stopping progress? What are the B^2 beliefs that would replace those you need to discard and would move you forward in achieving R^2?

FIGURE 5-5
A² ACTIONS FROM THE B² BELIEF OF
THE FOOD-AND-DRUG COMPANY

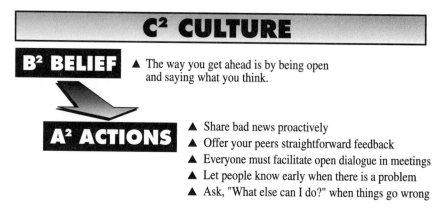

C² CULTURE

B² BELIEF

▲ The way you get ahead is by being open and saying what you think.

A² ACTIONS

▲ Share bad news proactively
▲ Offer your peers straightforward feedback
▲ Everyone must facilitate open dialogue in meetings
▲ Let people know early when there is a problem
▲ Ask, "What else can I do?" when things go wrong

In Figure 5-6 identify B¹ and B² in terms of shifts from B¹ and to B².

FIGURE 5-6
DESCRIBING YOUR NEEDED SHIFTS FROM B¹ TO B²

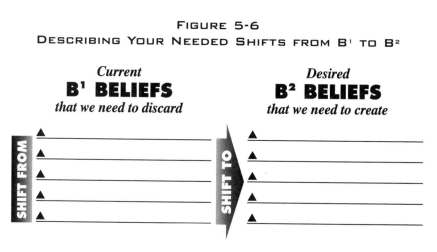

Current
B¹ BELIEFS
that we need to discard

Desired
B² BELIEFS
that we need to create

SHIFT FROM

SHIFT TO

What will happen if you do not bring about these shifts in beliefs in your organization? What will happen if instead you can create an environment where these beliefs are embraced and become an institutionalized part of the "new hire" dialogue? Defining the shift in beliefs that needs to occur is an essential step in creating a successful cultural transition. Our research and observations reveal that every successful, rapid cultural shift does this in one way or another. The more consciously and deliberately you approach the task of identifying beliefs, the more effectively you will accelerate the shift.

CREATING THE ROAD MAP: A CULTURAL-BELIEFS STATEMENT

With our imaginary new hire in mind, imagine that you could actually script what people would say when the newcomer asks, "How do things *really* work around here?" What would you want people saying to this new employee? What beliefs do you want promulgated? We advise management teams that are serious about accelerating their cultural shift to capture this "new hire" dialogue in the form of a Cultural Beliefs Statement—a cultural road map, if you will, for how you need people to think and act in order to get the desired R^2 results.

This Belief Statement is not written by one person nor must it set forth lofty ideals (although it if does, that's fine with us). It should be the product of group interactions in which the management team describes the key B^2 beliefs that the organization needs to create. Your Beliefs Statement may also include any key beliefs that already exist in the organization that you feel are critical to perpetuate your success. It must, however, capture what's missing that, if it weren't, would cause your organization, department, group, or team to progress toward the R^2 results.

The statement is written in the form of beliefs as people might state them to someone like a new hire. They should describe "how things work around here." Better yet, the statement can be written in the first person as you might say it to someone *as if you believed it.* Remember, the statement is a description of things as you would like them to be. Almost all the beliefs that the team will articulate are, by definition, not widely shared in the organization at this point. It's a description of your desired state, a description of C^2.

Although it is management's job to develop this cultural road map, there is no sense in management trying to shift toward beliefs that the organization will either reject or find useless. The goal is to develop beliefs to which almost everyone can personally commit. If the culture truly shifts and a strong culture results, those who cannot commit to these beliefs will ultimately leave the company, be asked to leave, or do such a good job of "making believe they believe" that their lack of commitment becomes immaterial (we will talk about this comply-and-concede Level of Ownership in Chapter Eight).

Figure 5-7 is the Belief Statement developed by the retailer for whom we examined the B^1 to B^2 shifts:

FIGURE 5-7
ONE COMPANY'S BELIEF STATEMENT

Company #1   A Retail Food and Drug Chain

DECISION MAKING	I step up to the plate and make decisions I should make, and I take accountability for the results.
PEOPLE ORIENTATION	I treat customers, employees and suppliers as I want to be treated-- with honesty, courtesy and respect.
COACHING AND FEEDBACK	I invest time seeking, understanding and giving honest feedback to people I work or associate with.
PURPOSE AND DIRECTION	My daily activities are aligned with the purpose and direction of our organization.
INVOLVE AND SHARE	I look everywhere to involve the right people, inside or outside my unit, in developing and implementing the best ideas and solutions.
CUSTOMER FOCUS	I seek to understand and to meet or exceed customer expectations 100 percent of the time.
COMMUNICATION	I communicate what's going on and why within my area of responsibility so that all people hear the same message.
OWNERSHIP	I own my budget. I focus my priorities to exceed my budget regardless of the obstacles that come up.
ACCOUNTABILITY	I operate *Above the Line* by seeking opportunities to accept challenges and solve problems, realizing that I own the responsibility for the outcome.

This Cultural Beliefs Statement describes this particular company's *Culture of Accountability*. Recall that a *Culture of Accountability* is defined as a culture where people think and act in the manner necessary to achieve the result. Creating an environment in which people buy into and believe in these things is the process of leadership.

Creating accountability for thinking and acting this way is a key management responsibility.

You'll notice that many of these beliefs are action oriented. That's fine. If the company will respond best to action-oriented beliefs, great. If a set of more philosophical beliefs will serve people better, that's fine too. It is important only that the beliefs be aligned with one another and with the actions people must take to get the results the company needs to produce. Also, as we mentioned earlier, we've found it useful for each belief in the Belief Statement to begin with the pronoun "I" because each member of the team must own the beliefs. Using "I" to express a belief helps this process. Remember, culture changes one person at a time. Thus, anything you can do to promote individual buy-in will assist the transition. Belief Statements, particularly those crafted in a participative manner with an eye toward getting people to sign on, are an extremely powerful tool for culture change.

Beliefs do not exist in isolation, nor do they function in one dimension. Organizational culture is made up of a system of beliefs. You can't come up with just one belief, promulgate that belief, and expect it to motivate the right actions. You need a set of beliefs that work together as a system. The aforementioned retailer wants people to believe that it is their responsibility to step up and make decisions, but they also want those decisions to be aligned with the organization's and customer's needs. In addition, people must communicate what they are doing and involve the right people in the process. We could go on—all of the beliefs relate to one another and work together to guide behavior and action. They are a system of thinking that will drive different actions within the organization.

Culture is not a one-size-fits-all proposition. So every company must go through its own journey of self-discovery in order to understand its current beliefs and to develop new, needed beliefs. One useful product of that process is generally a Belief Statement, which we recommend that every company develop before undertaking a culture shift.

Many of the words chosen in Beliefs Statement have a specific meaning to the team that created it. That's why it is important that the statement not just be placed on the wall, or handed out to everyone, once it is created. There is an effective process for getting people to understand, buy into, and own this statement. In the next chapter, we will describe how to use experiences to create the beliefs you have identified in your Cultural Beliefs Statement. In Chapter Ten we will further examine the Beliefs Statement and answer specific questions such as:

- How do you present the Beliefs Statement to the rest of the organization?

- How do you use a Beliefs Statement to fully integrate the culture
  change in your organization?

- How many Beliefs Statements should you have in your organization? One for each management team? One for the organization?

- How do you effectively use the Beliefs Statement on a global
  basis?

Creating the road map that will chart your journey to a new culture is an essential step in accelerating the transition.

BELIEFS AND THE FOUR STEPS TO ACCOUNTABILITY℠

The shift in beliefs usually begins with management. This means
managers must *See It* by getting feedback from all areas of the organization, listening to the perspectives of others, and hearing the hard
things that may arise in that process. Managers *must* cultivate the ability to "see things as they really are." Understanding what people *really*
believe is the vital first step in the process of shifting beliefs.

Similarly a company's managers must *Own It* by personally step-
ping up to the plate, taking the transition process seriously, and
immersing themselves in creating the new B² beliefs. It is only by getting every member of the team engaged in this process that you will
get the traction you need to accelerate the shift. Engagement.
Involvement. Ownership. When you get this from the management
team, you will produce beliefs that mean something and drive action.

Regarding *Solve It*, the process usually demands actively redefining boundaries and creatively dealing with obstacles. It is essential to
stay focused on results to ensure alignment among beliefs, actions, and
results. In addition, the *Solve It* question—What else can I do?—can
be valuable in forming beliefs. Simply paraphrase it slightly: *What do
we need to believe* in order to achieve the results, hit our targets, and
accomplish our objectives?

Once the beliefs are formed, the team must focus their efforts
and *Do It*. They must work together to ensure ongoing alignment and
implementation of the beliefs by reporting proactively, following up

relentlessly, doing what they say they will do (that is, what they believe), and measuring progress toward the result. All of these will reinforce the beliefs and help align the company around them.

Everyone in the company must execute each of these *Steps To Accountability* in order for a shift to new beliefs to occur. Everyone must see and own the beliefs, and *Solve It* and *Do It* for the beliefs to become part of the culture and find expression in action.

THIS PIECE OF THE PYRAMID: THE CONTINUING CASE OF CPI

Let's again return to the case of Jay Graf and the culture shift at Cardiac Pacemakers, Inc. Having targeted new results and identified exemplary actions that would produce these results, the company had to develop a set of beliefs that would motivate actions necessary to achieve those results. Probably the most basic challenge Jay faced was that of shifting the company, including some prominent members of management, away from the belief that the next acquisition would fix things and to the belief that sound product development was the path to sustainable growth.

There were, of course, other beliefs that were not serving the company well, other beliefs that the company had to shift away from, as well as others they had to shift toward, if they were to succeed, as shown in Figure 5-8.

FIGURE 5-8
THE SHIFT IN BELIEFS AT CARDIAC PACEMAKERS, INC.

FROM **B¹ BELIEFS**	TO **B² BELIEFS**
▲ There's nothing really wrong, we're still in good shape.	▲ We need to start doing things differently or we might not survive.
▲ Each of us can just hunker down and do his job and we'll be OK.	▲ The company must function as a team.
▲ Communication is to be avoided; it's useless anyway.	▲ We need to talk honestly with one another.
▲ Nobody is really accountable for anything.	▲ People must be accountable for their commitments and performance.
▲ Customers still believe in our products.	▲ We will lose customers if we don't constantly win them.
▲ The next acquisition will fix things.	▲ Superior product development is the key to our future.

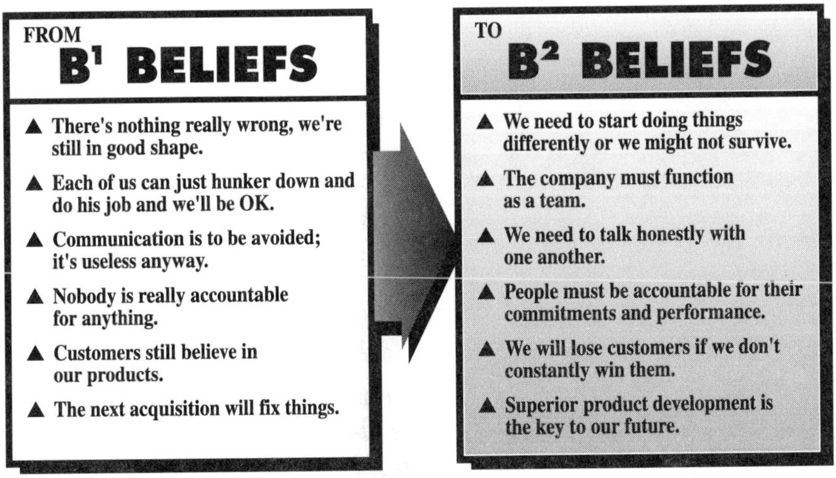

These beliefs, with further development, formed the basis of CPI's road map, their Cultural Belief Statement. Figure 5-9 lists CPI's Belief Statement, which ultimately consisted of seven corporate beliefs:

FIGURE 5-9
THE SEVEN CORPORATE BELIEFS AT CPI

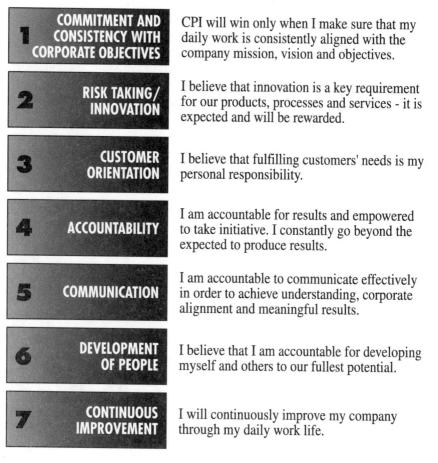

1	**COMMITMENT AND CONSISTENCY WITH CORPORATE OBJECTIVES**	CPI will win only when I make sure that my daily work is consistently aligned with the company mission, vision and objectives.
2	**RISK TAKING/ INNOVATION**	I believe that innovation is a key requirement for our products, processes and services - it is expected and will be rewarded.
3	**CUSTOMER ORIENTATION**	I believe that fulfilling customers' needs is my personal responsibility.
4	**ACCOUNTABILITY**	I am accountable for results and empowered to take initiative. I constantly go beyond the expected to produce results.
5	**COMMUNICATION**	I am accountable to communicate effectively in order to achieve understanding, corporate alignment and meaningful results.
6	**DEVELOPMENT OF PEOPLE**	I believe that I am accountable for developing myself and others to our fullest potential.
7	**CONTINUOUS IMPROVEMENT**	I will continuously improve my company through my daily work life.

These seven corporate beliefs comprise CPI's *Culture of Accountability* and underscore the importance of having a set of beliefs rather than one or two beliefs. For instance, CPI needed to believe in risk taking and innovation. They had suffered due to their reliance on outside technology, and they had developed a culture that discouraged taking risks and innovating. An aversion to risk and innovation can hobble product development. However, you don't want people taking unwise risks or innovating just for the thrill of it. A belief in risk taking and innovation could motivate unwanted action if not tempered by beliefs such as communication, accountability, customer orientation, and consistency with corporate objectives. Together, these beliefs say, "I am willing to take risks and innovate in order to move us forward. But I will tell others what I'm doing and get their feedback, and I'll be accountable for the results. Also, I'll take only risks that serve our goals, and I will not let customers suffer in the process."

Today, Jay sees these seven beliefs as critical to the turnaround of CPI. "There was power in the consensus we created around the seven beliefs," he says now. And that is the key to shifting a culture—changing the way people think so that they'll change the way they act and thus produce new results.

Jay and the rest of management did not just present the seven corporate beliefs to people and ask them to adopt them. They did, after working at various levels to develop these beliefs, present them as the beliefs of the company going forward. But they did not tell people to start believing these things. Instead they created experiences, including the manner in which they introduced the beliefs, that helped people to shift their beliefs from those of the C^1 culture to those of the new, C^2, culture. We will learn about these experiences in this section of the next chapter.

MILESTONES ALONG THE YELLOW BRICK ROAD

In this chapter we've seen the importance of beliefs both in leadership and in culture change. Effective leaders understand the power of beliefs to change people's actions. Working with people's beliefs is central to their leadership practice. They understand that beliefs drive the actions that people take. They realize that if they are seeing actions that don't work or not seeing actions that would work, then the beliefs underlying those actions must be discovered.

Understanding that there are different *Levels of Beliefs* can help a leader assess how much effort and energy will be required to create the new culture. A Level-One Belief is tentatively held relative to the other levels and does not engender a high personal investment in the associated positions. These beliefs are relatively easy to change with better information. A Level-Two Belief has been embraced as a function of repeated experience or a single significant experience and has been adopted as the *preferred* viewpoint. These beliefs are not so easily changed and require significant experience to shift. A Level-Three Belief is a deeply rooted belief based upon significant and meaningful experience that is considered a foundational value and concerns judgments of moral or ethical right and wrong. These beliefs are almost unchangeable and require significant experience to alter. Culture change, in most cases, deals with Level-One and Level-Two Beliefs.

So culture change involves getting people to adopt a new, B^2, set of beliefs about "how things are done around here." Creating clarity around the key beliefs that need to shift will help to accelerate the transition to a new culture. Posing and answering the following two questions can help you develop the beliefs that will best serve the company:

> What are the current beliefs that *will hold us back* from achieving the desired results?
>
> What are the needed beliefs that *will help us* achieve the desired results?

To effect a culture change and set the organization on a new course, leaders must identify, honestly and completely, the beliefs that are hindering the company from achieving the targeted results and those that would help the company achieve them. This often calls for individual and collective soul searching and open feedback about how things *really* are.

A Cultural Beliefs Statement describes a *Culture of Accountability* for that organization. It is not to be drafted by the corporate communications department for public consumption. Rather it should be drafted by management, with input from employees, as a practical tool to produce results and create alignment.

Remember, too, that beliefs exist as a system. Adopting one belief could skew people's behavior or otherwise put the organization out of alignment. If people share a set of beliefs and are aligned with the sought-for results, then the company is well on its way to changing its culture and achieving the results.

Beliefs, however, cannot be changed simply by asking people to change them. Shifting beliefs is not a matter of just developing new and useful beliefs and posting them on the company bulletin boards or distributing them on e-mail. Management must create experiences that will cause people to change their beliefs. At the action level, as opposed to analytical level, this is the greatest challenge leaders face, and we come to grips with it in the next chapter.

CHAPTER SIX

CREATING EXPERIENCES THAT INSTILL THE RIGHT BELIEFS

The cyclone had set the house down, very gently—for a cyclone—in the midst of a country of marvelous beauty.

The Wonderful Wizard of Oz
L. Frank Baum

Dorothy finds the strange, colorful Land of Oz quite different from her familiar home back in Kansas. Dorothy's home in Kansas had been populated with people like her. She was used to the customs and, although there were no doubt things about her home that annoyed her, at least the place made sense (until that tornado came along). But Oz is a different story. You could unwittingly eliminate the Wicked Witch of the West and be declared a hero by the most peculiar group of townspeople you ever saw. Although most people seem helpful, it is tough to get a straight answer out of them. Plus, unlike Kansas, where nothing seems to change, in Oz you never know whom you are going to meet or what is going to happen next.

Despite the radical differences surrounding her, despite having been dropped suddenly into an other-worldly environment, despite having acknowledged that she and Toto are not in Kansas anymore, Dorothy at times acts as if she were still at home. She still reverts to her old ways of thinking and acting, even though she is in, let's say, a very new culture. How can she possibly forget that she is in such a radically altered situation and place?

The answer is found in her experience, at the very foundation of *The Results Pyramid*.

Dorothy's lifelong experience back in Kansas created strongly held beliefs—ways of thinking and acting that would persist even in another world. She carries her old ways of thinking and mental models into her new surroundings. Of course, with enough new experiences she does finally get the hang of things in Oz. Her view of her world changes only as her experience does, and it takes a good number of new experiences to bring about this change.

Because experiences are such strong determinants of culture, when you want to shift an organization's culture, you must create new experiences for everyone in the organization. And they must be the right experiences. They must be experiences specifically targeted at fostering the needed beliefs, those beliefs that will motivate the required actions and ultimately produce the desired results. Like Dorothy's view of the world, the current culture will persist until enough new experiences cause it to shift.

Creating experiences is nothing new in the process of managing an organization. Managers create experiences for everyone around them every day. Every interaction between a manager or supervisor and an employee amounts to an experience that will either foster and promote or undermine and erode the desired B^2 beliefs. The question is whether or not the experiences that leaders are creating are the ones that will cause people to shift the way they think and act so that they achieve the results the organization seeks. Our experiences with clients have led us to believe that managers must consciously think about, plan for, evaluate, and create the right experiences for people throughout the company in order to develop a *Culture of Accountability*. This chapter will illustrate the foundational role that experiences play in creating that culture.

For starters, let's look at a small, but very effective organization. This company, Amy's Ice Creams, has purposely focused on creating experiences to manage their culture and produce the results they seek.

EXPERIENCES DRIVE RESULTS

Under the hot sun of East Texas, an ice-cream shop has to offer customers something more than ice cream if it's going to compete. Amy's Ice Creams has found an entertaining way to offer something more. Amy Miller, owner of the seven-unit chain, understands the power of experience, not only for her employees, but for her customers as well. She sells an experience with every scoop. Even more than ice cream, Amy sells fun.

In the November 1996 cover story of *Inc.* magazine, John Case describes the employees of Amy's Ice Creams as performers. Customers watch them juggle their ice cream scoops, toss balls of ice cream around, and even dance on the freezer tops. He notes, "If there's a line out the door, they might pass out free samples—or offer free ice cream to any customer who will sing or dance or recite a poem or mimic a barnyard animal. They wear costumes. They bring props. They pop trivia questions. They create fun."

The entire culture at Amy's Ice Creams is a culture of fun. The company has achieved competitive advantage by understanding that they're selling something most of us associate with good times and childhood—ice cream. Amy Miller saw that a plain-vanilla approach to this business would not differentiate her product. But selling fun would.

The article points out, "Her way to sustain that difference—to ensure you'd encounter the experience that sets her stores apart—was to create and nurture a culture that makes that experience inevitable. She had to get the right people and get them to behave in the right way. And because their behavior had to be inventive, unflagging, and self-initiated, she had to get them to know what the right way was without being told." In other words, the Amy's Ice Cream way of thinking and acting had to become a part of the culture.

There are companies that have developed environments where people look to be told what to do by their boss. But you cannot tell employees how to be creative and entertaining. You need to create a culture that encourages them to be that way. At Amy's Ice Creams, employees know what to do because the signals the culture sends are clear. That culture, and the beliefs that are part of it, have been consciously created and then sustained one experience at a time.

For an employee, what might be termed the Amy's experience begins before that person is even hired. Instead of an application form, an applicant to Amy's is handed a plain white paper bag and told to take it home, do something with it, and bring it back in a week. "Those who just jot down a phone number will find that Amy's isn't really for them, but an applicant who produces [according to Amy] 'something unusual from a white paper bag tends to be an amusing person who would fit in with our environment.'" Right from the start, Amy's Ice Creams creates an experience—Here's a bag— Now show us you can sell ice cream. This experience begins the process of defining, differentiating, and transmitting the Amy's culture to all new employees.

Every experience that the employees have thereafter is created with the intent of reinforcing the belief that Amy's sells more than ice cream. Amy's sells fun! That's the Amy's experience. On the foundation of experience Amy has built her company culture, differentiating her stores from her competitors' throughout her market. What about the results? Amy's Ice Creams, with annual revenue of $2.2 million, is growing at 20 percent a year. That's a lot of ice cream and a lot of fun.

The question for every leader is: How can I create the experiences that will drive the beliefs we need to have through the organization? Keep in mind that the issue is not whether you should create experiences and beliefs and a culture. You're already doing that and will continue to do so, whether you want to or not. The question is whether you consciously manage the experiences you create so that they work for you and the organization, and not against you. As a leader, being conscious of what you're doing and not doing on a daily basis is fundamental to creating a *Culture of Accountability*.

Alex Markels, in a 1991 article that appeared in *Fast Company*, told the story of AES, a large and successful worldwide builder of power plants. When AES first issued shares to the public, the company also made public its unique business philosophy. Markels stated that the Securities and Exchange Commission was curious about that philosophy, and a little skeptical. The SEC required AES to state that philosophy as a risk factor in the IPO prospectus: "If the company perceives a conflict between [its] values and profits, the company will try to adhere to its values—even though doing so might result in diminished profits or forgone opportunities."

Every year AES conducts an employee survey to gauge how well the company has adhered to its stated values. The data from this survey is used as a management tool to determine a portion of the salary increases and bonuses of top executives. Each year the plant-by-plant results on the values survey are considered a leading indicator of performance. Without question, executives at AES are taking accountability for the experiences they create.

True to their philosophy and conscious of the experiences they create, AES's cofounders, Dennis Bakke and Roger Sant, have taken their lumps when things have gone wrong. In the *Fast Company* article, Markels reports that in 1992 workers at the company's Shady Point, Oklahoma, plant falsified emissions reports. (They said they feared for their jobs if they failed to meet pollution-reduction goals.) AES managers uncovered the wrongdoing and reported it to the government, which administered a $125,000 fine. Bakke and Sant took personal responsibility for the values breakdown at the Oklahoma plant. In doing so, they created an experience that words alone could not convey. In addition to delivering a sincere public apology, they reduced their annual bonuses by 65 percent and 85 percent respectively. Think about this. If you were an employee of the AES company, what beliefs would you take away from this experience?

REFLECTING ON THE IMPACT OF EXPERIENCE

Each of us can no doubt relate to the impact of experiences on our own lives. The following questions provide a useful reflection on the depth of this impact. Try this quick exercise:

1. Think of the strengths and weaknesses of your boss. We know everyone has them. Consider your perceptions of what he or she does well and how he or she could be more effective.

2. Think specifically about the experiences that led you to form these beliefs about his or her strengths and weaknesses. Make a firm connection between the experiences and the beliefs. Get that clear in your mind before going on with the exercise.

3. Now, think about whether any of your beliefs about your boss's strengths and weaknesses changed for you in any way over time. If a belief did change, think about the experiences that led to that change. If no belief changed, think about the ongoing experiences that have sustained the belief up until now.

4. Finally, consider a weakness and ask yourself what experiences you would need to have in order to adopt a new belief about your boss's effectiveness. What would the boss need to change in the way he or she does do things in order for him or her to be more effective in your eyes. What would tell you that the boss is improving?

An experience vivid enough to remember typically leads to a belief. When a belief forms it is because of an experience. Over time, meaningful experiences will either create new beliefs, reinforce current ones, or cause current beliefs to shift to new ones.

Sometimes there is a gap between the experience people are having and the experience you want or need them to have. The "experience gap" can be the difference between producing, or not producing, essential A^2 actions that will yield R^2 results. To be effective, leaders must recognize a gap when it exists. By not understanding the experience people are having in the organization, managers can remain unaware of gaps and leave them open. Closing gaps when they are recognized will accelerate changes, moving the organization toward C^2 and R^2 more quickly.

THE POWER OF SHARING EXPERIENCES

People like to share the experiences they have. They relate these experiences to peers and co-workers and summarize, usually unknowingly, the beliefs they've formed from these experiences. Often, these experiences are retold by listeners to others and are passed along as evidence of "the way things are." Call it gossip. Call it telling stories or sharing experiences. Whatever you call it, it happens. People tell one another stories. These stories perpetuate culture by transmitting, albeit informally, beliefs about how things work.

Stories provide vicarious experiences. They allow people who are new to an organization to quickly learn and absorb the organization's culture without having to experience it all firsthand. They become the oral history of the company and the common experience of the organization. Eventually, the telling of these experiences can transcend the individuals themselves, which is one reason that you can sometimes change all the people and still have the same culture.

As you've heard, bad news travels fast. Negative experiences prompt people to talk. The rumor mill churns hardest and the grapevine grows wildest when people hear of experiences that go contrary to the B^2 beliefs you are trying to establish in the C^2 culture. In the absence of consciously created positive experiences, negative experiences will become the main determinant of culture. This feeds a vicious cycle of negativity because people tend to recognize experiences that reinforce their existing B^1 beliefs rather than those that promote the new B^2 beliefs. To counteract this cycle, managers must tell positive stories that reinforce B^2 beliefs and A^2 actions. It takes more energy and effort to relate positive experiences than to tell negative stories, yet it is certainly worth the expenditure.

Effective leaders take their role in managing culture seriously. They consciously provide experiences that foster B² beliefs. They look for people who are providing these kinds of experiences and create an environment where these positive stories are told so that everyone in the organization hears them.

TYPES OF EXPERIENCE

How do you create an experience that leads to a change in beliefs? Many leaders we've worked with have found that at first the experiences they created did not change people's beliefs. In some cases, the experience backfired, producing beliefs they had not intended to foster. Why is this? Most experiences need to be interpreted for people in order for them to form the beliefs you want them to have. Few experiences stand on their own. In this context, it helps to understand the kinds of experiences you create for others and the effects of these different experiences. We have found it useful to think in terms of four types of experiences. These are depicted in Figure 6-1.

FIGURE 6-1
THE FOUR TYPES OF EXPERIENCES THAT DRIVE BELIEFS

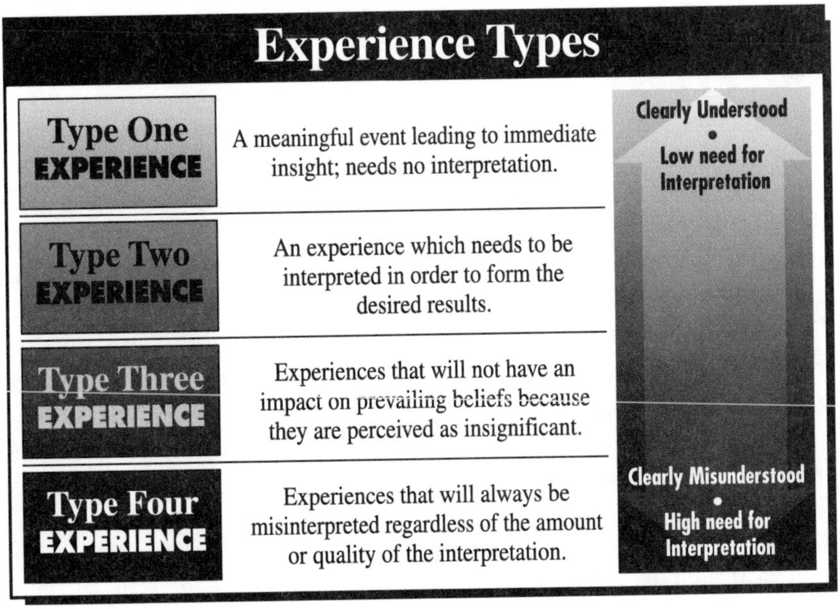

Experience Types

Type One EXPERIENCE	A meaningful event leading to immediate insight; needs no interpretation.	**Clearly Understood** • **Low need for Interpretation**
Type Two EXPERIENCE	An experience which needs to be interpreted in order to form the desired results.	
Type Three EXPERIENCE	Experiences that will not have an impact on prevailing beliefs because they are perceived as insignificant.	
Type Four EXPERIENCE	Experiences that will always be misinterpreted regardless of the amount or quality of the interpretation.	**Clearly Misunderstood** • **High need for Interpretation**

This figure is based upon our observations of leaders creating experiences intended to shift beliefs. It focuses on the types of experiences that managers create for others, including other managers, and illustrates a way of thinking about the clarity and meaning of these experiences.

A Type-1 Experience is a clear, meaningful event leading to immediate insight. It needs no interpretation by management in order to foster the desired belief. For example, at Daimler-Benz, prior to the leadership of Jürgen Schrempp, controversial matters never made it to the management board. They were always settled privately in meetings beforehand and then ratified by the board. When Schrempp took over as chairman he immediately created a Type-1 Experience for board members. He arrived at his first board meeting and at each subsequent one ready to openly debate everything. The message to the members of the board was clear and required no interpretation: Come to board meetings prepared to be challenged. No more meetings beforehand to ensure noncontroversial board ratification. This chairman was going to be involved, not only in strategic direction, but in the operational details of the company.

Many leaders have found that when they create an experience quickly in direct response to feedback, that experience most often becomes a Type 1, needing no interpretation to foster the desired belief. Certain experiences, such as being open to feedback, expressing willingness to collaborate, offering resources to those outside of one's area, and asking clarifying questions while listening to a presentation can all be Type-1 Experiences when they are created in direct response to feedback from others.

A Type-2 Experience needs to be interpreted by management in order for it to foster the intended B^2 beliefs. In general, most experiences are Type 2. Most experiences require interpretation. For example, a leader who is perceived as not open to feedback or as unwilling to collaborate may find it difficult to create a new experience, because people may see such attempts as strange or out-of-character behavior. This highlights the fact that many decisions, actions, and policies require interpretation primarily because people's frames of reference can distort their meaning.

During a cultural transition, experiences often need more interpretation than might otherwise be given because old C^1 habits, perspectives, and beliefs persist. By definition, new experiences need more interpretation than do familiar ones. Ensuring that experiences are interpreted in light of B^2 beliefs will ensure that A^2 actions and R^2 results follow.

For instance, in 1992, AES teamed up with a Belgian utility to purchase two power plants—one in Kilroot and one in Belfast. AES has over 6,000 employees, and yet it has never established corporate departments for human resources, operations, purchasing, or legal affairs. Its headquarters staff includes fewer than 30 people. Lots of companies talk about grassroots teams, but few give teams more power than does AES. The joint venture with the Belgian company, according to Alex Markels' *Fast Company* article, has been a financial success but also a cultural struggle. Mel Bacon, who has spent more than 23 years at the Belfast plant, describes a key B^1 belief in the plant's culture as "a fear of relinquishing control." On the other hand, the AES culture suggests that "the best way to exercise power is to give it up." To transplant this and other company values into the Belfast plant, AES dispatched a U.S.-based employee, Chris Hollingshead, to Belfast.

Not long after Hollingshead arrived in Belfast one of the generators went down. Hollingshead, working with Bacon, suggested that managers vacate the facility while workers got the turbines back on line. Bacon, firmly entrenched in the B^1 beliefs and C^1 culture, resisted, stating that if managers vacated the plant the best people to supervise the work would be leaving. With the C^2 culture in mind, Hollingshead prevailed. The repair was done without the supervision of the managers, and to the astonishment of Bacon, it was done without a hitch.

But old attitudes and beliefs die hard. Markels states that soon after the generator outage, the plant operators suggested replacing an expensive steel pipe with an inexpensive plastic one. Bacon feared that the plastic pipe would last only a few days. Yet the operators made the decision to trust their judgment and install the pipe. After a year the pipe continued to show no signs of wear.

In the Belfast plant Hollingshead worked hard to interpret the experiences for Bacon and others in light of the AES belief: "The best way to exercise power is to give it up." Both the experiences *and* the interpretation of those experiences instilled the AES beliefs at Belfast. The interpretation was constant: "We're all creative, capable of making decisions, trustworthy, able to learn, and perhaps most important, fallible. We all want to be part of a community and to use our skills to make a difference in the world. At AES, we've shifted to giving advice rather than giving approval. And we have moved ahead faster than we would have otherwise."

When AES raised $350 million to invest in a joint venture in Northern Ireland, two control-room operators led the financing team. Occurring in isolation or left unexplained this and other AES experiences might be misunderstood. But at AES the experience is constant, as is the interpretation: People at AES are trustworthy and capable and everyone is fallible. AES is faster and more nimble because "its leaders renounce rather than consume their own authority." They have effectively created the B^2 beliefs they feel are necessary to their success.

Type-3 Experiences are perceived as insignificant. They have no impact on beliefs because they are perceived as events that fit into the normal pattern of things. Type-3 Experiences have no real impact—either positive or negative—on beliefs. Many day-to-day experiences fall into this category.

An example of a Type-3 Experience, unfortunately, can be the posting of company vision-and-values statements to the general employee base. Due to the experience created in the way they are usually introduced, these documents have little if any impact on people's beliefs. Leaders should be on the lookout for Type-3 Experiences when they think they are creating an experience that will shift a belief. If you discover that you have created a Type-3 Experience, then go back and begin again to identify potential Type-1 or Type-2 Experiences that will foster or reinforce the desired beliefs.

A Type-4 Experience will always be misinterpreted regardless of the amount or quality of the interpretation that management provides. Go ahead, hire your son-in-law. If you do, a large proportion of the people in your firm will view it as nepotism no matter how qualified he may be or how much interpretation you provide. This is not to say that a competent son-in-law cannot create experiences on the job that enable people to view him as a solid contributor, maybe even as a business genius of astonishing productivity. However, his *hiring* will no doubt always be viewed by most employees as nepotism. This brings up a good point—even though it is a Type 4, it may be the right thing to do. If it is, then understand how the experience you are creating will negatively impact the beliefs you want to reinforce and then mitigate that negative impact to the extent that you can.

A client of ours related an occasion in which they witnessed a Type-4 Experience firsthand. This company was dealing with significant budget cuts that led to work-force reduction for the first time in its history. Everyone was being asked to cut back, downsize, and do without. People at all levels felt stressed because despite the cutback in resources, they had to deliver the same results.

In this context, and as these cutbacks were hitting hardest, a very expensive modern-art painting was hung in the lobby of the headquarters building. Employees described walking into the lobby one morning and viewing the artwork for the first time. Rather than appreciation for its beauty, the painting evoked angst and incredulity as people considered the pressure they were under, the long hours they were working, and the friends who were leaving, all due to the cost-cutting initiative. Yet here was that painting. Clearly, management had "lost their minds."

What was initially intended to improve the work environment *for* employees (and commissioned almost a year before the drive to lower costs) became a Type-4 Experience that undermined management's credibility and eroded the belief that the company was serious about reducing costs.

No amount of explaining on the part of the management could convince people to see this experience any differently. It was a Type-4 Experience.

In general, try to avoid Type-4 Experiences. They typically foster undesired beliefs. To avoid them, you must identify them before the fact. Getting feedback from others is the key to doing this. Seeking the perspectives of others on how an experience may be interpreted will help you avoid unwanted Type 4s—that is, if you listen to what people tell you.

For instance, if management had checked out the potential reaction to hanging the artwork prior to doing it, they would have understood that a Type 4 was in the making. They would have seen that the emotional response created by hanging the painting at that time would suggest another course of action. They could have donated the artwork to a charitable organization and taken the write-off as a cost savings or at least stored the piece until a more appropriate time.

Notwithstanding the need to avoid Type-4 Experiences, managers sometimes, after weighing the costs and benefits associated with the prospective Type 4, must still move forward and implement the decision, policy, or direction.

After just three years at Daimler-Benz, Schrempp, 53, was being hailed as the leader of Germany's hottest company. Alex Taylor reports in the November 10, 1997, issue of *Fortune* magazine that "Since taking over in May of 1995, he has lopped off money-losing operations, eliminated a layer of top managers, and tried to instill a culture of responsibility and entrepreneurship. Long viewed as stodgy and arrogant, Daimler is now seen as progressive and fast-moving." But since beginning the journey in May of 1995 Schrempp has consciously created a number of Type-4 Experiences.

Taylor describes some of the experiences that Schrempp created. "He sold off the electronics operation. He disposed of Daimler's 24 percent stake in Cap Gemini, the French software-services company. The divestitures, plus the liquidation of Fokker, created huge reductions in the work force. Aerospace alone lost up to 40,000 people through layoffs, attrition, and divestiture. Even Mercedes, which had employed 180,000 in 1991, saw its head count fall to 140,000 by 1995."

Taylor states that the Germans coined a name for Schrempp's actions: Über Leichen gehen—"to walk over dead people." Taylor also states that Schrempp was bothered by his reputation. He had prided himself on never firing anyone without first personally addressing the individual, either in a group meeting or face to face. Taylor quotes Schrempp as saying, "There was a time when I was not the most popular person and at times I wondered if I had overdone it." Clearly Schrempp was aware that many of these experiences would be misinterpreted. However, notwithstanding the misinterpretation, if it's the right thing to do and you must proceed with it, then you must. This, too, is part of leadership. Keep in mind—and the experience at Daimler-Benz confirms this—that as time goes on people often see the "right thing" in perspective.

Viewing experiences in the context of one of the four types described here can help you create experiences that will lead to B^2 beliefs.

WORKING WITH THE EXPERIENCE TYPES

The following exercise will help you see how the four types of experiences might work in your own organization.

Using a key B^2 belief that you need to instill in your organization, identify an experience you could create in each experience type in Figure 6-2. What could you do that would potentially fall into each category?

Experiences create beliefs that drive actions that produce results. The more clearly people interpret experiences as supporting B^2 beliefs, the faster you will achieve R^2 results.

FIGURE 6-2
WORKING WITH THE EXPERIENCE TYPES

A key B² belief you want to create:

Experience Type	Experiences that you could create to instill the B² belief
Type One A meaningful event leading to immediate insight; needs no interpretation.	
Type Two An experience which needs to be interpreted in order to form the desired beliefs.	
Type Three Experiences that will not have an impact on prevailing beliefs because they are perceived as insignificant.	
Type Four Experiences that will always be misinterpreted regardless of the amount or quality of the interpretation.	

INTERPRETING EXPERIENCES— MOST ARE TYPE 2

Culture change is not just a matter of crafting a Belief Statement and distributing it throughout the organization. That has been tried often and has failed almost as often. Changing a culture requires leaders and eventually everyone in the organization to create experiences aimed at shifting, creating, or maintaining desired beliefs.

Many of the experiences you create will of necessity be Type-2 experiences. In these cases you must take extra steps to ensure that those experiences drive B^2 beliefs. This means that you have to understand how people are interpreting experiences. For example, suppose people in your company are not used to offering and receiving open and candid feedback. To move toward a culture characterized by the free flow of feedback, you may decide to set the example and create the experience of asking for and offering feedback. You know this will be a Type-2 Experience given your past actions. To succeed you must make it clear to everyone that this is what you are doing. This would involve preparing people for their feedback sessions with you by explaining what you are doing and why, ensuring that you will openly receive their input, and following up in a positive manner so that they know it *really* was okay.

As you know, if a company has been remiss in sharing feedback, it will take far more to change that than a company-wide memo calling for greater willingness to share perspectives. It will require creating the experience of exchanging feedback and—key point—proper interpretation of that experience. For instance, at the end of every staff meeting, you could go around the room and talk about the experience members of the team are having in coaching others and in being coached. By taking steps to make sure people understand why we are starting to give feedback—to improve performance rather than to point out problems—people will more readily adopt the desired B^2 belief, that feedback improves performance.

This is about creating the right kind of experience and fostering the right belief. Think about it: Without that kind of checking-in regarding experiences people can easily develop contrary beliefs, such as: They're trying to catch people doing things wrong, or They don't think I'm doing a good job.

To avoid such unwanted beliefs you must provide interpretation—help people see why you are doing what you are doing and what you want others to get from it. Then, if the feedback you receive indicates it is not working you may need to adjust your approach.

Here is the best part: People will begin to look for these experiences and notice them. They will share their observations and insights about these new experiences with others. When you learn something new, don't you want to tell someone about it? When you see something new in your environment, don't you want others to see it too?

Once again, culture changes one person at a time. When people go through several belief-changing Type-1 or Type-2 Experiences, they become missionaries. They become missionaries because their beliefs have changed. They become agents of change because of the human tendency to share new beliefs with others. So in a true cultural transition, these agents of change create and interpret experiences in ways that influence the beliefs of others.

EXPERIENCES CREATE BELIEFS FOR MANAGEMENT TEAMS TOO

Almost invariably we find that the team at the top, when facing the need to shift their organizational culture, also must shift the culture of their own team. Tougher results, a changing business environment, and a new managerial focus can all generate a need for greater alignment, clarity, and accountability in management's own C^2 culture. Given this, the right experiences at the right time will create the beliefs needed to bring the team together in a way that drives R^2 results.

One management team of a European company had just such a need. The assessment of their management revealed a fragmented team focused solely on their own individual roles and engaged in finger pointing to justify lackluster performance. The new president, Claude Guillame (again, we have camouflaged the name to protect client confidentiality), had come into the organization to set matters straight. Immediately, he created the experience for the team that things had to change. He openly confronted performance issues in management-team meetings and demonstrated his business savvy in making strategic decisions without getting the input of others on his team.

The early experience of the team was negative, but the beliefs were clear: Current performance was unacceptable, things needed to change, and the president didn't trust the members of his team. One year later, after considerable performance improvement, they met together as a team to evaluate what they needed to do to improve the culture and achieve next year's plan. Each of them believed "they had to come together as a team." Claude recognized that it was time to shift his approach. While he had intentionally created early experiences for the group that got their attention, he now needed to bring the group together and forge a team.

As the team worked together to define the management culture, they developed a Cultural Belief Statement that described the environment they now felt they needed. They also discussed the experiences needed to create C^2. Based on feedback that he received on how he could demonstrate the new B^2 beliefs more completely, Claude realized that *he* needed to create a different experience for the team by recognizing more vocally and visibly the achievements of the group. As Claude shared this potential experience with his team, everyone agreed that this would be a Type-1 Experience that would clearly drive the belief that they were all in this together—succeed or fail. Claude also received feedback from the group that he should confront less and listen more. He was a brilliant strategist, but the team felt he gave little space to them in these decisions. He committed to hear them out in his routine meetings and truly seek to understand their perspectives. Just the willingness to hear this feedback and respond to it showed the team that Claude wanted to shift the team culture still further.

The team discussed the perception in the organization that management was not really a team. They wanted to create a Type-1 Experience that would begin to shift this belief toward a new one—that management worked collaboratively for the success of the organization. They decided that they would begin having lunch together in the employee cafeteria. In the past, rarely did any one of them show up in the cafeteria at all, let alone come together to eat. The effect of this was immediate because the experience was visible and the intended meaning clear: We are a team that enjoys working together and we want you to know it.

To further create the experience of working together as a team, the group agreed to change the seating configuration in their staff meeting. Before, Claude had been seated in the front of the room facing the team (they explained it was a small conference room that accommodated only this seating arrangement). Now, they would move to a different room where they could sit around a table so everyone could see everyone else.

These experiences and others began to create new B^2 beliefs in the management team, just as they did in the organization. Consistently reinforced, the experiences they created for one another led to the management-team culture they felt was essential to achieving R^2 results.

Experiences give you leverage on the beliefs and actions of your employees. Usually, you can't get people to change their beliefs or, in the long run, their actions just by asking them to. We've all seen that. But you can change beliefs and actions by creating new experiences. The process of changing culture is akin to moving a stone too big to budge with your bare hands. You need leverage in a situation like that. To move people from their current beliefs, particularly *Level-Two Beliefs*, to new ones, you need the leverage of experiences. Continual, conscious, consistent experiences that reflect and reinforce the beliefs you want people to hold will create the changes you want to create.

THIS PIECE OF THE PYRAMID: THE CONTINUING CASE OF CPI

Let's return to our ongoing example of Cardiac Pacemakers, Inc. One major experience for CPI came as Jay openly disagreed with an acquisition strategy. He convinced other key players in management to agree that CPI should not acquire a company they had been pursuing that would have required them to shut down their own larger in-house pacemaker-development effort, which supported their best-selling product line.

Jay remembers saying, "Do we all recognize the experience we're about to create for this organization if we shut down a major product-development program because we're buying a little pacemaker company?" There is no question that for the people who staffed this specific development program, and perhaps for R&D as a whole, this action would have been a Type-4 Experience. Management reached an accommodation: They would not shut down the product-development effort even if they did acquire a company.

This represented a serious turning point for CPI, but it was only one of many key experiences created on their journey to a *Culture of Accountability*. To spur product-development efforts and to demonstrate their seriousness about "fixing the engine," CPI created Heavy Weight Product Development Teams comprised of key players from the functional organizations. In addition, the functional jobs left open by this move were never filled, as all available resources were directed to product development. This was a Type-1 Experience for everyone in the organization. It communicated to everyone that CPI had established an aggressive new product development strategy and was going to make it succeed. Additionally, a new VP of R&D was promoted to provide strong technical leadership.

Furthermore, rewards were tied closely to performance. The top 10 percent and bottom 20 percent of management were ranked in terms of potential promotability. Not only were the top 10 percent identified, but the reasons they were identified as top talent were widely communicated. Interpretation made this Type-2 Experience powerful because it established clarity around the expected criteria for advancement at CPI.

The senior management team, comprised of Jay, the VPs, and the directors, identified and established B^2 beliefs. After doing so Jay and several VPs, along with an additional 28 CPI directors and managers, signed on to become facilitators of workshops designed to move the change forward. Every member of the organization participated in a one-day workshop designed to communicate the needed cultural shift and to create ownership for the shift at all levels of the company. The fact that senior managers, including Jay Graf, would spend their time leading these meetings created a Type-1 Experience for the organization: Management was serious about achieving a full-fledged cultural transition at CPI.

As we mentioned earlier, CPI chose over 160 people to receive President's Awards for outstanding demonstrations of actions consistent with CPI's seven cultural beliefs—another experience that reinforced management's ongoing commitment to making sure the shift happened. The success of CPI's cultural transition is, like any successful cultural shift, rooted in the right type of experiences, the foundation of *The Results Pyramid.*

MILESTONES ALONG THE YELLOW BRICK ROAD

Experiences are the foundation of an effective culture incorporating B^2 beliefs and A^2 actions. Leaders lead by creating useful, consistent, powerful experiences for people at all levels in the organization. Managers who cannot manage the experiences they provide find themselves at the mercy of their culture, particularly when conditions get rough. You will either manage your culture or your culture will manage you. Experiences that consciously reinforce the beliefs you need will deliver actions that yield results. That's how it works.

To transform an organizational culture or to add new elements to a fairly solid one, you need to start creating new experiences consistent with the beliefs you want. An understanding of the four types of experiences can be invaluable in this regard. Remember: Type-1 Experiences are clear and need no interpretation in order to foster desired beliefs. Type-2 Experiences need interpretation in order to foster desired beliefs. Type-3 Experiences do not impact beliefs. Type-4 Experiences will always be misinterpreted.

To shift people to new beliefs, you must generate Type-1 and Type-2 Experiences. Type-1 Experiences establish beliefs powerfully and unmistakably. Most cultural shifts will require that you generate at least several of them. However, you will of necessity be creating many Type-2 Experiences. We say "of necessity" because you have fewer chances to create Type-1 Experiences and because the filter of B^1 beliefs will lead people to incorrectly interpret some experiences. Thus, you must interpret most of the experiences you will create to ensure that people are developing the desired beliefs.

Type-3 Experiences are a nonissue in culture change. Just be certain that people are not seeing what you see as a Type-1 or Type-2 Experience as a Type 3. Remember the example of the Belief Statements that are hung on walls and ignored.

Avoid Type-4 Experiences because they will be misinterpreted. If, however, doing the right thing will create a Type-4 Experience and there is no other way to serve that end, then by all means do it and trust that time will show people that you did, indeed, do the right thing.

Finally, management teams themselves must usually shift their culture as an organization does. This, too, requires new experiences. Leaders must create experiences to foster useful beliefs for one another as well as for the rest of the organization. The leaders' beliefs do not automatically undergo a permanent shift just because they create the Beliefs Statement, as powerful as that experience can be. Rather, managers must create and sustain their own effective culture by generating Type-1 and Type-2 Experiences among themselves just as they do for the rest of the organization.

With this chapter we conclude our examination of the four elements of organizational culture and of the specific shifts needed to bring about a cultural transition. In Part Three, we introduce you to some practical tools that will help you move your organization to a new culture as quickly as possible.

PART THREE
ACCELERATING CULTURE CHANGE

They had hardly been walking an hour when they saw before them a great ditch that crossed the road. It was a very wide ditch, and when they crept up to the edge and looked into it, they could see it was also very deep, and there were many jagged rocks at the bottom.

"What shall we do?" asked Dorothy, despairingly.

"I haven't the faintest idea," said the Tin Woodman; and the Lion shook his shaggy mane and looked thoughtful. The Scarecrow said, "We cannot fly; neither can we climb down into this great ditch. Therefore, we must stop where we are."

"I think I could jump over it," said the Cowardly Lion, after measuring the distance carefully in his mind.

"Then we are all right," answered the Scarecrow, "for you can carry us all over on your back, one at a time."

"Well, I'll try it," said the Lion. The Scarecrow sat upon the Lion's back, and the big beast walked to the edge of the gulf and crouched down.

"Why don't you run and jump?" asked the Scarecrow.

"Because that isn't the way we Lions do these things," he replied. Then giving a great spring, he shot to the other side. They were all greatly pleased to see how easily he did it.

The Wonderful Wizard of Oz
L. Frank Baum

ACCELERATING CULTURE
CHANGE

All leaders shape organizational culture every day of their careers. While the culture is largely the result of the experiences that leaders either provide or do not provide, it typically develops over years and is often the result of unconscious effort on the part of management. The practices covered in Part Three enable you as a leader to consciously accelerate the cultural transition by using some proven tools that focus effort and speed the journey.

The first tool is feedback. The practice of asking for and giving feedback to one another keeps a team moving forward rapidly because they can continually adjust their experiences, beliefs, and actions to ensure that they are properly shifting them so that they reinforce and demonstrate the desired cultural beliefs. With the right kind of feedback, specifically focused on the cultural shift, people waste almost no time on the wrong road or in blind alleys.

A second tool is alignment. If people in an organization are aligned with the need for the change and with their understanding of the characteristics of the new culture, they will move toward that culture much more quickly than if they are not. The greater the alignment, the faster the movement forward. Alignment puts everyone on the same track, moving in the same direction with coordination and commitment. We show you how to create alignment around the culture change and how to maintain it throughout the process of transition.

Everything in this book relates to leadership, because leadership is the act of managing culture. Leaders must embody the culture change, make the change in themselves, and get others involved in their change process. This kind of leadership is a tool that accelerates the speed of the transition like nothing else because people see the change in their leaders. We describe what leaders must do in times of transition in order to move the change forward and bring the organization with them into the new culture.

Finally, we review several aspects of the implementation of the process that serve as tools for enrolling everyone in the organization in the culture change. Experience has shown that these elements, properly managed, will significantly enhance the success of the change effort and speed up the process of integrating the culture throughout the organization.

CHAPTER SEVEN

USING FOCUSED FEEDBACK TO ACCELERATE CHANGE

What shall we do now?

The Wonderful Wizard of Oz
L. Frank Baum

Dorothy, the Scarecrow, the Tin Woodman, and the Cowardly Lion leisurely strolled (or, when the mood struck them, skipped) down the Yellow Brick Road to get to the Emerald City. But in our increasingly competitive world, organizations cannot afford a leisurely pace on their journey to the Emerald City. In this chapter we look at the first of several accelerators that can assist organizations in moving quickly to a *Culture of Accountability*.

In identifying accelerators of cultural transition we begin with feedback. Feedback is to successful cultural transition what Dorothy was to her traveling companions. When Dorothy applies the oil to the rusted Tin Woodman, she gets him to move. Feedback can have a similar effect on an organization. Without feedback, movement toward a C^2 culture is limited at best. With feedback, particularly when it is employed in the manner we describe in this chapter, movement toward a *Culture of Accountability* is accelerated.

Feedback of various kinds exists in many organizations, but rarely is it employed as the tool for change that it can and should be. There are reasons for this, which we examine in this chapter. We also examine how people at all levels of the organization can give and receive useful, actionable feedback in a way that generates change.

While there are other kinds of feedback, we concentrate on feedback focused on whether or not individuals and teams demonstrate the B^2 beliefs and A^2 actions necessary to achieve the R^2 results. For example, we worked with the global manufacturing services group of a large company that needed to create a significant shift in its culture. This was a service group, a huge, sophisticated facilities management group, whose very existence was at risk. Their internal customers believed that the group's services were dictated to them, and were overpriced to boot. This services group needed to shift from a culture of entitlement to a customer-driven team, and they needed to shift quickly.

After they crafted a set of customer-focused beliefs, they used feedback to help them align their actions around those beliefs. As the executive director of the group put it, "Once we established the beliefs, we exchanged open and honest feedback on how we were doing as a team, began practicing the beliefs, and then expanded them throughout the organization. Through feedback at all levels of the organization we learned to live by those beliefs. Without constant commitment to give and get open and honest feedback we could not have made this change happen as quickly as we did."

When people in the group went out to the company's divisions and tried to change by creating a new experience and demonstrating the beliefs, they naturally encountered problems. The internal customers still held the same old beliefs and expected the same old approaches: You'll tell us what you'll do, whether or not we want it, and then you'll allocate the costs to us. When people in the service group encountered this resistance they would come back to the team and talk about it: "Here's what I'm facing. Here's what I'm up against . . ." This would begin a conversation that included feedback, coaching, and encouragement. Collectively, people in the group pooled their knowledge and asked each other, "What else can you do?"

The executive director points out that, "Open feedback specifically around our B^2 belief of accountability stands out as the one thing, more than any other, that accelerated the transition. We used to be very directive. We changed that behavior to requesting honest feedback about problems, and we continually pushed ourselves back to the accountability approach. Feedback gets people unfrozen from their old behaviors. Continual feedback has helped us get aligned around a common language centered on our cultural beliefs and organizational results and on accountability for upholding the beliefs and achieving the results."

WHY FEEDBACK DOESN'T WORK

Most management teams recognize the value of feedback, but find it hard to practice. While most organizations have some sort of feedback mechanisms, ranging from on-the-spot critiques to annual performance appraisals to occasional 360-degree surveys, these approaches often do little to implement cultural change. There are three reasons that feedback doesn't work for many companies: There is too little given. The feedback lacks context. And when it is received, it is often ignored. Let's examine how these barriers can be overcome so that feedback can be used as a true accelerator of culture change.

WHERE'S THE FEEDBACK?

In most companies there is far too little feedback of any kind. In talking with thousands of managers and professionals, we've never heard anyone say that they receive too much feedback. Instead, most people say that they receive too little feedback, that they want and need much more than they get. Feedback should be a big part of communicating on any team.

Feedback is countercultural to most organizations. We have seen this wherever we've gone in the world. Many U.S. companies have told us that their overseas affiliates would be less open to feedback. At times, we've been told that certain cultures, for example, those in Latin America, are particularly reluctant to give or receive feedback. Yet our experience has been that organizations everywhere—Latin America, Europe, Asia, and North America—are all equally devoid of frequent, useful, focused feedback and that all of them are receptive to learning how to do it when it is properly presented.

Because feedback is not typically a cultural strength yet is essential to cultural transition, many organizations create Cultural Belief Statements that include a specific B^2 belief about feedback.

In many companies people virtually never give or receive feedback, except in annual performance appraisals, and then they are often surprised at what they hear. Many companies, particularly very small ones, don't even do appraisals. Appraisals are often not completed in a timely manner or are given a fraction of the time and thought they deserve. Superiors don't like giving them. Subordinates don't like getting them. Even when given, annual performance appraisals tend to work poorly. We have a firm belief: *Once-a-year feedback doesn't work.* Such an interval is too long for the feedback to be of any real value. Feedback that infrequent is usually either too watered down to be effective or so hard-hitting that the person being critiqued becomes defensive, goes into a tailspin, and winds up *Below the Line*. While annual performance appraisals can play a role, they don't provide enough feedback to speed up culture change.

The fact that too little feedback is shared in a company should not suggest that the potential for it does not exist. We believe most companies hold vast storehouses of valuable feedback waiting to be tapped. As an experiment, ask yourself the following questions:

- First, if your boss or one of your subordinates or colleagues were to ask you openly and candidly, "What feedback do you have for me?" would you have any for that person?

- Second, do you think that if the person took that feedback to heart, it would help him or her improve his or her results?

- Third, have you actually ever given the person this feedback?

A great majority of the people answering these three questions acknowledge that they have not provided that feedback. Finally, ask yourself:

- Do you think there are people on your team who may have valuable feedback for you, but are hesitant to share it with you?

Consider these questions, and your answers, and see if you don't agree that people have potentially valuable feedback for one another, if they can just learn to give it and receive it. This is even truer when you begin practicing the Cultural Beliefs. The people around you will be in a position to give you helpful feedback that will strengthen the experiences you create and help you interpret these experiences for others.

You have to make time for feedback. It doesn't have to be a lot of time, particularly if you make frequent feedback part of your culture, which is essential for rapid change. But it does require some time. *Above the Line* organizations make time for feedback. In contrast, the *Below the Line* mentality, which fails to place priority on feedback, slows down change and perpetuates C^1 behavior and actions.

FEEDBACK WITHOUT CONTEXT

Feedback is often given without an overall context. In other words the feedback may or may not move someone forward in emulating the C^2 culture. In actual practice a lot of feedback addresses so-called strengths and weaknesses (let's face it, usually weaknesses). Telling people that they have to handle themselves better in meetings or that they have to get organized is not the kind of feedback we're talking about here, at least not when it is expressed that way. Feedback, to be useful, needs to be much more specific. To be an accelerator of cultural transition it needs to be given within the context of *The Results Pyramid.*

We believe that feedback is most powerful when it is tied to the B^2 beliefs and A^2 actions necessary to create the C^2 culture. To create organizational culture, you must guide the person getting the feedback toward the desired beliefs, actions, and results. This lifts the entire feedback transaction to a higher plane, one well above personal strengths and weaknesses, and gives it context and direction.

This entails using statements such as, "We believe in treating one another with respect in this company, Helen, and I know you hold that belief. But that was not the experience I had in this morning's meeting when you spoke to Jim about the idea he presented." A statement such as, "Will you please tone it down in meetings from now on?" isn't as effective, certainly not in the long run. It is vague, critical, unfocused, and, to the person hearing it, probably all too familiar. Unfocused feedback is perhaps better than no feedback at all, but it is characteristic of organizations that have not defined their culture. In these organizations feedback lacks context because context has not been established.

FILTERING OUT FEEDBACK

The third reason feedback doesn't work is that even when people get useful, focused feedback, they often rationalize and externalize it. They find ways to label it "inaccurate perception" rather than "applicable observation." They dismiss it. They defend against it. They look for ways to invalidate it. They don't *Own It.*

People externalize feedback by running it through filters, which usually screen out much of the feedback they receive. For instance, we worked with an engineer (whom we'll call Mark) who rose to vice president of manufacturing. Mark had an interesting approach to feedback. He told us that he would consciously and successively apply a set of filters to any feedback he received on the job. If he heard feedback, he would ask himself, "Is it accurate or not?" If the feedback made it through this first filter he would then ask, "Is there a basis for this or not?" If it made it through that one he would ask, "Is it relevant or not?" and, finally, if it made it through all of the preceding filters he would ask, "Is it right or wrong?" Mark told us (and his team) that he would respond to any of the feedback that made it through all four of his filters.

Figure 7-1 below depicts these filters—and the ultimate result.

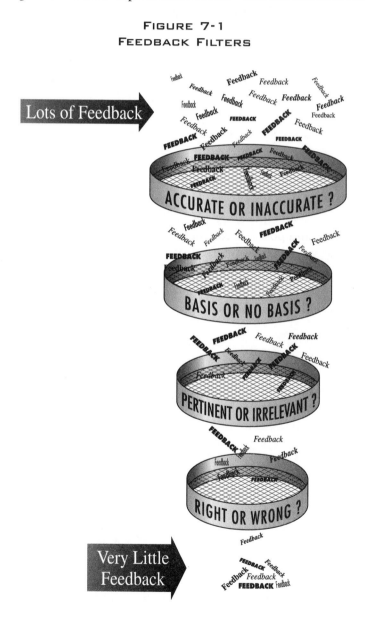

FIGURE 7-1
FEEDBACK FILTERS

After Mark described this process to us we asked him how much feedback he actually responded to. He replied, "That's just the problem. I don't get any good feedback!" In truth, by the time he was done running the feedback through his filters, there was precious little of it left.

Many, perhaps most of us, take an approach similar to Mark's. Here are some filters people commonly apply when receiving feedback:

You're not my boss. (Who died and left you in charge?)

He's new around here. What could he know?

He's been here forever. He's totally out of touch.

Why should I listen to headquarters staff? They never sold for a living.

Why should we listen to salespeople? They don't see the big picture.

I used to think like that when I was at their level.

Why should I listen to him? He doesn't do it either!

The expatriates just don't understand how things work here.

Given this, you might think it's a miracle that any feedback ever gets through to anyone. People in every country and in every industry, company, and position use filters.

By the way, Mark's filtering of feedback created an interesting experience for his people. We interviewed some members of his team, asking them to tell us about Mark and feedback. They said, "That's just the problem. Mark doesn't listen to feedback." In fact, they had stopped giving it long ago.

Filters not only reduce the feedback you get to mere crumbs, but eventually reduce the amount that you're initially given to nothing. If you don't respond to feedback, you stop getting it. When that happens, you're much more susceptible to unpleasant surprises. When people in the company stop telling you things that you need to hear because they think you're not open to hearing them, you're on your own. And when people in the company stop telling one another the things they need to do to better demonstrate B^2 beliefs and A^2 actions, the change process stalls.

During the cultural transition, Mark decided to abandon his filters and adopt two new questions. Upon hearing feedback, he simply asks:

Is that a belief I want people to have?

Will that belief get in the way of getting results?

Try applying these questions to the feedback you receive. For instance, if someone tells you that the meetings you chair are unproductive or that the company's prices are too high or that people don't have the resources they need to get their jobs done, they're expressing a belief, aren't they? If you ask yourself, "Is that a belief I want this person to have?" and, "Will that belief get in the way of getting results?" aren't you going to embark on a more fruitful line of reasoning than you would by screening out the feedback?

If someone has a belief that will lead him or her to actions that are not aligned with R^2 results, then we say, "Change it." How you go about that will depend on the belief and the situation. But the key question—however you ask it—is: "Does that belief work?" "Will it move us to C^2?" If it doesn't, you have to change it in order to get the results you want.

In our experience these belief-based questions supercharge the feedback process so that it leads to a change in behavior. You get more feedback and you act on more of it, with better outcomes. You feel better about responding to feedback. This is because you are not filtering out feedback, or ignoring it, or discounting the source, or making value judgments on it. You are simply taking the feedback at face value—viewing it as information, as a point of view—and considering the key point: "Since this belief exists, what should I do?" If the belief drives A^2 actions, great. If it doesn't, then the question becomes, "What do I need to do to shift this belief—how do I change the experience I am creating?"

These belief-based questions *must* become part of the way you think and act if you are serious about accelerating the shift to a new culture. They are extremely useful replacements for whatever filters are currently operating in your culture. Filters have kept entire organizations in the dark when feedback from competitors, customers, and internal innovators was there for the taking. Filters impede behavior change, the key to any cultural transition. Ultimately, openness followed by ownership represents the only useful posture toward feedback.

GIVING AND RECEIVING FEEDBACK

People benefit most from feedback when they are open to it. Openness impacts both the giver and the receiver. When giving feedback it is best to do so in the spirit of sharing a point of view or a perspective that you believe might be helpful. People respond more favorably to feedback when it is given without a sense of absoluteness or "this is the way it is." When receiving feedback it is best to view it as something potentially helpful, and feel neither threatened by it nor reflexively reject it or become defensive.

People who give or receive feedback in the context of "perspectives being shared," rather than "truth being declared," tend to manifest greater openness. They understand that a variety of perspectives—including their own—have value. Nobody's perspective is correct, or even useful, 100 percent of the time.

An example from Federal Express lore captures incorrect feedback from a Yale University management professor who graded Fred Smith's paper on a reliable overnight delivery service. "The concept is interesting and well-informed, but in order to earn better than a 'C,' the idea must be feasible." Now this professor truly believed that an overnight delivery service would not work. But Fred Smith listened to the feedback and, while probably finding it hard to hear at the time, evaluated what he heard and went on to found Federal Express, which he leads today as its CEO.

When giving feedback we must all remember that we are offering just one perspective—our own. However, if we wait to give feedback until we are 100 percent certain that it is 100 percent correct, we will limit ourselves to giving feedback rarely, if at all, or to merely stating the obvious.

ATTITUDES TOWARD FEEDBACK

The attitudes of openness that foster the right approach to feedback warrant examination, as do the opposite, closed attitudes. The simple matrix in Figure 7-2 brings together a range of attitudes toward feedback.

In this matrix, the horizontal axis through the middle represents a continuum of attitudes that people hold toward getting the perspectives of others. This continuum ranges from "Open to others' perspectives" to "Closed to others' perspectives." The vertical axis through the middle represents a continuum of attitudes toward sharing one's own perspectives. This continuum ranges from "Openly shares perspectives" to "Does not share perspectives."

The attitudes that any person holds toward feedback can be plotted on this continuum. Or you can plot your own attitudes. Here's how: Start with the left-hand end of the "Open to others' perspectives"

FIGURE 7–2
ATTITUDES TOWARD FEEDBACK: FOUR DIFFERENT PROFILES

Openly Shares Perspectives

Open to Others Perspectives · **Closed to Others Perspectives**

Inviting Open to feedback from others and willingly provides feedback.	**Intimidating** Openly shares their own perspectives but relatively closed to others' perspectives.
Influenceable Open to feedback from others, but less willing to share their own perspectives.	**Immovable** Closed to others' perspectives and sparingly shares their own views.

Does Not Share Perspectives

continuum and mark the spot on the line that represents your relative openness toward the perspectives of others. The exact center would be average, while points to the left or right of that would be above or below average. (Be honest!) Then go to the vertical, sharing-perspectives continuum and mark the point that represents your relative openness toward sharing your perspectives with others. Again, the exact center would be average.

The final step is to use the marks on each axis as coordinates and to plot the point defined by these coordinates (as shown in the figure). That point will tell you which quadrant you fall into. We have labeled each quadrant with the corresponding attitude toward feedback: Inviting, Intimidating, Influenceable, or Immovable. Here is a description of each of these postures:

Inviting: Open to feedback from others and willingly provides feedback. This is the most desirable approach to feedback, so efforts to move oneself and others toward this attitude will be rewarded.

Influenceable: Open to feedback from others, but less willing to share their own perspectives. This attitude often characterizes those who need extra direction or who lack confidence in their own judgments. They should be encouraged to share their views, and those views should be acknowledged as valuable.

Intimidating: Openly share their own perspectives but relatively closed to others' perspectives. In extreme forms, this is the posture of the "know-it-all." People who willingly share their viewpoints can have valuable perspectives. Yet if they reject others' views they cut off communication and create an intimidating air about them. They generally need to "tone down" the presentation of their views and become much better listeners.

Immovable: Closed to others' perspectives and sparingly share their own views. This attitude cuts off communication in both directions. Immovable people lack confidence in their own views *and* feel threatened by the perspectives of others. They must learn to trust that others are interested in their perspectives and that others' views are not going to undermine them.

The best attitude toward feedback, as toward so many things, is a balanced one. This does not imply a position at the just-average dead center, but rather one in the upper-left-hand quadrant. An inviting posture characterizes people who willingly accept the perspectives of others while openly sharing their own views. This attitude facilitates the sharing of feedback during culture change. Leaders should take steps to create this attitude toward feedback by modeling and personifying the approach. This will do more to move the organization toward an open posture than any other single thing.

Ron Whitcomb, manager of field services for Oakley Aircraft Equipment, oversees technical support for the North American region. (The situation is real, but the name is fictitious.) As part of his job he works with airlines to get planes out of circulation long enough for his team to get in and make seating repairs. To an airline, avoiding down time is crucial, so they must coordinate schedules with Oakley, based in Britain, to make sure that they have the correct parts on hand in, say, Minneapolis.

Ron told us that he learned long ago that the best way to establish a good working relationship is to be willing to receive feedback from your employees, subcontractors, and customers. He then related the following story: "A few years ago I had an assignment to begin the modification of the seats for one of our account, a major U.S. airline. As part of my job I am accountable if anything goes wrong in the installation of the seats. Every nut and bolt has to be scrutinized for size, weight, strength, and torque. The potential liability is enormous, and because of the exacting nature of the business, I like to be on site for the first few days. I had been in the habit of dictating exactly how the job was to be done, regardless of what the rest of the team thought. After all, it was my neck on the line. I knew that if the team followed my direction there would be no mistakes. Besides, doing it my way produced very good results!"

Ron continued, "As time passed, I sensed that some of the subcontractors were frustrated with me. I halfheartedly asked for some feedback one day and was surprised at their response. Some of the things they said were hard for me to hear. The team members were very frank about the way I was managing them. They suggested that I relax and listen to what they had to say once in awhile. They indicated that I didn't give them enough credit. The team felt that if they could make a few changes in the order of the repair and the assembly, without compromising aircraft safety or FAA regulations, they would be able to increase productivity and take some pressure off all of us.

"Because I started to listen, I began to *see* what they had been trying to tell me. The way I had been doing things worked, but what they had proposed could work better. Feeling a little skeptical, I finally agreed to the changes. The employees were right! Because of the changes, minor as they may seem, productivity increased and the workers are happy. Moreover, they feel valued. The airlines and Oakley save money, as many of our subcontractors bill on an hourly basis. I learned that listening to the ones who do the work makes a world of difference. While we cannot always implement what employees want, it is very valuable, even profitable, to listen. Now when I get on a job site, I invite suggestions as well as offer my own thoughts. Our working environment is better because people know that I will listen and gain their perspective first, before I make major decisions."

That's the balance to strive for, because it does the most to accelerate cultural transition and improve your ability to achieve the results you have targeted.

After you plot your own attitudes toward feedback, you might find it interesting to plot those of your boss or some of your colleagues as well. Finally, and perhaps most usefully, you might want to explain the matrix to a trusted colleague and ask him or her to plot *your* attitudes on the matrix. Just remember to be open to that feedback!

THANKS FOR THE FEEDBACK

That reminds us—when you get feedback the best response is direct and simple: *Thanks for the feedback!* When most people hear feedback, they act as if they must accept, reject, or act upon it immediately. Yes, there may be urgent or high-pressure situations where you have to act on the feedback instantly. But generally all you need to say is, "Thanks for the feedback!" You're not thanking them for being accurate, or right, or insightful. All you're thanking the person for is his or her willingness to provide the feedback he or she had for you. At the same time, "Thanks for the feedback!" expresses no judgment of the feedback itself or commitment to any specific change in action.

This response is not the only answer that we recommend. If the feedback is obviously useful, the better response might be, "Great idea! I'll do that." However, there's usually no need to evaluate, accept, or reject feedback on the spot. It's best to take time to think it over, and saying, "Thanks for the feedback!" buys you that time.

PROVIDING FOCUSED FEEDBACK

Feedback focused on shifting the organization to a *Culture of Accountability* will accelerate the transition to C^2. As we've noted, this feedback focuses on the B^2 beliefs and A^2 actions that produce the R^2 results you're committed to achieve. This feedback should help people see when and where they are, or are not, demonstrating the cultural beliefs. This kind of feedback accelerates behavior change because it ties beliefs to actions in the context of the cultural transition.

Specifically, focused feedback should be provided around the Cultural Beliefs along two dimensions: reinforcing and constructive. Reinforcing feedback is feedback that addresses how someone is positively demonstrating the Cultural Beliefs and actions. It is important to provide reinforcement when people live the beliefs, particularly during cultural change, so that they keep on demonstrating the desired behavior. Constructive feedback provides the recipient with suggestions and guidance on what else they can do to demonstrate the beliefs more fully. Both reinforcing and constructive feedback are important to helping people live the Cultural Beliefs.

Consciously tying feedback to beliefs enables leaders to work with people's beliefs, instead of just at the level of actions. We mentioned in Chapter One that many managers mistakenly focus on changing people's actions by simply and solely asking them to change their behavior. It is far more effective and lasting to reference the Cultural Beliefs and, if necessary (and it often is), to help the person receiving the feedback to relate those beliefs to their actions. Feedback becomes a powerful accelerator of cultural change when it is framed in terms of the beliefs, in terms of promulgating them throughout the organization through the right experiences.

Feedback couched solely as criticism geared to correcting mistakes when people are not demonstrating C^2 beliefs and actions will cause them to avoid giving and getting feedback. It focuses attention on the wrong things—the mistakes people make as they move into the new culture.

Instead, any step in the direction of C^2 should be genuinely encouraged. Any attempt, even a failed attempt, to demonstrate the cultural beliefs should be reinforced. While constructive feedback is essential we believe strongly in the power of reinforcing feedback as a tool for motivating people to demonstrate the desired beliefs, actions, and results. Positive feedback will do much to reinforce the culture shift.

IF YOU WANT FEEDBACK, YOU MUST SEEK IT

Leaders must assume accountability for creating the environment of trust and teamwork in which feedback can flourish. Leaders can do this best by asking for feedback themselves. In fact, making feedback part of the culture requires leaders to begin asking for feedback, from one another and from subordinates. When interpreted correctly and done consistently over time the experience of leaders asking for feedback will promulgate a belief that asking for and offering feedback is "the way we do things around here."

For instance, a major consumer packaged-goods company found that employees believed their managers weren't "doing enough for them." According to the company's internal organizational-effectiveness consultant, people felt their managers weren't giving them enough guidance and weren't seeing to their development. A lot of complaints were aimed at management, but when we asked employees whether they had requested feedback, their reply was, "No, it's not my job to ask for it."

This attitude was widespread in the organization. People took no accountability for seeking feedback. As we have mentioned, this is not unusual. The internal consultant went on to explain, "The big change [after making feedback part of the culture] has been that employees now see they have a key role to play and that they don't have to wait for someone to give them something. They are, in fact, accountable to seek out feedback and to manage their own development and to engage their manager in those areas." Creating a culture in which people become accountable to ask for feedback places them in the driver's seat regarding their jobs, performance, and advancement. Somewhat paradoxically, asking for feedback from others empowers the person who is doing the asking.

Leaders must initiate this endeavor. They have to be the first to ask for feedback on how well they are demonstrating the Cultural Beliefs because they must model the behaviors and create the experiences that they want people to have. Assuming accountability for receiving feedback begins with asking for it. Simply asking, "What feedback do you have for me?" begins the process. Getting people to ask this question accelerates the cultural transition. Getting everyone in the organization to ask it will speed the journey to C^2.

You cannot get feedback by wishing or hoping for it, nor can you control the amount that people will spontaneously give you. You can, however, control the amount you request. We purposely phrase the question as an open-ended one: "What feedback do you have for me?" It is not a yes-or-no question but rather one that assumes that the person does have feedback for you. If the person answers "None," or "None at the moment," that's OK. The question is still more thought provoking than, "Do you have any feedback for me?"

FEEDBACK AND ACCOUNTABILITY

A key point: *If you don't do anything with the feedback, then it will not accelerate culture change.* Aside from the sheer lack of feedback in most organizations, the greatest problem is that so little of what there is gets used. To be an accelerator of culture change, feedback must be acted upon by those who receive it (including management). Our point is not simply that people should get feedback. Our point is that when people get feedback and then act on it, they accelerate cultural change.

A friend of ours, who is a pilot, recently told us of a time when he ignored valuable feedback, which almost cost him and three other people their lives. Here's the story in his own words.

I made plans with my fiancée (whom I married a year later) and her sister and boyfriend who were going with us to fly to Vacaville, a 20-minute flight from San Jose, and have dinner at a nice restaurant next to the airport. I had to return in time for a mandatory meeting at work later that evening. During my preflight on the plane, I noticed there was not enough fuel to make the round trip. I didn't want to waste time and knew we had plenty of fuel for the trip to Vacaville— we could refuel while eating in the restaurant and not affect the schedule at all.

We boarded the plane and headed for Vacaville, where, after a smooth landing, I parked near the fueling area. Unfortunately, the fuel operator had closed for the day. There was a note to call the operator at home and he would come out for an enormous fee. I reasoned that we could fly to Livermore Airport, which was halfway between Vacaville and San Jose, and get fueled without paying this ridiculous fee. I was able to convince everyone that we didn't need to worry, that we would have just enough fuel to get us to Livermore.

After a wonderful dinner, we hurried to the plane and departed Vacaville. When I called Livermore from the air, I was informed that all fueling operations had closed for the evening. At this point my passengers were seriously concerned. I told them we had just enough fuel to make it to Hayward Airport, which is just over the hill by the bay.

I called Hayward Airport and their fueling service was open. I notified Hayward tower that I would like to land there. They informed me that the fog had just rolled in and would prevent our landing there.

I turned the airplane toward the San Jose Airport where I knew the weather would be clear. This had become my only choice. My future sister-in-law asked me what we were doing now! Everybody in the plane was upset. I could hardly blame them. At this point I was upset with myself.

The extra flying over Livermore and then Hayward had burned even more fuel. I was approaching San Jose Airport from the north. The control tower told me to use runway 30. This meant that I would have to fly past the airport, turn around, and approach from the south. I told the tower I was low on fuel and would appreciate no delays. The controller then suggested I use runway 12 and told me he would divert all other traffic so I could do so. However, not wanting to interrupt the landing pattern, I told him that I would just use runway 30.

With the right fuel-tank gauge below the E, and the left one on the E, everyone was yelling at me to do what the controller suggested and get this plane on the ground. This time was the only time during the entire trip that I acted on feedback. I called the tower back and told them that I thought I needed to use runway 12. The tower immediately diverted all other incoming traffic and then cleared me to land. The landing was considered an emergency, and fire trucks were positioned in case we didn't make it.

The landing was smooth and uneventful. My friends were ecstatic when the wheels touched the runway with the engines still running. To be honest so was I. Just for the fun of it, the fuel service operator drained the right tank and found about one quart of fuel. That is about 15 seconds of engine-operating time in flight. I let out a nervous laugh and learned a valuable lesson about what it means to really listen and take advantage of the feedback you receive.

As this story shows, if you don't hold yourself accountable to act on the feedback you receive, you will likely pay a price. During cultural transition you must take accountability to act on feedback received.

Feedback is the way we tell one another whether or not we are manifesting the cultural beliefs and getting the results we want. It tells us where to make adjustments in order to demonstrate our beliefs more completely and achieve our results more fully. Feedback enables us to adjust the experiences we are creating.

Sometimes feedback is hard to hear. We have heard it referred to as "the truth that can't be spoken" or "the 800-pound gorilla that we're trying to ignore." The little boy who said that the emperor had no clothes was providing hard-to-hear feedback. None of the adults in town would dare to point it out. Often people will speak the hard-to-hear truth to one another, but not to those who need to hear it. One of our clients shared an insight that is true of many companies: "We are a lot better at talking *about* people than we are at talking *to* people." Imagine how clearly the people in your company could *See It* if simple "truths" could be communicated in a positive, constructive manner. That is the first step toward implementing a *Culture of Accountability* and the fastest way to get a transition moving, or moving faster.

People who have truly assumed accountability for demonstrating the organizational beliefs and for achieving the desired results seek the perspectives of others. This enables them to *See It*. This in turn enables them to offer their perspectives to others, which will help more people to become accountable. Those people will then seek the perspectives of others and more clearly *See It*, and so on. A key point here warrants emphasis: The leaders set the virtuous cycle in motion by seeking the perspectives of others. (Over 50 years ago, Dale Carnegie noted that the most interesting question you could ask someone is: "What do you think?" That's asking for feedback.)

The next step is to *Own It*. Anyone who sees the feedback and then thinks that it doesn't apply to him or her is in trouble. To *Own It* you must acknowledge your involvement. The famous quote from Eldridge Cleaver says, "If you're not part of the solution, you're part of the problem." But to *Own It* you must realize that "If you're not part of the problem, you're not part of the solution." You have to acknowledge your role in creating the current culture of your organization—and this is particularly so if you're in a leadership position—if you're to play a role in shifting the culture. To play that role effectively, you must consistently ask, "What feedback do you have for me?" Then you must own the feedback by making the tie between what you're hearing and what you have done.

Feedback works as a tool for culture change only when people respond to it. This means that after saying, "Thanks for the feedback!" you must *Solve It* by asking "What else can I do to demonstrate our beliefs?" Finally, you must *Do It* by reporting proactively on your progress in implementing the feedback and doing the things you say you'll do.

You must *See It*, *Own It*, *Solve It*, and *Do It* with regard to giving feedback as well. To model the behavior, you must assume accountability for giving feedback when you've got it, not just when you're asked to provide it. The organization must value feedback (there must be a strong cultural belief in its importance) or you will not make time for it. The experience you create when you make time for feedback will accelerate your transition to a *Culture of Accountability*.

Companies that use feedback as a tool for creating a C² culture find that they spend more time discussing the important things in an open and candid manner and embrace accountability for helping others succeed. They also find that they can change their company faster than they ever thought possible.

Think about it: Two people cannot move a piece of furniture down a staircase without giving each other feedback. How can a company hope to move its culture if its people don't give one another constant feedback in the process?

MILESTONES ALONG THE YELLOW BRICK ROAD

Feedback represents a powerful vehicle that can speed your organization to a new, more effective culture—if you use the right kind of feedback and use it well. Unfortunately, in most organizations there is far too little feedback and what little there is tends to lack context. Much feedback is simply ignored by the receiver. To accelerate culture change, feedback must be frequent, focused, and unfiltered.

By frequent, we mean daily, continual, ongoing. When you are shifting an organization to a new culture, it is impossible for people to request or receive too much feedback. By focused, we mean focused on the beliefs the organization has agreed to adopt and the results it has committed to achieve. By unfiltered, we mean that people must be open to feedback. The most open posture to adopt to feedback is an inviting one.

As we have seen, the way in which you give and ask for feedback is important. Asking for and offering both reinforcing and constructive feedback will do the most to encourage positive efforts while correcting shortcomings. That kind of feedback focuses on what is working *and* what could be better. Ask for feedback by saying, "What feedback do you have for me?" and when you receive some say, "Thanks for the feedback!"

To evaluate feedback ask yourself, "Is this a belief I want people to have?" and "If people have that belief, how will it affect their actions and our results?" Our approach is to see input from others as just that—input, information, a point of view. It is merely someone expressing a belief. If that belief works for the organization, great. If it doesn't work, then you need to change the belief, rather than deny that it exists or shoot the messenger.

This brings up the last key point about feedback: You have to use it. The most important point of this chapter is not that people should give one another feedback, it is that you must get feedback so that you can act on it. Feedback, no matter how good it is, will not be a tool for accelerating culture change unless you put it to use.

By using feedback in the context of the cultural beliefs, people will gain a clear sense of how they are demonstrating those beliefs and what they can do to further demonstrate them. In this way, they can adjust the experiences they are creating in order to accelerate the transition to a *Culture of Accountability*.

CHAPTER EIGHT

ALIGNING A CULTURE FOR RAPID PROGRESS

I am everywhere, but . . . I am invisible

The Wonderful Wizard of Oz
L. Frank Baum

Frank Baum's book, *The Wonderful Wizard of Oz*, explains that the wizard himself created the Emerald City. The people of Oz take him to be a great and powerful wizard because, as an Omaha-based circus balloonist brought in on a strong wind, he came to them from a faraway place. As a "wizard" he is able to get the people of Oz to build the city, complete with lots of greenery, hence the name the Emerald City. He keeps order and happiness by claiming that his magic extends to all reaches of the city.

Unfortunately managers have no magical powers, or even the appearance of them, to bring about change. But they do have something equally powerful—the concept of alignment. And while alignment itself is invisible, you know whether or not it is present when you see how people act in an organization. When practiced, alignment can significantly increase the pace of progress.

The dictionary defines alignment in terms of adjusting the parts of something, in relation to one another, so that they are properly positioned. For the purposes of accelerating the transformation from C^1 to C^2, we are concerned with adjusting the parts of a culture so they are positioned properly in relation to one another. Unless experiences, beliefs, and actions are aligned with and reinforce R^2 results, useful culture change cannot occur. A lack of alignment, as shown in Figure 8-1, undermines the pursuit of organizational results.

When an organization is out of alignment, progress toward any result, particularly culture change, will be slower and the risk of failure higher than in an aligned company. Without alignment people work at cross-purposes. They do so not because they are incompetent or lazy, nor because they want to undermine the organization. Rather, they are out of sync and uncoordinated, pursuing their own objectives without building on the synergy found in working with one another. The solution is to get everyone—every person, function, department, and division—aligned around the C^2 culture. Everyone's experiences, beliefs, and actions must be aligned with the results that the leaders have decided to pursue. The leaders must initiate this process, but everyone in the company ultimately becomes accountable for maintaining it.

Please do not let the mechanical connotations of the word alignment throw you. You can, for instance, align the wheels of your car and forget about them for a while. Carpenters can align the joists of a house they are constructing and the building can stand straight for decades. This is not the case when you are aligning an organization.

FIGURE 8-1
A CULTURE OUT OF ALIGNMENT

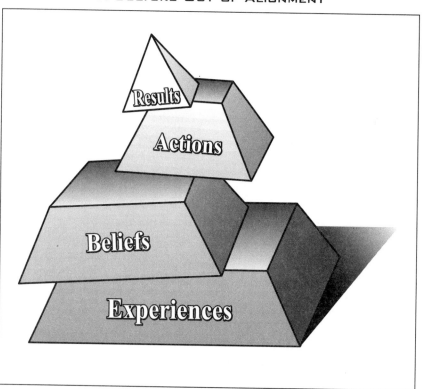

In this chapter we examine alignment—what it is and how to achieve it—in depth. In its various forms, alignment represents your second accelerator (after feedback) for speeding your journey down the Yellow Brick Road.

GETTING ALIGNED AROUND ALIGNMENT

Let's spend a moment examining the importance of alignment. Remember, everything we've discussed in this book has one overarching purpose: to help people get results. Leaders shift a culture in order to achieve R^2 results. Either the culture is not producing the desired results, or it will not be able to continue to produce them given a coming change in the environment.

Consider the case of Remedy Corp., a manufacturer of computer help-desk software in Mountain View, California. Marianne Detwiler wrote of this company's success in creating alignment in the fall 1997 issue of *Entrepreneurial Edge*. Remedy has grown to $104 million in annual sales just five years after its formation. From the beginning, Remedy's founders established the philosophy and "belief" that being the "customer advocate" should drive all business decisions and processes. Detwiler reports cofounder Mahler's belief: "Our philosophy is that every employee is a sales-and-service person." She states that Remedy Corp. noticed that "most vendors who were trying to sell a product would set up appointments with potential customers, pretend to listen to the customers' problems, then redefine the customers' problems in terms of their product's features."

Remedy wanted to do it differently. Mahler continues: "We wanted to be the champion for the customer's problem in the vendor community and really establish a warm relationship with customers." To get everyone aligned with this approach, Mahler says, "Every employee is responsible for answering customer questions and complaints; it doesn't matter if they are in finance, sales, marketing, or engineering. We tell them it's their job to take the question—even if they can't understand it—write it down, own it, and get back to the customer because from their point of view, the employee is Remedy."

Remedy's been happy with the results. Not only has this approach produced incredible sales growth, it also earned the company the top listing on *Business Week*'s hottest growth companies. Remedy created a clear result that everyone could buy into. Then they drove a philosophy and set of cultural beliefs that were specific and well articulated and paid constant attention to them. They created alignment among all the pieces of the pyramid: they created experiences that drove the desired beliefs to motivate the needed actions and produce results.

We define alignment as: *common beliefs and concerted action in collective pursuit of a clear result*. The first part of this definition—common beliefs and concerted action—encompasses culture (that is, what people think and do.) The final part—a clear result—covers the outcome produced by the culture. Again, you change the culture to get a new and better result. So you need alignment around both the C^2 culture and around the results you expect that culture to produce. If people hold common beliefs, they will act in concert. If people hold common beliefs, engage in concerted action, *and* are collectively pursuing a clear result—that's power! That's the power of alignment.

The commonality of belief and the concertedness of action must occur from person to person, function to function, and across the organization. As people enroll in the process of change and sign up to the C^2 culture, a collective energy emerges. People must hold common beliefs, and those beliefs must drive concerted action. The more closely aligned the people are, the faster they can accelerate change and produce new results. For this to occur, however, you must first understand what causes people to get out of alignment.

FORCES THAT PUSH YOU OUT OF ALIGNMENT

Unfortunately, a company's culture does not stay in alignment by itself. *Alignment is a process, not an event.* It is a process because the forces working to push the company out of alignment are constant. They are the same forces working to pull people *Below the Line* and to draw a company back toward the C^1 culture. Some of the key forces that work to push a company out of alignment during culture change are shown in Figure 8-2.

During a shift to a new culture vestiges of the old C^1 culture will work hard to throw the company out of alignment. This always happens. A change in culture is always accompanied by experiences that reinforce the old beliefs, experiences that are interpreted as C^1, and as

FIGURE 8-2
FORCES THAT PUSH YOU OUT OF ALIGNMENT

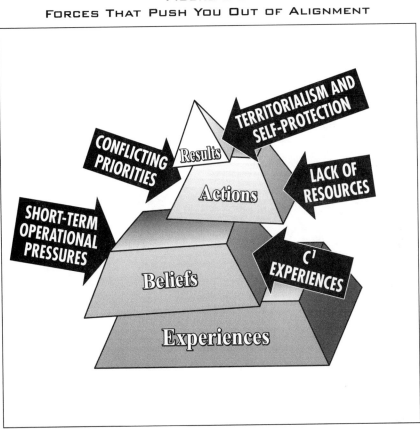

Type-4 Experiences that push the organization in the wrong direction. Then, once you gain alignment, you must maintain it. Leaders must understand when they know when they have failed to create alignment or when they have lost it. Figure 8-3 lists some telltale signs of a lack of alignment.

Recognizing that you lack alignment enables you to do something about it. Based on their actions, many leaders must think there is not much to be done about lack of alignment: It's just a fact of organizational life. But lack of alignment in adopting C^2 beliefs and performing A^2 actions will halt the culture transition. That is why you must be vigilant in identifying any lack of alignment and then move quickly to correct the problem.

FIGURE 8-3
HOW TO TELL WHEN YOU'RE NOT ALIGNED

Signs of a Lack of Alignment

People remain silent and don't voice their opinion when you call for a decision.

You keep being surprised by the actions people take because they are inconsistent with the agreed-upon direction.

You don't see tangible progress on an issue when by all rights you should be moving forward throughout the organization.

In meetings, people keep bringing up issues that you thought were resolved.

People complain, make excuses and blame others for lack of progress.

You observe a lack of ownership and enthusiasm for implementing a course of action that has been set.

People state that they disagree with a decision or a direction that has already been taken.

ALIGNMENT IS NOT AGREEMENT

Many management teams confuse agreement and alignment. Our view is that alignment means that you have some measure of agreement but not necessarily total agreement. This means that you can have some disagreement and still be aligned. In fact, our experience has been that you can't have true alignment without disagreement. True alignment does not occur until people have had the opportunity and assume the accountability to say what they really think in a manner that lets them work issues through and gain some buy-in. Disagreement inevitably accompanies this process, and that can be good.

A major manufacturer we worked with had what the president called a "culture of consensus." On the face of it, this might seem like everyone's dream organization. How wonderful—a company where people must agree with a decision before they take action. That's the way it was in this company. There was only one problem: chronic inaction. The management team could never reach consensus, so nothing ever happened. They traded the power to act for veto power, and it was a poor bargain.

All of us have seen the best idea owned by one person fail miserably while a good idea owned by many succeeded. Alignment does bring agreement—the agreement to move forward, the agreement to support the direction or decision, and the agreement to speak up if you become unaligned. However, in all of that there can be a level of disagreement that acts positively by prodding people to keep reviewing, to keep considering, and to keep looking to ensure that the direction in which they are headed is the right one.

ALIGNMENT AND OWNERSHIP

The close commonality of belief and tight concertedness of action that characterize strong alignment also generates emotion, the kind that leads to personal ownership for the result. Emotions—ranging from affiliation to loyalty, from professional pride to personal passion, from teamwork to self-sacrifice—can lead to high levels of ownership. Effective leaders know how to tap these emotions, how to get people to form emotional bonds to the organization and its goals. They engage people's hearts and minds in the pursuit of results.

Too many managers appeal only to the intellect. Often this works. The links between culture and results and between beliefs and action hold strong intellectual appeal. An intellectual understanding of alignment may be enough in many instances. However, accelerating the change to C^2 and consistently producing outstanding results generally calls for emotional commitment as well as intellectual agreement. Emotional commitment generates a deeper sense of ownership than that created by intellect alone. In general, the more that people *Own It*, the stronger the culture.

LEVELS OF OWNERSHIP

First, let's review what it means to *Own It*. Our definition includes (1) being personally invested in the situation, (2) acknowledging your involvement, (3) creating and maintaining a sense of alignment, and (4) committing to your personal and team objectives.

People's failure to *Own It*, to invest personally, to become involved and committed to the C² culture, works against alignment. But the corollary is also true. Think of the power your organization would have if everyone in it were fully, deeply, personally committed to the cultural beliefs statement. Personal commitment—ownership—lies at the heart of accountability and thus at the core of a *Culture of Accountability*. Ownership is essential. It occurs at various levels, however, as illustrated by Figure 8-4.

As the model shows, ownership for organizational or departmental results, or for any situation, can vary from "none" to "high." As we walk through this model, consider a time when you have seen someone, perhaps yourself, demonstrate a low degree of ownership in implementing a corporate effort and a time when a high degree of ownership was manifested.

Starting with a low degree of ownership—resist/resent—at the bottom of the figure, you see people behaving in ways that reflect resistance or resentment. People disagree intellectually with the course of action or desired result and are not emotionally involved, at least not with positive emotions. So they have committed neither their minds nor their hearts to the endeavor. It is at this level that people entrenched in the old C¹ culture, who do not recognize a need to change, typically resent being asked to do things differently and may openly resist efforts to move forward.

At the top of the diagram—buy-in/invested—we see the high degree of ownership that occurs when people agree with a course of action intellectually and have an emotional desire to participate. Both their minds and hearts are engaged and they are thoroughly invested and vigorously involved. These people are probably already demonstrating C² behavior. They find it easy to "sign up" and readily see the advantages that the company will gain by shifting the culture.

In the lower middle range—exempt/excuse—people are figuratively saying, "I don't own it." They agree intellectually but are uninvolved emotionally. They will either hold themselves out as being

FIGURE 8-4
LEVELS OF OWNERSHIP

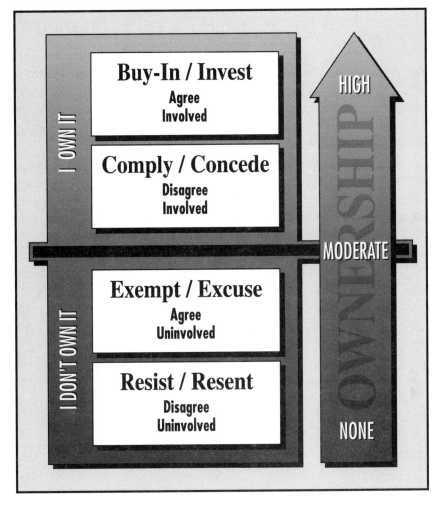

exempt because they're "too busy," or they'll make excuses because they "can't get to it." People at this level of ownership will not move forward. They think that a culture shift is a good idea but that it applies to everyone except them. They think they are exempt because of market conditions, organizational needs, functional requirements, or any number of other things.

In the lower of the two "I-Own-It" boxes—comply/concede—people disagree with or are uncertain about the endeavor from the intellectual standpoint, but they're emotionally invested enough, on the grounds of loyalty, professionalism, or other considerations, to take action. You've no doubt seen that level of ownership. It's not necessarily bad and, realistically, it's all you can achieve in certain situations. Very often people who simply comply with requests and concede to move forward produce solid results. Yet people at this stage can be aligned with a direction and still lack what it's really going to take to get the result.

In a cultural transition, many people, perhaps the majority, reside at this level of ownership. They exhibit A^2 actions, but with wavering commitment. At the first sign of wavering on management's part, they can revert to the C^1 way of doing things. Because there is some uncertainty about the direction in which they are headed, it may not take much for them to disengage.

Not long ago a friend we'll call Bill told us of his experience in building an addition to his home that illustrates the potential impact of comply/concede. In working with his roofer, Bill asked that at the end of each day he place a tarp over the exposed room so that the expected rain would not cause water damage during the night (this was an El Niño spring). The roofer said that it wasn't his job to cover the roof and that someone else ought to do it. Bill persisted, however, explaining that he needed the roofer to do it because he was the last one up. At the end of each day the roofer "mumbled and grumbled and in a halfway manner spread the tarp over the roof"—each time reminding Bill that "it wasn't his job."

During this project, our friend took a trip out of state. He met with the roofer before he left and asked him to please remember to put the tarp over the roof because rain was predicted. Two days later Bill received a phone call from home. The report was bad. The ceiling over the existing rooms where the roofing was being done had caved in and destroyed furnishings and much of the completed interior work. Bill couldn't believe it. He asked if the roofer had put the tarp up before he finished for the day. And he had! But he had not spread the tarp out over the entire roof and fastened it securely. Clearly, this roofer may have aligned himself to doing what he was asked, but he didn't "buy in."

Getting people to *Own It* is among the key tasks and greatest challenges of management, particularly during culture change. It's a key task because one committed person is worth ten who are interested. It is among the greatest challenges because our current social climate works against ownership and commitment. Yet effective leaders work to move people to high levels of ownership.

Moving to a Higher Level of Ownership

Moving people from the comply/concede level of ownership, or from any of the lower levels shown in Figure 8-5, to the highest level will accelerate culture change. A critical mass of people at the buy-in/invest level will produce enough alignment and positive momentum to keep the change effort energized and moving forward. To achieve this critical mass and true buy-in, key people in the organization—and you know who they are—*must* get on board. The experiences these people create galvanize those who are "watching" to see what happens.

Figure 8-5
Creating Buy-In: Alignment Leads to Greater Ownership

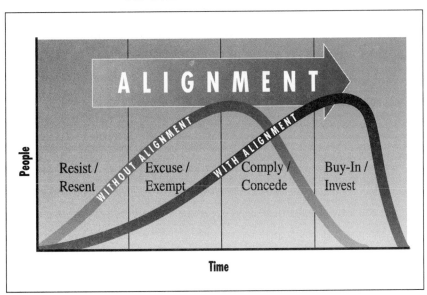

Expending effort to move people from one level of ownership to the next is essential in creating alignment. As the Levels of Ownership suggest, those efforts will primarily take two forms:

1. Working with people through persuasion to create greater understanding of the change

2. Getting people personally involved in the change itself

Working with people to develop some level of agreement about where you are headed and why is essential. People who entirely disagree with a course of action will find it difficult to stay in alignment for long. That is why you have to do everything you can, early on, to involve key people in creating the culture change. Then you need to continue to involve them with experiences by showing them positive examples of A^2 actions that drive R^2 results. You should expend every effort to get them on board, persuading and convincing them, so that you create the broadest possible agreement.

Getting them involved in demonstrating aspects of the change will go a long way in helping them see why it is important. Helping people create firsthand C^2 experiences will convince them that this course of action is the right thing to do. Experiences, both those you provide for them and those they provide for others, drive beliefs.

Moving the majority of people in the organization to one of the top two Levels of Ownership as quickly as you can will accelerate the transition and generate A^2 actions throughout the organization. Certain steps in the alignment process described in the next section will enable you to move the maximum number of people to the higher Levels of Ownership early in the transition.

THE ALIGNMENT PROCESS

We've developed a formal model of the alignment process for use in your early efforts to outline C^2 and draft the Cultural Beliefs Statement. In practice, though, every team is different and will require some piece of the model to be different for them. Broadly, the model has five key elements, as shown in Figure 8-6:

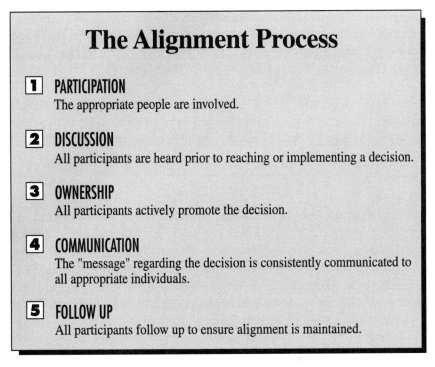

FIGURE 8-6
STEPS FOR CREATING ALIGNMENT

The Alignment Process

1 **PARTICIPATION**
The appropriate people are involved.

2 **DISCUSSION**
All participants are heard prior to reaching or implementing a decision.

3 **OWNERSHIP**
All participants actively promote the decision.

4 **COMMUNICATION**
The "message" regarding the decision is consistently communicated to all appropriate individuals.

5 **FOLLOW UP**
All participants follow up to ensure alignment is maintained.

In the following sections we examine each of these elements. As you'll see, each element is itself a process, and each comprises an essential step toward achieving alignment.

As you read the following sections, think of alignment as an accelerator that speeds up the transition. Like feedback, it's a tool for speeding up culture change geared to generating new and better results. Alignment accelerates change because if it is employed correctly, people will more readily think and act in the ways that will produce results.

PARTICIPATION: HAVE THE RIGHT PEOPLE INVOLVED

Many managers wrestle with the issue of who needs to be involved in a decision. A lot of management teams operate as if everyone needs to participate in every decision. But sometimes it's obvious that not "everyone" needs to be involved in certain decisions. People are often willing to get aligned, particularly when they know that good process has been used to determine the proper course. To ensure alignment, the *appropriate* people should be involved in the process. In addition to the decision makers this may include:

- People who will have a major role in the implementation of the decision
- People who could potentially pay a price for the decision
- People who will be asked to do something extraordinary to make the decision work

The number of people involved should match the scope and significance of the decision. At the outset, you should ask, who are the right people to involve in light of implementation? Gaining the perspectives of others not only produces a better decision, but also sets the stage for obtaining alignment as the decision is implemented. Involving the right people in the process, in the right way, can improve the chances of success for any venture.

As you consider who should participate, be explicit about the decision-making process you will employ: leader-led, consensus, or majority view. Each approach has its place. Each may require a different level of participation. Understanding how the decision will be taken beforehand can help you determine who should be involved.

The element of participation can itself involve a cultural shift. If too many people typically participate in decisions there's usually some underlying element of mistrust. An atmosphere of mistrust characterizes companies in which people feel they must be present for every discussion on every decision, whether or not they're directly involved. In this environment, people not involved don't trust that those who are will make a correct or fair decision. Creating an environment where people are not worried that others will "sell them down the river" because they're not participating is essential to alignment.

On the other hand, if too few people are invited to participate in decisions, it may signal that the leader does not trust the input of others. That's bad, because it can lead to suboptimal decisions as well as to poor implementation. Many managers who avoid seeking input from others fail to help them distinguish between participating in the discussion and participating in the decision. Since alignment is not agreement and the goal is not consensus, participants must realize that they are involved in the discussion but not in the decision. Randy Tobias, former chairman at Eli Lilly and Company, and before that vice chairman of AT&T, put it best when he said, "Committees don't make decisions, leaders do." His point is that you don't hold committees accountable for decisions; you hold leaders accountable. Ultimately someone has to step up and assume full accountability for what has, or has not been done.

In culture change, involving the management team in creating the Cultural Beliefs Statement is essential to obtaining alignment. However, it is equally important to involve others in the expanded management team by asking for their input during the initial assessments. Deciding what kind of culture you need is best done with the various perspectives clearly in mind. As you will see in Chapter 10, even when you introduce the Cultural Beliefs, it is best if people can participate in discussions similar to those that led management to their conclusions.

In the alignment process, the goal of participation is not merely to have people involved or even to have the appropriate people involved. It is to have the appropriate people involved in the right way. You need the right people engaged. You must help them to understand their roles. And you must get them to say what they think, which brings us to the next element in the process.

DISCUSSION: ENCOURAGE PEOPLE TO SAY WHAT THEY THINK

For discussion to lead to alignment, all participants must feel that they have been heard before a decision is made. When describing the kind of participation that leads to alignment, we like to use the term "council" instead of committee. We also like the term "counsel," which is what a good council has to offer. The participants in a council need to understand that they are there to offer their counsel, their advice, input, views, and the benefit of their experience. They are not necessarily the decision makers. This must be clear. If they believe they are participating in the decision, they may be disappointed and go *Below the Line* or out of alignment when another decision is made. If they are actually participating in the decision, the result may be a suboptimal, consensus decision.

Many, perhaps most, of us tend to feel that we have not been heard unless others agree with us. It's human nature to think, "If you really heard me and really understood what I was saying, then certainly you would agree with me." In practice, agreement is the test people often use to determine if they have been heard. We have spoken with countless managers who have left team meetings unsatisfied because their view was not adopted; they felt as if no one was listening. Yet, having been in some of those same meetings, we observed that the individual amply and ably argued their perspective to no avail. The team or the leader just didn't agree.

The common practice of preparing your rebuttal while other people talk undermines alignment. People know whether or not they're truly being heard. We have been in many discussions in which people thought they understood another person's position and, when asked to state that position, could not do it. A discussion defined by presentations, speeches, or lectures without an equal dose of interchange and reflection often leads one to perceive alignment where none exists.

The ultimate test of whether or not people feel that they have been heard must be their own feeling on that point. Discovering this involves checking in with them, restating what they said to ensure that you understand it, and explaining how their concerns can be addressed or why they cannot be. Restating and then interactively correcting your understanding develops the true comprehension that is essential to alignment.

When working with a cultural transition, people must have forums for discussing the change. Talking about the changes in the business environment, the problems with the present culture, and the experiences that drive current beliefs is all part of the process of helping people shift to the C^2 culture. Open discussion, free expression, and healthy debate enable people to "be real" about the necessary changes. In a sense, management must create a dialogue with the organization about the change, and that dialogue should occur at all levels. While these discussions may unleash some emotion, this emotion will create a passion for making things the way they need to be.

FOSTERING POSITIVE CONFRONTATION

Let's face it: Reasonable people can have deep and legitimate differences of opinion regarding a decision or course of action. *Positive confrontation is the practice of openly discussing those differences without cre-*

ating interpersonal or organizational damage. Effective leaders realize that discussion of differences is going to occur one way or another. They also realize that it is far better for that discussion to occur openly in conference rooms rather than secretly in hallways and offices. Secret discussion, often accompanied by personal attacks as well as unrelated grievances, work against alignment. Properly conducted, open discussion limits damage and creates alignment.

It is up to the leader to create the environment in which positive confrontation can occur. The technique for creating this environment involves three things:

1. The leader setting the tone

2. The group agreeing to ground rules

3. The people holding themselves accountable for following the ground rules

The leader sets the tone of the meeting by creating a positive experience that drives the belief that open dialogue and positive confrontation is desirable and can occur without negative consequences. The leader must tailor the experience for the group, but it will include having an agenda, ensuring that the right people are participating, announcing the focus of the meeting, and initiating the discussion of ground rules. Through all of this, the leader will create the right experience, and interpret it when necessary.

Listed in Figure 8-7 are ground rules for positive confrontation. These can be used as a guide, but the leader should have the group generate its own.

The leader should create accountability and see that the *group* enforces its ground rules. To do this, he or she should invite the team to police itself rather than assume the role of enforcer. The leader should be a facilitator rather than a director. For any given group, there will certainly be ground rules specific to the organization (for instance, "No mention of reorganization!"). The ones suggested here contribute to positive confrontation, but we encourage you to develop your own as well.

Positive confrontation is missing from the culture of many organizations. When people shift the way they think and act, some emotion and passion accompanies the change. Management cannot drag the organization kicking and screaming into the new C^2 culture.

FIGURE 8-7
CREATING ALIGNMENT IN THE TEAM

Ground Rules for Positive Confrontation

1 Focus on issues, not personalities -- avoid personal attacks.

2 Separate your own opinions from the facts as you know them.

3 Acknowledge your own "hidden agendas."

4 Make sure you can restate the views of others before you debate them.

5 Don't interrupt.

6 If you think someone is "hiding out," check in with the person and ask them what they think.

7 No "hallway" discussions, openly share your perspectives with the group.

8 Wear all of the hats you should be wearing during the discussion.

9 Remember, the goal is to move forward as a team -- we will not advertise the disagreement, but we will demonstrate our full support of the decision.

Rather, they must facilitate an open forum that allows people to vent their frustrations and confront the realities that make change difficult. In such an environment, people are more able to move on to a new way of doing things.

Ownership: Assume Accountability

Perhaps you've heard the expression, "When all is said and done, more is said than done." Once a decision is made, once a course of action has been determined, then everyone in the group must own the decision and promote it as if it were his or her own, even if it wasn't. Otherwise, more will be said than done.

While not every member of the management team must agree with a decision, everyone must actively promote it. In this context, promoting a decision means owning it as though it were actually yours *even if you disagree*. Bottom line, that's what it is. So let's look at exactly what we mean by "own" and "promote."

Various decisions require various Levels of Ownership, as depicted in Figure 8-4. The highest level of ownership—buy-in/invest—is necessary in some, but not all, situations. Recall that at that Level of Ownership people agree intellectually with the decision or course of action and are emotionally involved. Both their hearts and minds are committed. In other situations, however, the next Level of Ownership—comply/concede—will produce results. At that level people disagree with the decision, but are involved emotionally because they are part of the team, possess professional pride, or, simply, need a livelihood. Because this Level of Ownership produces action, it will often produce results.

Leaders must decide which Level of Ownership will be necessary to produce the actions that will achieve the desired results. Then they must bring people to those Levels of Ownership. If that is not possible then they must replace those people with others who can develop the necessary Level of Ownership. This can be a tough decision. You have to ask, "Can I get the result with people who are at the comply/concede level?" You also must face the facts when people "don't own it." Leaders who attempt to get results through people stuck in the exempt/excuse or resist/resent levels and refuse to move forward are engaged in a futile exercise. By definition, uninvolved people will not move forward. They may make excuses. They may pretend they're moving forward. But they will not actually move forward and produce results. Instead, they will throw the organization out of alignment.

Now let's turn to "promote." After management has made a decision, they must promote it throughout the company or at least in the relevant segments of the company. In the sense that we use the term here, leaders promote a decision in one of four ways, as shown in Figure 8-8: They can support, advocate, sponsor, or champion the decision or course of action.

FIGURE 8-8
PROMOTING THE CULTURE CHANGE

Four Ways to Promote the Culture Change

SUPPORT	ADVOCATE	SPONSOR	CHAMPION
Actively promote the new culture.	Vigorously and proactively support the decision to create C^2.	Actively and vocally take ownership of the culture change. Play a leadership role in the change effort by going first with bold strokes.	Very actively and vocally lead by making extra effort to be among the few to move the issue of the culture change forward on the agenda for the entire organization.

Showing *support* is one way of actively promoting a decision or direction. This means actively agreeing with the logic of the decision to move to a C^2 culture and taking reasonable measures to remove obstacles and assist others in bringing it about. Another way is to be an *advocate*, which indicates more vigorous and proactive support of the decision to create C^2. A third way is to *sponsor* the decision by actively and vocally taking ownership such that one's own success or failure becomes intertwined with the success or failure of the decision. This involves playing a leadership role in the change effort and might entail "going first" with some bold strokes. Finally, to *champion* a decision is to actively and vocally lead people in efforts to make it a success. Here, a leader makes an extra effort to be among the few to move the issue of the culture change forward on the agenda for the entire organization.

From a practical standpoint, not everyone needs to champion the change. The manner in which one chooses to promote the culture change depends upon many factors. However, all participants must either support, advocate, sponsor, or champion the change in order to feel that they are demonstrating their alignment and actively promoting the shift.

COMMUNICATION: GET THE WORD OUT

If leaders employ each of the first three elements of the alignment process—participation, discussion, and ownership—they stand a good chance of communicating a consistent message to the organization. However, communication will not happen by itself.

Here's an example of what we mean. A company we know wanted to motivate and reward their employees for a particular result, so they offered them a stock-option program. The management team was enthusiastic about it. They clearly saw it as a great way to get employees involved and excited. Yet, when it was introduced it was a disaster. Employees totally misunderstood it. Believing that they had to spend money on the options in order to make money, they saw the program quite negatively. Rather than being an incentive, it came across as a penalty.

Many employees did not understand how stock options work. Once the communication program was fine-tuned and the options were properly explained—how they worked, what everything was tied to, how much money people could make—the employees bought in. In fact, many came to appreciate the program and the long-term payoff it would likely bring. But when it was first introduced it was a Type-4 Experience.

We mentioned that every company we have worked with—every single one—has cited a need to improve their communication. We've also mentioned how often we have seen a lack of clear, really clear, communication on the results the organization has targeted. When members of the team walk out the door after a decision is made, each one must be prepared to create a common experience in his or her area to reinforce the right beliefs, actions, and results. Time spent on what and when you are going to communicate is time well spent.

Communicating about the culture change to the organization is critical. This is where you will signal that the process is either another "program of the month" or a bona-fide effort to change. The communication plan has to convey the "why's" of what is happening. Too often, leaders miss the opportunity to tie changes in culture with changes in the business environment and the R^2 results that need to be achieved. In the absence of this connection, people ascribe the effort to the personality of the leader. When this happens, people say, "We're changing because Frank is at the helm. Just wait, when he's gone, things will change again or go back to normal." We have heard more than one middle manager resisting culture change with the comment that they are "waiting out" the leader.

Follow-Up: Make Alignment Permanent

Maintaining the alignment you have achieved involves continually giving and receiving feedback regarding where people are, creating experiences of alignment, and applying the four *Steps To Accountability*. This amounts to strong follow-up.

Culture change cannot succeed if management doesn't follow through and ensure that there is accountability for doing what people say they will do. There is too much at stake for management not to follow through. We have found that checking for alignment around specific points can be useful in following up, so let's take a quick look at some of these points.

Alignment Checkpoints: In your experience, you have surely seen situations where your company or team failed to get the result it pursued because people were not sufficiently aligned. To help you avoid this, Figure 8-9 lists some checkpoints to review with the team to ensure that alignment is maintained during culture change.

For maximum effectiveness you must develop your own specific checkpoints and use them in a group setting. Your team must be aligned in order to move forward, and the more aligned they are in relation to both the goal and the means to achieve it, the faster their progress will be.

As a leader you must create an environment that allows people to speak up if they are not aligned with a direction or decision. Alignment is a process, sometimes an iterative one. Managers resist checking in because they don't want to go back and reopen an issue.

FIGURE 8-9
MAINTAINING ALIGNMENT AROUND THE CULTURE CHANGE

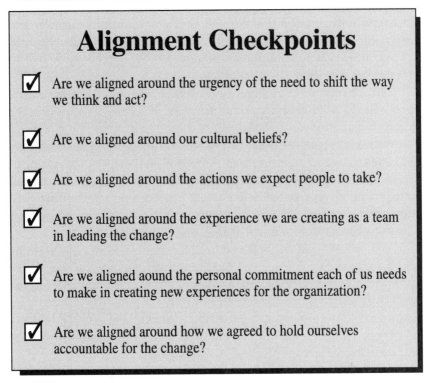

Alignment Checkpoints

✓ Are we aligned around the urgency of the need to shift the way we think and act?

✓ Are we aligned around our cultural beliefs?

✓ Are we aligned around the actions we expect people to take?

✓ Are we aligned around the experience we are creating as a team in leading the change?

✓ Are we aligned aound the personal commitment each of us needs to make in creating new experiences for the organization?

✓ Are we aligned around how we agreed to hold ourselves accountable for the change?

Yet while you cannot keep rehashing a decision, you must constantly create the dialogue necessary to maintaining alignment.

Of course, if you are not aligned with a decision, then you owe it to the group to speak up. After a fair hearing, you need to be willing to move forward with the group. Naturally, how strongly you feel will determine your ability or desire to move forward. Sometimes the single voice can be right. You may agree as a team to keep discussing the concern and to check in periodically to ensure you are on the proper course. Or, someone may feel that he or she cannot get aligned and that he or she is not a good "fit" for where the organization is headed. Whatever the case, alignment is not a one-time thing—leaders must continually ensure that people are aligned with the cultural transition.

MILESTONES ALONG THE YELLOW BRICK ROAD

Creating and maintaining alignment during a cultural transition and during any other effort is essential to success. Leaders must continually pay attention to alignment because forces continually work to push the organization out of alignment.

The strongest alignment occurs when people operate at the highest Level of Ownership, buy-in/invest. While a large percentage will reside in comply/concede, leaders should help all the people move to one of the top two Levels of Ownership by helping them understand the change and getting them involved in it.

When people buy in and invest they engage their hearts and minds in the change effort and actively promote it. Their efforts will range from showing support, to sponsoring the change, to advocating it, or even to championing the cause to the organization.

As a leader, you must know how to create and maintain alignment around the C^2 culture and the organization's efforts to get there. In this chapter we've presented an alignment process that has proven useful to hundreds of managers in not only creating the culture they need, but also in implementing a broad range of decisions, initiatives, and programs. The elements of the process are participation, discussion, ownership, communication, and follow-up.

When properly used, each of these elements works to produce alignment. Participation calls for the appropriate people to be involved in the process. Discussion generates input and enables all the participants to feel that they've been heard. Ownership calls upon each team member to be accountable for promoting the change and for working to achieve the transition. Communication involves establishing a dialogue with everyone in the organization. Through follow-up, accountability is established and all participants ensure that alignment is maintained.

When cultural transitions and other worthwhile business initiatives fail, the cause can often be traced to lack of alignment. In such cases, management has failed to properly employ one or more of the elements in the alignment process. Somewhere, most often in the ownership or communication stages, there was poor execution. In contrast, when these five elements are properly employed, the probability of moving the organization to a C^2 culture—and doing so quickly—improves dramatically. In the next chapter, we examine the role of effective leadership in accelerating the shift to a new culture.

CHAPTER NINE

EMPLOYING LEADERSHIP TO MOVE THE CHANGE FORWARD

We must get back to the road in some way.

The Wonderful Wizard of Oz
L. Frank Baum

The character in the Wizard of Oz who arguably exercises the strongest leadership is, indeed, the newest arrival on the scene and the one who has to be the most open to new beliefs in order to survive—Dorothy. The little girl from Kansas also helps those who had been stuck in old, worn-out ways by helping them develop new beliefs that will work better for them. By following Dorothy's example and adopting her beliefs about the possibility of change and the path toward it, the Scarecrow, the Tin Woodman, and the Cowardly Lion find new lives for themselves. Like any good leader, Dorothy leads others to change as she works on changing herself.

In this chapter we more closely examine things leaders can do to move the transition forward and accelerate the process of change. Traditional leadership skills, such as developing and sharing a vision, communicating effectively, and defining and upholding standards, certainly have their place in this framework. But leaders who create a *Culture of Accountability* accomplish this by doing the things that they're already doing—planning, communicating, delegating, and so on—in ways that foster the B^2 beliefs. Much of leadership as we conceive it involves simply becoming aware of what you are already doing and of the experiences you are creating and whether or not they are moving others to adopt the C^2 culture.

LEADERS, AWAKE!

The mystical philosopher Georgi Ivanovitch Gurdjieff said that most of us are sleepwalking. When it comes to creating culture, many managers are indeed sleepwalking, and for that matter, sleeptalking as well. If leaders move unconsciously through the organization, they fail to create experiences consistent with the culture they desire. Yet when managers clearly see the effects of sleepwalking or sleeptalking, they often awaken and begin to lead their teams to the beliefs they want them to have.

A manager of a large manufacturing operation sent a memo to his staff announcing that he was going on vacation but that they would still be able to reach him. He told them he was taking his laptop and would be checking his e-mail, as well as his voice mail, every day. He made this announcement giving no thought to the experience he was creating for his team. He didn't consider the fact that he had never before told his team they'd be able to reach him while he was on vacation. Without interpretation from the manager about the experience he was creating, members of his team began to fill in the blanks: They, too, were supposed to remain accessible during their vacations.

One of his direct reports sent him an e-mail before he left asking if this was really the experience he wanted to create. The question "awakened" him and he acknowledged, "That's neither the experience I want to create nor the belief I want people to have." Now fully alert, he sent everyone an e-mail saying that he had received feedback concerning his announcement. He apologized for the message he had unintentionally sent and told them that he did not expect people to be reachable while on vacation. Furthermore, he told them all that he had decided to leave his laptop home and would not be checking his voice mail while on vacation—he would be inaccessible.

This last message cleared up the confusion about what was expected on vacations. The team also came to see that their manager was entirely open to feedback. Perhaps most important, the manager saw how easily he could create experiences that impacted beliefs. Simply stating that he was going to stay in touch during his vacation led his team to believe that this was probably a new feature of the culture. Once he awoke to the power he had to create experiences, foster beliefs, and change behaviors, he became more conscious and more effective in his leadership.

This simple example validates a belief we hold: Leaders, consciously or not, are always creating experiences. Being conscious of the experiences you are creating allows you to accelerate culture change. In an article in the February–March 1997 *Fast Company*, Dee Hock, founder and CEO emeritus of Visa, observed, "Control is not leadership; management is not leadership; leadership is leadership. If you seek to lead, invest at least 50 percent of your time leading yourself—your own purpose, ethics, principles, motivation, conduct. Invest at least 20 percent leading those with authority over you and 15 percent leading your peers. If you don't understand that you work for your mislabeled 'subordinates,' then you know nothing of leadership."

Our model of leadership puts this kind of influence within the reach of every manager and employee. It requires understanding that experiences foster beliefs, beliefs drive actions, and actions produce results. It does not require an outsized personality, arcane manipulation of others, inspirational speeches, or wild lunges at "greatness." Instead, it calls for honest motives, conscious thought, and focused effort.

LEADERS, MODEL THE C^2 CULTURE

Leaders have the visibility and authority to spearhead or undermine the transition to C^2. Hatim Tyabji, president and CEO of Verifone, Inc., was quoted in the February–March 1997 issue of *Fast Company* as saying, "The first principle of leadership is authenticity. If you want your company to exude a sense of urgency and a drive to get things done, then act that way on a daily basis. If you want your people to put the needs of the customers first, then do that too—in every situation. If you want your people to be frugal, then don't spend money on perks designed to make your life more comfortable."

One or two managers who don't adopt the C^2 culture can throw the whole organization out of alignment as they continue to think and act in a C^1 manner. Their actions send a clear message to employees that it is OK to not change and instead to continue their C^1 beliefs and behaviors. The experiences created by leaders who don't buy in and who are not invested in achieving the cultural transition often seem to be the most visible experiences. They tend to have a strongly negative effect on those who are themselves struggling to "buy in."

In contrast, leaders who use their visibility and authority to promote the new culture have a powerful, positive effect. This is especially the case over the long haul, as management continues to model the beliefs and behaviors over weeks, months, quarters, and years. As the process moves along, people begin paying attention to all the cultural signals and not just to the few that suggest that the leaders are not really committed. Ultimately, people realize that management is serious about the change. With time, as people recognize that the organization's new focus is permanent and that the leaders are committed to creating the new culture, they respond accordingly.

As Linda Grant and Richard Hagberg point out in their June 1996 *Fortune* article, "Rambos in Pinstripes: Why So Many CEO's Are Lousy Leaders," GE's CEO Jack Welch "insists on evaluating GE executives according to how well they embody the corporate value of 'boundarylessness.' That value is about overcoming the barriers that inhibit a free market for ideas within GE—such as overbearing bosses, people unwilling to work with others outside their function, or timidity about speaking openly with customers and suppliers. Spend too much time applying shoe leather to the necks of your subordinates, and you're out." In the same article GE's human resources senior vice president William Conaty states, "The people we are putting in key leadership slots are those we deem to be terrific role models. That means embracing the values, being able to motivate and energize, and having that infectious enthusiasm to tap people's potential and generate the capacity of the organization beyond what it otherwise would do."

When the role models that leaders have portrayed in the past are inconsistent with the C^2 culture then a first and vital step is for the leaders to acknowledge the changes they personally need to make. This acknowledgment, in and of itself, accelerates change. People genuinely need to know that leaders are aware that they were part of the C^1 culture and that they played a significant role in its creation. The leaders' acknowledgment provides a needed platform from which all others can acknowledge their involvement in the C^1 culture.

Beyond acknowledgment, leaders must sign on as active participants in the cultural transition. Cultures change as leaders change. Some managers are reticent about leading others through culture change. That's natural. Some leaders fear the task of developing new expectations and holding people accountable to achieve them. After all, what will people think? How will they respond?

People know they need good leadership. When they see it, they typically respond positively to it. Most employees at all levels develop new respect for leaders who take the four *Steps To Accountability* and acknowledge their involvement in the current performance of the company. Leaders who own their company's current results find that people are more willing to be jointly accountable to move the organization in new directions and make lasting improvements in performance. Typically, the collective reaction is, "Thank goodness management has snapped out of it. Now we can get somewhere."

Often, managers simply don't know what to do to create experiences that cause people to adopt a different belief. In the following section, we offer a methodology that you can use as a leader to effectively create experiences for others.

A METHODOLOGY FOR CREATING EXPERIENCES

We have seen many successful leaders create experiences that help people adopt B^2 beliefs. These observations have revealed a Methodology for Creating Experiences that works either with individuals or groups. This methodology is also useful for leaders who are working with people who feel the leaders are not demonstrating the B^2 beliefs.

It's natural for a leader to "slip up" occasionally and manifest old A^1 actions, particularly as the cultural transition gets underway. After all, the leader is only human and he or she is making the transition too. When these slip-ups occur, it is also natural for those who observe the leader's failure to point it out. People watch leaders closely, anticipating signs of slippage or backsliding. There are people in every company who justify their own unwillingness to move forward by pointing out any A^1 action manifested by the leaders.

So leaders face the challenge of not only demonstrating the new beliefs but of doing it in a way that demonstrates them even to those who are steeped in the old C^1 culture. The methodology we present here helps leaders establish a dialogue with these observers, usefully redirect their attention, and create the E^2 experiences needed to reinforce B^2 beliefs. There are five steps to this methodology, as shown in Figure 9-1.

FIGURE 9-1
METHODOLOGY FOR CREATING EXPERIENCES

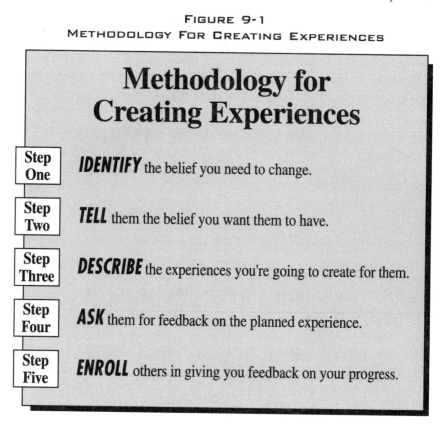

Methodology for Creating Experiences

Step One — *IDENTIFY* the belief you need to change.

Step Two — *TELL* them the belief you want them to have.

Step Three — *DESCRIBE* the experiences you're going to create for them.

Step Four — *ASK* them for feedback on the planned experience.

Step Five — *ENROLL* others in giving you feedback on your progress.

STEP ONE: IDENTIFY THE BELIEF YOU NEED TO CHANGE

When people point out that you have done something inconsistent with the beliefs, you must go beyond a simple "Thanks for the feedback!" Accurate or not, the feedback gives you an insight into the beliefs people are forming based on their experience with you. As we have said, you must ask, Is that a belief I want them to have? Will that move us toward C^2? If not and if it won't, the first step in creating a new experience is to clearly identify the belief you need to change. To do this you need to listen closely to what you're being told so that you can view the experience from their perspective. As you seek understanding, test the belief you think these people have formed by restating what you have heard. You may have missed valuable elements of the belief you need to change, and it's important to discover that now.

At this stage, remember to disengage your feedback filters and try to understand their perceptions. Then you can work to change the experiences they are having. You'll know you have successfully completed this step when you can restate the beliefs they hold to their satisfaction.

STEP TWO: TELL THEM THE BELIEF YOU WANT THEM TO HAVE

In step two you shift from identifying the belief you need to change to stating the belief you want them to have. While step one communicates that you sincerely want to understand their perception, step two lets them know that their current beliefs are not the ones you want them to hold. Acknowledging that the current beliefs are not desirable brings closure and rewards them with a sense of satisfaction that they spoke up and told you what they were thinking. And it reinforces the value of giving and receiving feedback on the journey to a C^2 culture.

Then, you need to tell them the belief you do want them to have. This new belief should be placed in the context of the B^2 beliefs. By making this connection, you reinforce the importance of the B^2 beliefs and communicate your commitment to them. Don't be shy in communicating about beliefs. Leaders who successfully instill beliefs talk explicitly about them. In this step, you are basically saying, "Oops, based on your feedback, I got it wrong. Let me get it right next time. Here's the belief I want you to hold . . ."

STEP THREE: DESCRIBE THE EXPERIENCES YOU'RE GOING TO CREATE FOR THEM

After creating the context of the belief you want them to hold, you should describe the experience you are going to create to reinforce that belief. Be as specific as you can about the experience(s) you want them to have. For example, use the situation that just occurred and state how you'll handle it differently in the future. By describing the experience you are going to create, you focus others on interpreting your future behavior in terms of the C^2 culture. Thus, when you behave in ways that reflect the stated B^2 belief, people will recognize it. This helps you break the pattern of people viewing E^2 experiences in terms of the persistent C^1 culture.

Resist any temptation to jump directly to step four and just ask others what you should do. This is important for several reasons: First, as the leader you are accountable for generating these experiences, so the plan should come from you. Second, it may seem that you are challenging the observers or putting them on the spot by asking them what to do before presenting your own ideas. Third, you communicate your commitment to making necessary changes by actively looking at what else you can do.

Consider this: If you're a right-handed golfer and you ask an observer to watch your swing to see whether you're keeping your left arm straight, where is she going to look? What is she going to watch for? She's going to watch your left arm and tell you whether you're keeping it straight, because that's where you directed her attention. That's the feedback you requested.

The Methodology for Creating Experiences aims at directing people's attention toward the beliefs and actions of the C^2 culture. If this process seems too detailed or strikes you as laborious, please understand that shifting people's focus from an old, existing culture to a new, as yet unformed one requires intense attention to details. The details in question are beliefs and behaviors. Culture change is a process that occurs one observation, one conversation, one belief, one person at a time. So leaders must think and work at this level of detail to accelerate the cultural shift from C^1 to C^2.

STEP FOUR: ASK THEM FOR FEEDBACK ON THE PLANNED EXPERIENCE

Leaders do not have to be the sole authors of their development. In fact, it's a mistake not to include others in your efforts to demonstrate the C^2 culture. By asking for input on your planned experiences, you draw others more deeply into the process. As you seek input, don't just accept at face value a statement of satisfaction. Ask what other experiences you need to create in order for them to form the belief you want them to hold.

This step is important because people usually have some idea of the experience they feel they *should* be having to support the desired belief. Usually, they can be quite specific about what they need to see. For instance, in order to believe that senior management is serious about cost containment, they may need to see senior managers flying coach. If they don't, it may not matter what else you do. If people have some idea of the experience they think you should be providing, you'd best know what that is.

Be sure to consider the practicalities of what people are telling you. If it's a good, usable idea and you're willing to do it, then say so. If it's something you do not think that you'll be able to accomplish, let them know that now. Remember they'll be watching you to see if you'll do the things you've agreed to do. That's good news! Half the battle is getting people to look for the new experiences that you are creating.

STEP FIVE: ENROLL OTHERS IN GIVING YOU FEEDBACK ON YOUR PROGRESS

The final step is to enroll others in giving you feedback on your progress. You do this by asking them for both reinforcing and constructive feedback. Ask them to look for those times when you demonstrate experiences that reinforce the desired belief *and* those times when you don't. Encourage them to give you the feedback as soon as they can so that you can act on it. You may have to convince them that you really want this, but the first four steps of the methodology will go a long way toward doing that.

Asking for feedback is essential because it directly involves the people you are trying to help to change. Because you've told them what to watch for in the future, and because they know that you will be asking for feedback on your progress, they will be looking for reasons to *think differently* about the beliefs they hold—a major step in creating a shift. Enrolling others in providing you feedback involves them in the process of change. Now you both have something to do, and the focus is right where it should be—on working collaboratively to establish the C^2 culture and achieve the R^2 results. Leaders and their subordinates are cocreators of the new culture. To bring this down to the day-to-day, action level, leaders must fully involve their subordinates in helping them demonstrate the B^2 beliefs.

While this methodology helps leaders demonstrate the beliefs, it also produces another interesting effect. It automatically and subtly focuses the observers' attention on their own beliefs and behaviors. When the leader takes each of the five steps of the methodology, he or she ignites the same thought process in others. People first hear the B^2

belief being reinforced and then hear that the leader, and by implication everyone in the company, is supposed to demonstrate that belief. As a result, observers will look for that behavior, think about that behavior, and seek that behavior not only in the leader but also in fellow workers and, perhaps most important, in themselves.

People do tend to focus on leaders' slip-ups and, if they look hard enough, they will catch leaders failing to demonstrate the B^2 beliefs. The Methodology for Creating Experiences enables you to enroll the people around you in helping you to demonstrate the beliefs you want them to hold. Using the methodology will help you accelerate not only your ability to live the Cultural Beliefs, but also your people's ability to do the same.

How the Methodology for Creating Experiences Works

Let's look at a couple of applications of this methodology. Suppose that an organization is committed to creating a culture in which people believe they can express themselves freely. Management wants to create experiences that manifest a commitment to the belief that they would be open to the perspectives of others, particularly the views of various functions. At a management meeting one of the attendees (Sue) experienced disturbing C^1 behavior from one of the leaders (Jim), who also attended the meeting. The following dialogue traces the steps of the Methodology for Creating Experiences and exemplifies what should happen when you get feedback that your behavior is not aligned with the B^2 beliefs.

Sue: Jim as you know, we've made a commitment to be open to the perspectives of others. But during the meeting this morning you were very defensive. Based on the experiences I have had with you I don't really feel that you're demonstrating our belief in being open to the perspectives of others.

Jim: So let me see if I understand what you are saying, Sue. You believe I'm not open to the views of others and that I'm defensive when I hear things that don't agree with what I'm saying. Is that right? (Step One)

Sue: Well, not exactly. You're not always defensive. And you're open to some perspectives. But when any of us from marketing says something, that's when I feel you close up and get defensive.

Jim: So what you're saying is that you do feel I'm open to most perspectives, but that I don't show that when marketing is involved. Is that what you believe? (Step One, continued)

Sue: That's right. I honestly don't believe that you're interested in the views presented by marketing.

Jim: Well, Sue, thanks for that feedback. I can tell you right away that's not the belief I want you to hold. And I can see that I've done some things that have led you to believe this. However, the belief I want you to hold is that I am open to the perspectives of others, and especially the perspectives coming from marketing. I really do feel that I need to know how marketing views these things. (Step Two)

I'll tell you what. I'd like to change the experience I'm creating for you. I can think of a couple of things I can do right away to demonstrate that I'm open to the perspectives of marketing and in fact value those perspectives.

At every meeting with marketing, I'll ask about the job we've been doing for them. In addition, I'll explicitly ask what we can do to support marketing better. Also, when marketing is offering their perspectives during other meetings I'll write down their views and make sure that my comments reflect the value I place on what I'm hearing. (Step Three)

Let me ask you, what other experiences could I create that would cause you to believe that I'm open to marketing's views? (Step Four)

Sue: Maybe soliciting our opinions of the job we're doing in some formal way. Maybe a written survey every now and then.

Jim: That's a good idea. We've never really gone out of our way to get feedback from marketing. Is there anything else? (Step Four, continued)

Sue: I don't think so. If you start asking for feedback and did the other things you mentioned I think that would do it.

Jim: Sue, I'd like you to watch for these things and let me know when you see me doing them. Let me know when you think I'm creating a negative experience that demonstrates a lack of interest in your perspective. Would you be willing to give me feedback—both reinforcing and constructive—on how I'm doing immediately after our weekly meetings? (Step Five)

Sue: Sure. That would be great.

This example demonstrates how a leader can use the Methodology for Creating Experiences to shift beliefs. But the real power of the methodology is demonstrated in actual application. We have seen countless instances where leaders have applied the methodology and shifted beliefs to accelerate culture change.

For example, Jay Graf at CPI told us of an occasion when the Information Systems and Services group was presenting a pilot plan at the senior staff meeting. This was a plan to evaluate the desirability of equipping sales people with laptop computers throughout the field. Jay admitted to having gone into the meeting somewhat prejudiced against the idea. Beforehand he had expressed doubts about the costs and benefits of this proposal. He wanted to know specifically how the laptops would save sales time or cut sales expenses.

During the meeting Jay was openly critical of the analysis. After the meeting, Dick Vogel, the vice president of finance, asked Jay if he could give him some feedback. At Jay's invitation Dick told him that he thought he had been a little harsh in the meeting. Jay's first response was that he needed to be critical at these meetings. Dick responded by saying that he thought some people were walking away with the belief that anything they said would be criticized at a senior staff meeting.

Jay immediately thanked Dick for the feedback and told him that this was not a belief he wanted him or anyone else to have. He told Dick that he would personally work on reestablishing the belief that while ideas get challenged, people are developed through supportive, positive coaching and feedback. Jay laughed as he told us how in the very next meeting a member of his staff heard something during a presentation that hit their hot button and caused them to become quite critical in their comments. Jay, acting on his feedback, created a new experience for the group presenting by shifting the critical tone of this meeting by offering support to the group, as well as some suggestions. After the meeting he gave his staff member the same feedback he had received from Dick Vogel.

Leaders who openly work on shifting the experiences they create when others see them as C[1] make themselves accelerators of the change process. People find it powerful when leaders shift. Leaders who shift are positioned to help others shift so that they live the culture beliefs.

ADDRESSING THE COMMON BLOCKAGES

All leaders play a key role in accelerating the cultural transition. But not all leaders find the process easy to implement personally. We have identified six common blockages that make it difficult for leaders to play their role in accelerating the transition.

1. Lack of flexibility of leadership style
2. Propensity to undervalue the "soft side"
3. Lack of skills essential to the change
4. Failure to make the change a priority
5. Failure to visualize the change
6. Poor timing of directing and facilitating

Some of these blockages may or may not apply to you, but some will apply to some people on almost any management team. We will briefly discuss each of these blockages and provide some suggestions on how they can be overcome. Evaluate yourself as you review each of these six items and, if they apply to you, determine "what else you can do" to remove them as an impediment to your progress.

NUMBER ONE: LACK OF FLEXIBILITY OF LEADERSHIP STYLE

Styles of leadership vary from leader to leader within a group or team. Effective leadership demands a certain level of flexibility in one's style, yet not all leaders can readily adjust their style to different situations. Never is flexibility needed more than during cultural transition. If leaders are locked into their leadership style and cannot adjust it, they will be seriously hampered in their ability to accelerate the cultural transition.

Certain shifts in the B^2 beliefs and A^2 actions will be difficult for a given leader to demonstrate simply because they are not consistent with that leader's style. For instance, a person who is very directive may find it difficult to facilitate open discussion. A person who tends to be softer spoken or heavily focused on pleasing others may find it difficult to give constructive feedback. Any cultural transition will typically require flexibility on the part of most leaders in terms of their style.

Suggestions:

- Recognize the strengths and weaknesses of your leadership style and how they either reinforce or conflict with desired A^2 actions and B^2 beliefs. Focus your attention on those weaknesses that will potentially hinder the culture change.
- Recognize that you are working with Level-Two Beliefs when it comes to style—be prepared to consciously change these beliefs.
- Look for those who may have compensating style differences to give you feedback along the way.

NUMBER TWO: PROPENSITY TO UNDERVALUE THE "SOFT SIDE"

We have noticed that many leaders tend to undervalue the "soft side" of business. While much has been done in the last decade to heighten awareness of the impact of organizational culture on business processes, many managers still find the concept difficult or foreign. Short-term operational realities crowd out their ability to see the relationship between what people believe, how people behave, and the results they achieve.

We remember one leader proclaiming to a group that rather than expending all this effort to work with the culture, "All we need is another product success" and things will be fine. Of course, the team asked the next question, "What do we need to do to create that product success?" Their discussion quickly turned to getting people to think and act in the manner necessary to drive the desired result.

Suggestions:

- Recognize who has the tendency to undervalue the soft side and take extra steps to help them buy in.
- Help people see how beliefs translate into behavior that will impact operational results.
- Make "soft-side" issues more concrete by creating sufficient accountability for follow-through.

NUMBER THREE: LACK OF SKILLS ESSENTIAL TO THE CHANGE

While some leaders have developed the necessary skills to facilitate cultural transition, others have not. There are a number of skills, such as facilitation, feedback, seeking others' perspectives, leading meetings, listening, public speaking, and so on, that a leader may need to improve in order to be effective at accelerating cultural change. The point here is not to identify all the skills that a leader may need, but to point out that not all leaders have all the skills necessary to maximize their impact on the transition. In addition, the Cultural Beliefs themselves may suggest behaviors and skills in which the leader feels personally deficient.

Suggestions:

- Specifically identify skills that you or your leadership team may need to improve and get formal training in those areas.
- Integrate the organizational training efforts to target skill deficiencies.
- Seek out people who are strong where you are weak and ask for their coaching and feedback.

NUMBER FOUR: FAILURE TO MAKE THE CHANGE A PRIORITY

No surprise here. Most leaders will say that they need more time before they start working on culture change, given competing priorities. Some may feel that they don't have time to change the culture and get results too. In the face of day-to-day operational realities, leaders often fail to focus on the role that culture plays in getting results.

Recently, we were with the senior management team of an affiliate of a *Fortune* 500 organization. We had spent a fair amount of time assessing the culture and planning the senior-management-team intervention. As we discussed the intervention with the affiliate's leader, he asked us if we could, given the business realities, shorten the senior-management-team intervention.

While we recommended staying with the proposed format, we worked within their time constraints. After the initial stages of the senior team work, the human-resources vice president called us and told us how pleased the group was with their progress. However, he said they felt they had short-changed themselves by not allotting more time to work together on the culture as a team. Many leaders underestimate the value of investing the time necessary to work the process of cultural transition.

Suggestions:

- Discuss how the cultural transition impacts day-to-day operational results with your management team.

- Look at what you're already doing—meetings you're already holding, tasks you're already performing, and ask yourself what you could do differently to accelerate the cultural transition.

- Apply the elements of the new culture to the results you are currently working to achieve: What should people be doing differently?

NUMBER FIVE: FAILURE TO VISUALIZE THE CHANGE

Some leaders have a talent for creating experiences that reinforce the needed shift in culture. They seem to intuitively sense what people need and when they need it. When it comes to culture, however, most leaders lack the ability to visualize either what they or their organization should do differently to demonstrate the C^2 culture. At some point (the sooner the better) everyone will need to visualize the change in order to make the change a reality.

Suggestions:

- Spend time talking with people about what should be different in what they do every day.

- Seek the counsel of other members of the team on the kind of experiences they feel you can create to reinforce the B^2 beliefs.

- Benchmark your efforts against other organizations who have undergone, or are going through, a similar change.

NUMBER SIX: POOR TIMING OF DIRECTING AND FACILITATING

Throughout the change process there is a time for the leader to step up and provide direction to keep the effort on track and a time to step back and adopt a facilitative approach to the change. Too often, leaders can miss the timing—directing when they should be facilitating and facilitating when they should be directing. People cannot "consense" themselves into a new culture. Creating alignment and maintaining it around the shift may require a healthy dose of direction. Getting people to enroll, sign up, buy in, and invest will require a facilitative approach that gets everyone involved. Knowing when to drive the process and when to let it be driven will hasten the overall speed of the transition.

Suggestions:

- Don't be afraid to hold the group to their commitments.

- Identify some trusted confidants and counselors who can help you gauge when to direct and when to facilitate.

- Don't hesitate to play the role of "champion" of the change—the leader needs to be seen that way.

These six blockages can be minimized by taking corrective action. However, this action demands a willingness to hear people who tell you when they see these blockages. That willingness, plus action along the suggested lines, will greatly enhance your ability to create lasting change.

LEADERS, HELP OTHERS THROUGH THE CHANGE

People go through various stages in adjusting to new ways of doing things. This is also true of culture change. We illustrate the stages people experience during cultural transition on the Culture-Change

Curve depicted in Figure 9-2. As the figure shows, initially there is a period of optimism and excitement, particularly when the Cultural Beliefs are first developed and promoted by the management team. The collective reaction is along the lines of, "Hallelujah, here's the change we've been waiting for. Let's get on with it!"

FIGURE 9-2
THE CULTURE-CHANGE CURVE

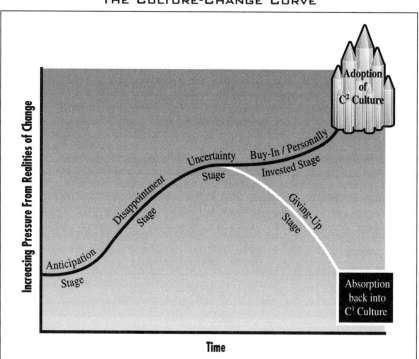

Next comes the disappointment stage, in which people who expected great things quickly don't get them. When they don't see instant change or radically new managerial behavior, when systems that were established to support C² ways of doing things are still reinforcing C¹ behavior, they begin to wonder if people are really serious about the culture change. They begin to feel the process is failing and and then, in the next stage, become uncertain as to whether it can succeed. They move to a posture of "wait and see" before they make any serious efforts to change. To a greater or lesser degree, every organization will go through this stage.

It is here that leaders themselves effectively decide whether the organization reverts to the C^1 environment or moves to the next stage and begins to adopt the C^2 culture. At this third stage we have seen leaders mistakenly begin to indulge their own uncertainty by sharing it with their staff. Obviously, leaders set the tone and focus the thoughts and actions of the people on either "giving up" or "owning it."

Typically, if leaders keep at it and don't despair, people will remain engaged and move the process forward. Leaders must understand where people are on the curve and take corrective action to keep them moving. Generally, the best managerial approach is one that runs somewhat counter to the prevailing mood. During the initial stage leaders need to express confidence and encourage everyone, but they should also be sure to stress that cultural change is a process that takes time and effort. The phrase "evolution, not revolution" is indicative of this stage.

In the disappointment and uncertainty stages people need plenty of reinforcing feedback about what's going right. If people are disappointed and focused on the negative, leaders must repeatedly cite the changes and gains that have been made, even if they seem small and few compared with people's expectations. The phrase "Let's look at where we were and at where we are now," followed by specifics, comes in handy at this point.

We are familiar with a large company that has for years been failing to grow at the rate of its competitors. The market has rewarded their performance accordingly. Morale is at an all-time low. Meanwhile, they are focused on changing their culture. They are currently in the second stage on the curve: disappointment. With this in mind management is focused on interpreting the positive shifts in leadership that are occurring. They are also emphasizing the company's current success in one of their key divisions, which will not be recognized by Wall Street for a few more years.

The buy-in/personally invested stage reflects the level of commitment of the management team to follow through on their agreed-upon changes. People either give up and are absorbed back into C^1 or they fully engage themselves at a level of buy-in and personal investment that ultimately leads them to adopt the C^2 culture.

At CPI, to move people along the curve the management team talked about their beliefs all the time. They constantly looked for opportunities to reference the beliefs whether they were at small on-site breakfast meetings or large-scale national sales events. In staff meetings they discussed decisions in terms of how they reflected the company's beliefs and what, if anything, they might do to more clearly demonstrate them. Before the end of each meeting, CPI managers also asked, "What kind of experience are we about to create for our people?" They wanted to ensure that every decision would instill or reinforce a B^2 belief, so they consciously worked on it together.

Another company we worked with that focused on helping people adopt the C^2 culture held an "awards ceremony" to honor people who most exemplified various aspects of *The Oz Principle* in creating a *Culture of Accountability*. They had a little statue they called "The Ozcar" and awarded it in various categories. There were individual and team awards for things such as Best Performance of *Above the Line* Behavior. The Lion Award for Courageously Speaking the Unspeakable went to a fellow who pointed out a tendency of senior management to be more invested in their own areas than in the whole company. The Tinman Award went to a woman who shared the most heartfelt thoughts during a monthly management meeting. When she accepted her Ozcar she said, "I've heard a number of people in the company say that if you say what you really think, you'll be punished. I've been rewarded instead."

In their book, *The 100 Best Companies to Work for in America*, authors Milton Moskowitz and Robert Levering researched the most unusual benefits that companies offer employees. While these benefits may not make sense in every situation, they have no doubt been inspired by people looking for what else they can do to reward and retain people who exemplify the behavior the company wants to reinforce. Here are some interesting examples from a number of well-know companies:

> **H. B. Fuller:** Every employee who graduates college receives $2,000.
>
> **Johnson & Johnson:** Newlywed employees receive one extra week's vacation.
>
> **Leo Burnett:** Employees receive unlimited sick pay.
>
> **SAS Institute:** All employees are entitled to free on-site child care.
>
> **Fel-Pro:** Free income-tax preparation and free tutoring for school-aged children.
>
> **UNUN Corp:** Employees receive 30 percent of their salary in one lump sum at the beginning of each year.

Behind any cultural transition lies a deep truth: The leaders who shift their companies to a new culture are those who get their companies to make the B^2 beliefs their own. They look at awards, rallies, and meetings; they look at promotion and compensation; they look at access to management or assignments to task forces; and they look at other forms of individual support. These companies are led by people who "own" the transition from B^1 to B^2 beliefs. Their leadership, which is visibly manifested in all of their actions, inspires ownership of the transition throughout the organization.

Leaders must also work hard to elevate the champions of the beliefs. Holding up the "true believers," who consistently exhibit behavior that demonstrates the desired beliefs and actions, as organizational heroes provides an unmistakable message. People see exactly what management expects. They see models of the behavior within their own ranks. They see this; they think about it; they discuss it; and eventually they strive to model it themselves.

Strong leaders provide clear messages through vivid group experiences. This does not mean "slash-and-burn" tactics. For instance high-profile "turnaround artists" often come into troubled companies and lay off people, cut costs, change suppliers, and dump assets. These moves do create vivid group experiences and, often, a quick, short-term boost in financial performance. However, equally often they leave in their wake a downsized, low-morale staff incapable of sustaining growth. In 1998, *The New York Times* reported that analysts believed that once-dominant Kraft Foods erred earlier in the 1990s in laying off senior salespeople who knew how to get retailers to stock and price the company's products. In June of that same year Al "Chain Saw" Dunlap, a manager known for turning companies around through particularly large and public layoffs, was himself very publicly fired by Sunbeam Corporation's board of directors. Under him the company failed to produce sustained growth.

In contrast, our leadership model calls for leaders who create experiences that drive home solid, useful beliefs that will serve the company over the long term. Helping others through the process of change so that the desired culture is adopted—and adopted quickly—is a key activity every leader of a cultural transition should be engaged in.

There will undoubtedly be those who refuse to shift, who stubbornly remain in C^1. For some of them, acknowledging that they do not fit in the organization is the right thing to do. Others may be important enough to the organization that you just have to work around them. Such situations are dicey because you can create a negative experience for others in the company by having these people around. If someone holds themselves out as exempt from the shift to the C² culture yet is allowed to remain in the company, leaders implicitly declare that person a "privileged character." Others ask, "Why not me?" to which some leaders bluntly reply, "Because you don't produce one point five million in revenue per year," or "Because he's the guy who has the technology this business runs on between his ears."

Some leaders dependent on someone with this kind of power over the organization deal with it by isolating the person. Difficult creative or R&D people or unruly major sales producers are often set apart—sometimes off site—ostensibly to remove them from the "bureaucracy" so they can "do what they do best." But the true goal is often to avoid a disruptive culture clash so the larger group can work undisturbed.

People don't shift their beliefs and behaviors when you tell them to. Some don't even when you create the "right" experiences. Thus leaders must shrewdly judge the type and depth of beliefs that people hold, then work with those beliefs and propel people toward the best resolution for all concerned. Most people respond well to sound leadership. Those who resist can often be won over. (Incidentally, turning around a popular, competent resister can enhance a leader's standing far more than firing him or her will.) However, some people will never make the change, and you must get them out of the company or out of the way.

TROUBLESHOOTING TRANSITION PROBLEMS

As you work to create culture change at all levels in the organization, you will likely encounter various problems in making the culture shift happen. Figure 9-3 sums up the common problems encountered by leaders during the transition and the potential remedies.

These quick hints will help you as the leader to identify the actions you should take to move the transition process forward. Leaders who understand what is happening with the transition process, the progress being made and progress that needs to be made, are positioned to take corrective action to keep the change process on track.

FIGURE 9-3
TROUBLESHOOTING PROBLEMS IN TRANSITION

Problem in Creating the Shift	Potential Remedy for Leaders to Use	
People not giving feedback	Formalize the feedback process Create time for feedback in meetings	see Chapter 7
People not following through on personal commitments regarding the change process	Hold them accountable	see Chapter 2
People not interpreting E^2 experiences correctly	Create Type 1 and Type 2 Experiences	see Chapter 6
People are *Below The Line* regarding their role in the change	Coach them *Above The Line* using the *Steps To Accountability*	see Chapter 2
People not living the Cultural Beliefs	Create alignment in the management team	see Chapter 8
People are confused and/or unclear about what they should be doing differently	Conduct a Stop/Start/Continue analysis	see Chapter 4
People keep asking leaders to tell them what to do	Coach from the Cultural Beliefs Statement	see Chapter 5
People feel you are demonstrating C^1 beliefs and behaviors	Use the Methodology for Creating Experiences	see Chapter 9
People see the culture change as just something management wants them to do	Connect the change with R^2 results and changes in the business environment	see Chapter 3
People who are not contributors are resisting due to their personal beliefs	Counsel them out of the company or increase intensity of experiences until they make a choice	see Chapter 9
People deemed to be irreplaceable contributors resisting due to their personal beliefs	Work around them or isolate them from the larger organization	see Chapter 9
People don't own the culture change	Work to convince them and get them involved in the change	see Chapter 8

MILESTONES ALONG THE YELLOW BRICK ROAD

Leaders must change along with everyone else in order for the culture to truly shift. The role the leaders play during the transition can accelerate the process when they pay particular attention to a few key areas that are listed in the chapter. Leaders have the unique challenge of leading the change while simultaneously making the change themselves. The best way for them to do this is to involve others in their efforts to model the beliefs.

To assist the leaders in doing this, this chapter provides a Methodology for Creating Experiences, which has the following steps:

1. Identify the belief you need to change.
2. Tell people the belief you want them to have.
3. Describe the experiences you're going to create for them.
4. Ask them for feedback on the planned experience.
5. Enroll them in giving you feedback on your progress.

This methodology, while effective in general, can be particularly useful when leaders receive feedback stating that they are not, in fact, modeling the beliefs.

Modeling the beliefs, that is, creating experiences that promote the C^2 culture, will be easier for some managers than for others. Common blockages for managers who find it difficult include their leadership style, a propensity to undervalue the "soft side" of business, or their lack of skills needed to promote the change. Others include a failure to make the change a priority, to visualize the change, or to understand when to direct and when to facilitate the change. We've provided specific suggestions for removing, or at least mitigating, each of these blockages.

In this chapter, we've also seen that people go through stages in a cultural transition, specifically, anticipation, disappointment, and uncertainty. This third stage, uncertainty, is marked by people's tentativeness regarding the change, and it represents a critical fork in the road for the leadership team. If the leaders handle this stage properly—by modeling the beliefs, maintaining enthusiasm, encouraging everyone, pointing out progress achieved, and keeping any doubts they may have to themselves—then the organization will proceed to the buy-in/personally invested stage. However, if the leaders fail to help people over this hump (depicted literally on the culture-change curve), the organization will likely devolve into a stage of giving up and see itself absorbed back into the C^1 culture. This potential turning point and these stages are common, almost predictable, so be prepared to lead people through what you know may lie ahead.

Leadership of a cultural transition calls upon leaders to help every individual and group within the organization to make the change. And we do mean *every* individual and group. We address the challenge encountered in enrolling the entire organization in the change in the next and final chapter.

ENROLLING THE ENTIRE ORGANIZATION IN THE TRANSITION

Never have I seen a more beautiful place.

The Wonderful Wizard of Oz
L. Frank Baum

A *Culture of Accountability* is indeed beautiful, but as we stated at the start, it represents more of an ongoing journey than an actual destination. Leaders, together with everyone else in the organization, must work continually to create and maintain the new culture. Among the toughest aspects of this process is moving beyond leaders to enrolling the whole organization in the change in a manner that speeds up the transition, particularly when the company possesses multiple functions, locations, and divisions and, perhaps, multinational operations.

In this chapter, we address nine important aspects of large-scale implementation of the processes we've examined in this book. While these challenges pertain mainly to managers of large companies, those in smaller ones, particularly those in companies that may partner with or be acquired by large companies, will also find useful ways of implementing culture change. This chapter deals with enrolling *everyone* in the transition so that you accelerate your progress toward the new culture, no matter how far-flung or diverse the organization. We will do this by reviewing the following nine aspects of large-scale culture change that will serve to accelerate the transition:

1. Use an integrated process.

2. Start a dialogue with the organization.

3. Allow for subcultures.

4. Start at the relative top.

5. Work with intact teams.

6. Create a process control.

7. Apply the change globally.

8. Assist the walking wounded.

9. Align the organizational systems.

These nine practices originate with the most frequently asked questions regarding the overall implementation of cultural change throughout the entire organization. We will take each, in turn, and examine how to effectively apply each of these practices.

We have found that when a management team has created the beliefs for their new culture, they often feel the urge to make one of two mistakes. The first mistake is to put the beliefs on paper and posters and placards and roll it out to the entire organization with the announcement that this is the way it's going to be. This approach can be characterized as "change by announcement," and, as we've seen, it doesn't work. The second mistake comes about as efforts are made to avoid the first mistake. It consists of confining the new beliefs to senior management. This approach aims to instill change through osmosis and assumes that when the leaders model the beliefs, the beliefs will then naturally permeate the organization.

Both approaches are well-intentioned, but misguided: The first stems from too much faith that the "excellence" of the beliefs will generate instant adoption. The second arises from managers overestimating their ability to express the beliefs consistently without their subordinates' help. Leadership goes beyond just announcing the change. Furthermore, it goes beyond just creating experiences at the top of the organization. Leadership consists of involving all people at all levels in the change.

To do this, leaders need an integrated process of implementing the cultural transition participatively throughout the company. All of the concepts, tools, and practices we've examined in this book come together in the process that follows. In this chapter we also examine specific issues that arise in implementation, such as fostering change in low-morale organizations and in international organizations.

USE AN INTEGRATED PROCESS

In Chapter One, we described the process of culture change in three phases: Deconstruction, Construction, and Reconstruction. Each of these phases occurs on both the organizational level and on a personal level. Deconstruction is the initial period when management initiates the change process and sends the signal to the organization that it is time to change. People become aware that a shift is in the making—management is spending time talking about the culture and people are working to understand the culture. Deconstruction is also the initial period when individuals get involved in the change process. Here, people come to understand the impact they personally have on the culture and the impact the culture has on them.

In Phase Two, Construction, the elements of culture—actions, beliefs, and experiences—are redefined in terms of C^2. People are engaged in a tentative period exploring new ways of doing things that may or may not be immediately successful. New experiences may backfire, new skills such as using feedback may not come easily, but people are nonetheless working on building C^2.

In the third phase, Reconstruction, the organization has begun to confidently pursue the culture change. Everyone creates the new culture by participating in the experiences, adopting the beliefs, performing the actions and achieving the results that characterize that new, C^2, culture. In this phase people understand that there is no turning back. They are committed to adopting the change.

As an organization implements the culture change, the steps shown in Figure 10-1 will help people move through these three phases of the transition. The model in the figure involves three practical steps for creating culture change: Formal Training, Experiences, and Organizational Systems Alignment. These steps apply to an organization of almost any size and are essential to creating the new culture and then making sure the culture endures.

Training involves the commitment of the resources necessary to schedule time in which people participate in a formal process of examining the culture, why it needs to change, what needs to change, and the roles they play in facilitating that change. While some of this can be done in regular staff meetings, true change requires a facilitated process that immerses people in the intellectual and emotional dimensions of change. The process must by highly experiential. It must

FIGURE 10-1
AN INTEGRATED PROCESS FOR CULTURE CHANGE

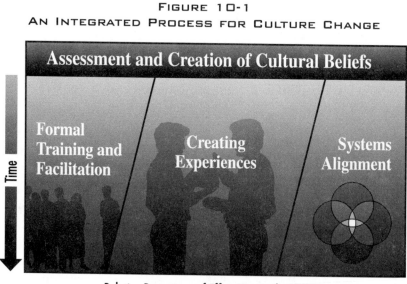

Relative Percentage of Effort Required to Sustain
the Culture Shift for Each Activity

engage people in open dialogue about how things are, and it must help them clearly understand what they can do to make the shift.

Systems refers to the informal and formal systems imbedded in the company's operations. Informal systems include things such as daily interactions and tasks, for instance, the ways in which people hold meetings, the firmness of deadlines, and the manner in which work is assigned. Formal elements include things such as hiring-and-promotion policies and reward systems. Ultimately, for the change to be complete, the formal and informal systems of the organization need to reflect the cultural beliefs. By aligning the systems with the beliefs, you institutionalize the culture: *First you shape the culture, and then your culture shapes you.*

Experiences are the modality for change we examined in detail in Chapter Six and again in Chapter Nine. They are the things that people do on a daily basis that either drive the organization toward adoption of the cultural beliefs or move it backward toward C^1. Experiences occupy most of the diagram in Figure 10–1 because they are the most important aspect of a cultural intervention. You can train people and work with the organizational systems, but if you do not provide experiences consistent with the beliefs, then you will not see the forward movement you want.

In phase one, formal training plays a greater role than does systems alignment. Systems should receive some attention in this first phase, for instance, management must understand the effects of the company's current systems, but they will not be a major focus of phase one. (Remember, as we said in Chapter One, it is a fallacy to think you can change people's beliefs and behaviors simply by changing the company's systems and structures.)

In phases two and three, the role of training diminishes while that of systems expands as B^2 beliefs and A^2 actions are integrated into daily operations. The role of training diminishes because as all the participants increasingly understand the new culture they want to create, they move from learning to doing. This is especially so in phase three. At that point, most people in the company know what they must do to make the shift to the new culture and are busy doing it. There may be some "footdraggers" or outposts that still require training, but in phase three most people actively use what they've learned from the training and experiences of phases one and two. They have the knowledge; now they are applying it. In phase three, training is used to bring people new to the organization on board more quickly with "the way things work around here."

The role of systems expands in phases two and three. An organization's informal and formal systems are imbedded in the operations and therefore affect, and are affected by, the way people think and act. Throughout the transition, management must ensure that the systems are aligned with and ultimately promote the C^2 culture. We will examine the role of systems more closely later in this chapter.

Thinking about culture change in an organized, step-by-step manner and taking the time to develop a plan significantly heightens the chances of success. We have found that many leaders take an overly loose and anecdotal approach to culture change. Such an approach may effect a culture change among the leaders because they sit on a single committee. But when you want to enroll an entire organization of tens of thousands of people in a change, a loose approach will not do the job. We've known several leaders who woefully underestimated what it takes to shift a large organization to a new culture.

A cultural transition plan must be designed specifically for a given company in light of its situation, goals, operations, people, and geography. Such a plan will—in addition to identifying the characteristics of the C^1 and C^2 cultures and employing feedback, alignment, and leadership—provide for training, experiences, and systems enhancements at each phase of the shift.

START A DIALOGUE WITH THE ORGANIZATION

Enrolling the organization in the culture change entails creating a dialogue with employees at all levels of the company about the culture. Getting people to openly talk about the beliefs they and others hold, the experiences they are having, and their perceptions of what people are doing will begin to engage both their hearts and minds.

Often in this dialogue, a certain amount of venting occurs as people describe their feelings about "the way things are" and "the way we would like them to be." We have found that when it comes to culture change, *where there is no emotion, there is no investment.* This doesn't necessarily mean negative emotion, but rather open and honest engagement. When you have this kind of dialogue, people are readying themselves to change.

There are a number of ways to launch these dialogues. Some senior managers hold formal "town halls" where people can talk more intimately with leaders they usually see from a distance. In these meetings, leaders have a prime opportunity to create Type-1 Experiences for the attendees. Undoubtedly, stories will then be told about what was said and done. We have seen many positive experiences created in forums.

In one company, the transition included moving to a compensation system called consensus pay. This approach incorporates the idea that your performance is best evaluated when your peers can participate. By including their perspectives you have to demonstrate teamwork and think beyond your own function—two beliefs that were central to the C^2 culture this company needed to create. At first, this program was seen as a morale buster. People did not like the idea of having their performance rated by others, particularly when it affected their pay. When the program was introduced, however, it was not put in the context of culture change.

Dialogues with management, such as town halls, provide the opportunity to interpret such experiences for people, get their feedback, and provide context for the change. Yet if you really want honest dialogue, town halls may not be intimate enough. That's why some leaders find other ways, for instance "breakfast with Bob." In this case, Bob, a plant manager, would have breakfast once a week with various employees at all levels and talk intimately about organizational issues. While smaller groups limited the number of people he could personally reach, these breakfasts were well received and had a positive impact. In fact, people got upset when they were canceled for any reason because they looked forward to their chance to give the boss their views. Some leaders have an open e-mail address where employees can candidly write to them. Bill Gates does this, and reportedly answers every inquiry he receives.

There are many mechanisms: management by walking around (MBWA), town halls, staff meetings, breakfast meetings, and e-mail, among others. However, during phases one and two formal training sessions or communication workshops can provide the best environment and, perhaps more important, the best process for creating open dialogue.

ALLOW FOR SUBCULTURES

Enrolling everyone in the change, particularly in a large organization, raises the issue of subcultures. Even small companies can have them. Subcultures naturally arise around the various functions. Each functional part of a business—sales, marketing, production, finance, accounting, human resources, and so on—tends to form its own somewhat unique culture driven by its own mission. Each function also tends to attract a certain type of person with a certain educational and business background. Subcultures also arise around geographic locations; for example, nonheadquarters sales offices and off-site R&D labs usually form cultures of their own. Subcultures can also be found in teams dedicated to some specific activity such as product development.

In the process of enrolling the entire organization in the transition, how should leaders deal with subcultures?

First, in the same way that culture change does not involve changing people's individual personalities, groups of people retain their collective personalities, their subcultures. The goal of the transition is, within the context of those individual and collective personalities, to have people adopt beliefs that will enable them to manifest who they are and what they do to the greatest benefit to the organization. The unique attributes and functions of each person and department do not disappear. Instead, the transition strengthens the bonds and workings among the functions. To the extent that these subcultures can modify and translate the culture change to their unique environment, they will more readily buy in to the transition and make it work.

The best way we've found to accommodate subcultures involves creating a Cultural Beliefs Statement at the top, but not foisting it on the rest of the company. In companies with one or more strong subcultures, for instance, specialized groups such as technical services or R&D, the most effective approach is to allow them to develop their own Belief Statements, *within the context of* the one promulgated from the top. In addition, most departments must devise their own A² actions to express the beliefs and thus create the right results. If senior management allows them to do this with some latitude, they will see greater buy-in and deeper ownership of the change.

In fact, we have found that the Belief Statements created across the organization will usually vary very little from function to function and from that which management crafted. While the differences can be quite subtle, however, they enable each group to *Own It* and drive the change in the best way for their specific function.

When working to effect culture change in various divisions, departments, and functions you should find two tactics particularly useful: (1) starting at the relative top and (2) working with intact teams.

START AT THE RELATIVE TOP

Successful culture change starts at the top, at least the "relative top." By this we mean that regardless of where you initiate the culture-change process—in a team, a division, a function, a subsidiary, or the organization at large—it must start at the top to be most effective. The relative top is the leader of that team, division, function, subsidiary, or organization, the leader relative to that group. By working with that leader and his or her management team, you create the necessary leadership and support to drive the change through the organization.

How far any senior management team should go in identifying relative leaders depends upon the culture, the organizational structure, and the relationships among the leaders. We have, however, found that in most groups true culture change cannot be generated "from the middle." It must come from the top, from the relative top.

Why? Because if the leader at the relative top does not support and promote the new culture, he or she will continually create experiences that hinder its adoption. Leaders have the position and power to create those experiences, and they will create them if they oppose the change. Attempting culture change in any group without the buy-in of the relative leader throws that group out of alignment and, essentially, dooms the effort.

CRAFT BELIEF STATEMENTS THAT WORK

In a larger organization where you are cascading the change effort, it is important to enroll the relative leaders in the process of leading the change. To win the support and buy-in of the relative leaders of any group, either have them participate in constructing the overall Cultural Belief Statement, or allow them to craft their own Belief Statement with their group within the context of the overall statement—or both. Then when they promote the process in their own group, they can more readily move from support and advocate to sponsor and champion. We have witnessed leaders who were not really engaged until they were actually in the driver's seat leading the change in their own group. As a sponsor, they begin to promulgate their own set of beliefs, which are aligned with those of the larger organization and provide experiences that truly get people's attention.

When using multiple Belief Statements within an organization, there are generally some *givens* that should be understood as the context within which those multiple statements are made. These givens may include emphasis on one or two beliefs that must be present throughout the entire organization. These relative leaders may also have some givens for their groups that they want to be sure are captured as their cultural shift is defined. We might suggest some givens as well. Every culture change is improved by a good dose of accountability and feedback. These two ingredients are essential to a *Culture of Accountability*, and we have observed them in some form on the list of everyone we have worked with. Making sure that givens are included on the list is a role the leader will likely need to play.

A small company, for instance, one in which everyone knows everyone else, should be able to buy in to one Cultural Belief Statement because everyone can take part in crafting it. Although there are various functions, people work together closely enough so they can discuss and understand the value of each belief. In a large company, the greater diffusion of people and functions warrants multiple Belief Statements and the process of creating them.

Geographical remoteness and international operations usually dictate multiple belief statements because those entities are, of necessity, strong subcultures. A remote sales office usually prides itself on being "in the field" and removed from the headquarters culture. A foreign subsidiary presents issues and differences unique to their own circumstances and local market conditions. If geographically remote or foreign operations craft their own Belief Statements, *within the context of* the overall Cultural Belief Statement, they will generate greater ownership and, indeed, a better road map.

Management must decide when, and to what extent, separate Beliefs Statements can be of value. We emphasize, however, that management must also create and maintain strong cultural context, including some givens, in which the relevant entities create these statements. When this context exists, senior management will usually find the resulting Beliefs Statements to be strikingly similar to the one they created.

Finally, any new relative leader—any senior or middle manager who joins the company during a cultural transition—*must* be formally brought on board. His or her buy-in is essential during the transition and after the new culture is created. Every new leader of a group, a department, or an entire organization must be aligned with the Belief Statement even if altering it is necessary.

WORK WITH INTACT TEAMS

If you want to speed up the change, work with intact teams. That is, work with teams that already exist within the organization, rather than with teams put together expressly for the purpose of culture change. While the latter may be desirable at some point in the process, such groupings are best used *after* intact teams have had the opportunity to work together on the culture. An intact team is a group of people who work together regularly to accomplish some objective. In most companies, the senior management team or the executive committee is an intact team (or aspires to be one). In many companies, the division heads or the regional managers are an intact team. Of course, in most companies a given department or function, such as accounting, sales, or product development, or a segment of a department, represents an intact team.

Culture change occurs most surely and quickly when you work with intact teams because each team already has its own culture and carries it with it into any endeavor it tackles. Culture change is itself a team endeavor. Each day the team acts out C^1 in the way they operate. Therefore the fastest and most effective method for changing the way that group thinks and acts is to keep the group together through the process. In this way, they use their everyday work experience as a vehicle for culture change.

Once enrolled, the team practices the new C^2 culture every day. Together, they give one another feedback and support in demonstrating the cultural beliefs. After creating the culture shift *within* the intact team, they are then better able to create the shift *between* intact teams. Who better knows where you demonstrate alignment with the Cultural Beliefs and where you don't than the people you work with every day? Working with intact teams supercharges the process by providing a real-life laboratory for change. It also creates ownership by having the relative leader lead the change and by immediately translating the new culture into day-to-day situations.

Less effective, slower alternatives involve having representatives from various teams (instead of intact teams) undergo culture change in waves or having only representatives from teams (instead of entire teams in waves) undergo the process. If you want to enroll the entire organization as quickly as possible, avoid these approaches and work with intact teams.

Using cross-functional teams to accelerate culture change is a flawed tactic when it is the only tactic employed. For instance, you cannot take midlevel people from finance, accounting, production, and so on, pump them full of the C^2 culture in a series of meetings, and then expect them to take the culture to their departments. It doesn't work very well, surely not very quickly. However, cross-functional work sessions on the culture can be an important part of the transition plan. Depending on the Cultural Beliefs you are promulgating, it may even be essential. But these work sessions are best done after intact teams have started the transition in their own environments.

CREATE A PROCESS CONTROL

In manufacturing, every process needs a process control. We find the same to be true of culture change. To move the organization forward during cultural transition, you must create accountability for following through with your transition plan. Perhaps nothing will do more to accelerate the transition than to create true accountability for demonstrating the experiences, beliefs, and actions that characterize the C^2 culture.

The process of cultural transition should not result in an inordinate amount of new meetings, new To Do's, or new processes. Rather, all of your efforts should focus on what you are already doing by asking the question, "Should these be done a different way?" By focusing on what you are already doing, you will find a ready forum for applying the cultural changes in a practical, effective manner.

One manufacturing organization has particularly impressed us with the rigor, discipline, and success of their model of process control. Dr. Ed Smithwick, former vice president of Biochemical Manufacturing for Eli Lilly and Company, was responsible for all of bulk-manufacturing operations worldwide. As an outgrowth of his work with statistical process control, he developed what he called the C_4I model shown in Figure 10-2. This model has been widely used within the corporation and helped them galvanize their thinking around process control. This model is also applicable to culture change.

The first "C" relates to the question, Is the process *capable* of producing what was intended? Is it capable of meeting the requirement? For our purposes, we would ask, "Is the transition plan and change process that you have established truly capable of producing the change you want?" Sometimes, in analyzing why a process failed to produce a result, leaders realize that the process was never capable of producing it in the first place. For example, if your plan does not include using experiences to instill beliefs, then your process is not capable of delivering accelerated change.

FIGURE 10-2
THE C_4I MODEL

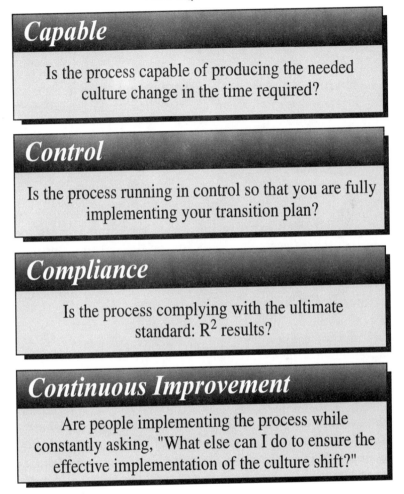

Capable

Is the process capable of producing the needed culture change in the time required?

Control

Is the process running in control so that you are fully implementing your transition plan?

Compliance

Is the process complying with the ultimate standard: R^2 results?

Continuous Improvement

Are people implementing the process while constantly asking, "What else can I do to ensure the effective implementation of the culture shift?"

The second "C" is the process in *control*. Are you doing the things that you said would need to be done in order to bring about the change? Are any key steps being skipped? By ensuring that the process is running the way it should, you will increase the probability of successful change.

The third "C" in the process is *compliance*. That is, does it comply with the standards that have been set and required? In manufacturing this may have to do with regulatory standards. In culture change, the standard is results. Is the process in compliance with the R^2 results that you have identified? As we have said, maintaining the connection between the process and the results is essential.

Finally, the last "C" has to do with *continuous improvement*. The question here is, "Are the people running the process doing so with the goal of continuous improvement?" For our purposes, are there ways to improve the process to make it more effective for relative leaders, subcultures, or international affiliates, or the overall change? Listening to feedback on what is and isn't working is important in this regard. Leaders should move forward with the expectation that they will likely make process improvements along the way—improvements that will make the change effort even more targeted and effective.

Perhaps the most effective process control is the commitment of the leader and the entire management team to ask these questions and to hold themselves accountable to answer them. Leadership, as we have described it throughout this book, will most surely do more to accelerate the effort and facilitate your organization's journey to a *Culture of Accountability*.

APPLY THE CHANGE GLOBALLY

International operations, particularly when they are numerous or in unfamiliar national cultures, can present the greatest hurdle to enrolling the entire organization in rapid culture change. Here we discuss the matter from the perspective of U.S. companies with foreign operations. However, these issues pertain to any company with foreign operations, regardless of the headquarter's nation.

Foreign operations add another dimension to the cultural landscape in that you have the company's C^1 and C^2 cultures, the foreign subsidiary's C^1 and C^2 cultures, *and* the national socioeconomic culture of each entity. Typically, a U.S. company starts up or acquires a foreign subsidiary and transplants American senior managers to establish the company culture there. This makes sense because, as we've pointed out, that operation is going to have a culture and from the standpoint of headquarters it should be closely linked to the company culture. However, we've observed another interesting phenomenon, one not particularly positive for the prospect of enrolling the foreign subsidiary in a cultural shift. The company culture is strong among people at the top in that foreign subsidiary, but as you travel down in the ranks, the company culture becomes less influential and less obvious.

Nowhere is it more important (and it is *always* important) to involve people at all levels in the transition than in a foreign operation. You may have to go to unprecedented forms of involvement, in which you turn large segments of the change over to those at various levels. This can demand a leap of faith. In "letting go" you risk that they will tear the cultural road map apart. You do this, however, anticipating the reward—that they will put it back together in a similar fashion, but in a way that will be truly theirs.

Nonetheless, the relative leader must ensure that the givens are maintained and that a close connection with the company's culture occurs. The Cultural Belief Statement provides indispensable context for these transition discussions. In the process, you must listen carefully to the native managers.

An experience we had with the Japanese affiliate of a U.S. company illustrates the value of this kind of listening. In Japan the affiliate's senior managers, mostly expatriates, discussed culture change, accountability, and *The Results Pyramid* and declared their buy-in to these as important elements in their own change.

Yet, as they began the dialogue within their own organization, there was a huge misunderstanding. The rank-and-file Japanese thought that alignment means doing what your boss tells you to do—"get aligned with your boss's directives and you'll be fine." They interpreted the meaning of alignment quite differently than their U.S. counterparts. This would hardly foster the kind of accountability and initiative that management wanted in the new culture. In response, senior management moved implementation efforts to very low levels in that organization, and it paid off. Native Japanese employees became very engaged in the process and devised superb examples and methods for creating accountability in Japan while maintaining a close connection to the overall company culture.

Culture can be quite "sticky." To produce needed adaptation when you're driving a culture shift in a foreign operation, get everyone involved. They are, in fact, the only people who can adapt it to their unique needs. Adopting a global view of the change early in the process will bring advantages later as you implement those changes.

ASSIST THE WALKING WOUNDED

While we work with numerous companies that want to raise their high levels of performance to still higher levels, we also encounter many that have been laid low by poor management or adverse external conditions. When an organization has achieved poor results over an extended period, morale naturally suffers. Change, in and of itself, can lead to a sense of loss as people yield to the natural tendency to focus on what they perceive to be the downside of the change: I have to learn new skills, I have to change old habits, and I have to step out of my comfort zone (which may be risky).

In one company, employees used the phrase "walking wounded" to describe those people who had not quite recovered from the impact of poor results or the perceived downside of the impact of a change. Clearly, the walking wounded were easy to spot, as they suffered from the effects of poor morale.

Low morale can occur throughout the organization or in "pockets." In large companies, a department or even an entire division can suffer poor morale relative to the rest of the organization. They may be in an especially tough industry. Whatever the case may be, we have noted three distinct but overlapping stages of decline in morale shown in Figure 10-3: questioning, doubting, and giving up.

FIGURE 10-3
STAGES OF DECLINE IN MORALE

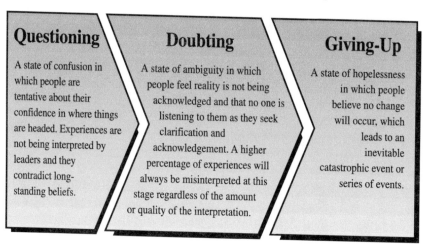

Questioning

A state of confusion in which people are tentative about their confidence in where things are headed. Experiences are not being interpreted by leaders and they contradict long-standing beliefs.

Doubting

A state of ambiguity in which people feel reality is not being acknowledged and that no one is listening to them as they seek clarification and acknowledgement. A higher percentage of experiences will always be misinterpreted at this stage regardless of the amount or quality of the interpretation.

Giving-Up

A state of hopelessness in which people believe no change will occur, which leads to an inevitable catastrophic event or series of events.

In the "questioning" stage, people have experiences that contradict the company's institutional beliefs. Simultaneously, leaders fail to help people interpret these experiences properly. This reflects the leaders' failure to assume accountability for developing a credible, practical plan for change. People may try to maintain optimism, or perhaps a false front. They may exhibit wait-and-see or other *Below the Line* behaviors when facing challenges. Ultimately, people question the credibility of those leading the organization, as well as the credibility of their decisions.

In the "doubting" stage of decline, people feel they are not being heard as they seek acknowledgment and clarification of what they're experiencing. In this stage, and as long as senior management fails to assume accountability and develop a remedy, people can misinterpret even positive experiences. As a group they have begun to doubt management's ability to see reality clearly and perhaps their competence or even honesty. Some of the more qualified and talented people, who typically have several career options, may exit the company at this stage. The leaders know they have a problem, but may see it only as a "morale problem" for which they feel powerless to develop a solution.

In the "giving-up" stage, contradictions between daily experience and stated beliefs and between actual results and performance objectives become institutionalized. They become part of the culture. Cynicism often becomes widespread, and people view the situation as hopeless, as one they are powerless to change. Senior management itself often shares these feelings and may discuss them privately. People give up on organizational objectives and pursue private goals, usually viewing their jobs as "just a paycheck" and holding on until they reach retirement, a child's college graduation, or some other financial goal.

Senior management is almost always aware of declining morale, particularly in the doubting and giving-up phases. However, they often feel powerless to change it. One common reaction during any of these stages is to "get tough" by raising performance expectations, issuing stern directives, or punishing failure. This led an employee in one company we know to anonymously post a sign on the bulletin board that read: "The beatings will continue until morale improves." The sign produced the only laughs people had experienced in some time.

GETTING OUT OF THE MORALE MORASS

Oddly enough, at any stage of a decline in morale, senior management can stop the slide and get back on the road to results. To do this, those at the top of the organization must do three things: First, they must let people vent and understand that they have been heard. Second, they must unambiguously acknowledge *and assume accountability for* the current situation and results. Third, they must present a credible plan, in which they call upon everyone to do his or her part to turn the situation around and achieve results. That is, everyone must start developing a positive, high-performance culture. Management must do all three of these things to enroll people in a cultural transition after morale has sunk.

In organizations where morale has declined to low levels, people need time to vent their views and feelings before they can move on. Of course, this should be done in a constructive manner. The goal is not to dredge up the past, launch accusations, and find fault. Rather it is to let people express their thoughts and emotions and then move quickly toward establishing hope that things can be different, because that hope is what they've lost.

People who have weathered persistent poor performance and situations that contradict institutional beliefs need to have the reality of their experience validated by the people at the top. If the leaders do not validate these experiences, people will feel that the leaders want to avoid the real issues. The leaders will lack the necessary credibility because people will think, You cannot lead us out of a situation that you cannot even acknowledge. This acknowledgment must be unambiguous and must come from the top. After that acknowledgment, the leaders must assume accountability for the situation clearly and publicly. When they do, they create a powerful experience, win credibility and goodwill, and set the stage for the next step, which is to develop a plan to remedy the situation.

Developing the remedy represents the best way to keep this entire process positive. The remedy, of course, is to identify and then begin to make the right shifts at each level of the culture. Involving the entire organization in a solution in which everyone has a role to play keeps the organization *Above the Line* and out of the Blame Game. Of course, the leaders must gauge the readiness of the organization to take the next step. You must carefully work through the process in order to bring the organization along in a timely manner.

So to exercise leadership and to create the right experiences for low-morale organizations, leaders must identify and acknowledge, that is, see and own the entire C^1 culture and help everyone else do the same. Equally important, they must *simultaneously* focus on the necessary shifts to the C^2 culture. This means that discussion of any negative aspect of the C^1 culture—an R^1 result, A^1 action, B^1 belief, or E^1 experience—should be followed by a discussion of the corresponding R^2 result, A^2 action, B^2 belief, or E^2 experience. This focuses the effort on the shift and the future, rather than on hopelessness and the past.

Few situations present tougher leadership challenges than declining morale. The demands differ markedly from those in which a solid company needs to improve or faces a new development in the environment. Low morale is endemic and internal. It can undermine the ability of an organization to affect their culture and change it. That is why you must simultaneously, with the three extra steps we identified in the beginning of this section, work on the low morale while you work on the culture.

ALIGN THE ORGANIZATIONAL SYSTEMS

The third part of the model that we introduced at the beginning of this chapter has to do with aligning the organization's informal and formal systems with the Cultural Beliefs. The reconstructing phase of the culture change requires that the B^2 beliefs and the A^2 actions be formally integrated into the business processes of the organization. For example, let's take the Cultural Beliefs of cross-functional teamwork and longer-term strategic focus. Informally, people might take extra steps to get input from someone in another function whom the decision might affect, but who would not be directly involved at that stage. Formally, meeting agendas would be structured to include time for discussion of longer-term, more strategic business issues. Working with the organizational systems allows management to institutionalize aspects of the culture so they become deeply imbedded as "the way we do things around here."

Because the organizational systems reinforce how people think and act, leaders must be certain to align the systems with the beliefs. A company's systems are inevitably going to drive a certain way of thinking and acting. Leaders must ensure that those systems reinforce the new C^2 culture rather than the old C^1 way of doing things. This entails looking at all of the systems in the organization—the social system, reporting system, decision-making system, hiring system, promotion system, compensation system, information system, and so on—and asking, "Are these systems reinforcing the beliefs that we have adopted?"

The compensation system represents a sterling example of a system that should foster and reinforce cultural beliefs, but often fails to. You are going to be paying people anyway. Why not pay them for thinking and acting in ways that benefit the organization? It may seem obvious, but people often fail to make the obvious explicit.

One CEO we worked with stunned his senior managers with the lucidity of his logic when, after many go-rounds on how to create true collaboration, he said, "Let's stop asking people to make sacrifices and start rewarding them for doing what we're asking them to do." To create this collaborative environment, one in which nobody wins unless the team wins, the company created a compensation system that tied most incentive pay to the team achieving its goals.

Every system in your company has the potential to work either for or against the culture you are trying to create and maintain. Leaders, and those charged with the upkeep of the systems in question, must ensure that these systems are properly aligned by auditing those systems to identify gaps and then bringing those systems into alignment with the Cultural Beliefs. Forming teams around each system to conduct this audit and to make recommendations is one effective way to accomplish this.

For example, after their acquisition, PCS Health Systems, headquartered in Scottsdale, Arizona, shifted their strategy from being solely a claims-processing company to a company focused on providing interventions for its clients. Under the direction of their new leader, J. P. Milton, PCS acknowledged that to achieve their strategy one of the many things that had to happen in order to be successful was to shift the company culture. Within the culture one of the key beliefs that needed to shift was the notion that pure, quantitative results were all that mattered. Instead, PCS needed people to believe that effective process was also integral to achieving long-term results for the organization. Early on people struggled with this shift.

In performance evaluations, the organization's leaders identified managers at all levels who were not making the shift. As the management team reviewed the performance evaluations, they noted that some of those same managers who were not making the shift were also given the highest rankings on their evaluations. When the department heads were asked why they were ranking highly the managers who were struggling to make the shift they said that the system forced them to rank the managers that way. The performance evaluations did not provide the department heads with enough opportunity to consider more subjective criteria that involved what they termed "the dimensions of what you do."

In order to align the organizational systems with the beliefs they needed to create, PCS adopted the performance evaluation system so that it gave equal weight to both achieving objectives and performing well on the eight PCS dimensions: customer focus, communication, teamwork/interpersonal, innovation, leadership, management, people development, and values. In addition to ranking the people on broader criteria that pertained to process, the PCS operations committee began to evaluate the company's leaders as a group. This change in the performance-evaluation system communicated the importance of achieving results and of doing so in ways that would maximize overall company results. Furthermore, the merit evaluations for these leaders were to be done collectively at the operations committee. This reinforced the importance of not only achieving functional objectives but doing so by working as a team.

At PCS, the systems changed to reinforce the culture. The culture changed to produce results that created a total turnaround in performance. The percentage increases in all the major categories of performance went off the charts. Today, PCS continues to experience significant growth in their market share.

Ultimately, a successful transition to a new culture causes the characteristics of the organization's culture to become imbedded in its informal and formal systems. These systems in turn perpetuate that new culture, constantly reinforcing the way people need to think and act to achieve the results the organization exists to achieve.

ONWARD TO THE EMERALD CITY

In this final chapter we have examined nine practices that help leaders implement culture change in large organizations. Many of these practices also prove useful in smaller companies. Depending upon the specific needs of your organization we recommend that you:

1. Use an integrated process for culture change.
2. Start a dialogue about the change with the organization.

3. Allow for subcultures.

4. Start at the relative top.

5. Work with intact teams.

6. Create a process control.

7. Apply the change globally.

8. Assist the walking wounded.

9. Align the organizational systems.

We present these practices under the rubric of enrolling the entire organization in the change because in any large-scale change the challenge is to get *everyone* on board. When you have strong sub-cultures, foreign operations, or low morale, that challenge becomes even greater. Also, we have found some leaders unaware of the value of certain tactics, such as starting with the relative leader and working with intact teams. Using at least several of these practices will accelerate your company's transition to the new culture.

And that is what our journey to the Emerald City has been about—learning how to accelerate culture change. No one in business today, or in any other endeavor for that matter, believes that organizations will be able to stop changing. In fact, the need for change can only increase.

In this book we have provided a practical approach to creating a *Culture of Accountability*, an approach that produces real change in the way people think and act on their way toward achieving results.

Every organization has a culture. Effective leaders know that they will either manage the culture or it will manage them. Shifting the culture toward a new set of beliefs and actions is essential for most companies facing the need to achieve new results or the need to perform at the same level in a dramatically different business environment.

Culture change happens one person at a time. You accelerate a change in the culture when you engage the hearts and minds of everyone in the endeavor and they begin to ask themselves: What are the results that are most important to achieve? How must I think and act in order to produce them? What do I want those around me to believe about how they need to think and act? How can I create experiences that foster those beliefs? Of course, that process begins with you.

Managers get results through others. Yet they cannot simply ask or order people to take the actions they should. Instead, they must lead people to do them. Leading people, in the true sense of the team, means creating experiences that reinforce a *Culture of Accountability*. We have tried to direct managerial attention to what we believe is most important: the effect that leaders have on those around them.

Applying the *Steps To Accountability* to your change effort will make all the difference in the world. These steps lead to what in our view stands as the first principle of business (and life): personal accountability. There is no power like the power of people who assume personal accountability for achieving a collective goal. They may fail, but far more often they will succeed.

For the characters in *The Wonderful Wizard of Oz*, the journey to the Emerald City ends with the realization that the journey itself was a process of personal change:

Then Dorothy exclaimed (to the good witch Glinda), "You are certainly as good as you are beautiful! But you have not yet told me how to get back to Kansas."

"Your silver shoes will carry you over the desert," replied Glinda. "If you had known their power you could have gone back to your Aunt Em the very first day you came to this country."

"But then I should not have had my wonderful brains!" cried the Scarecrow. "I might have passed my whole life in the farmer's cornfield."

"And I should not have had my lovely heart," said the Tin Woodman. "I might have stood and rusted in the forest till the end of the world."

"And I should have lived a coward forever," declared the Lion, "and no beast in all the forest would have had a good word to say to me."

"This is all true," said Dorothy, "and I am glad I was of use to these good friends. But now that each of them has had what he most desired, and each is happy in having a kingdom to rule beside, I think I should like to go back to Kansas."

"The Silver Shoes," said the Good Witch, "have wonderful powers. And one of the most curious things about them is that they can carry you to any place in the world in three steps, and each step will be made in the wink of an eye. All you have to do is knock the heels together three times and command the shoes to carry you wherever you wish to go."

"If that is so," said the child joyfully, "I will ask them to carry me back to Kansas at once."

. . . The Silver Shoes took but three steps, and then she stopped so suddenly that she rolled over upon the grass several times before she knew where she was.

. . . For she was sitting on the broad Kansas prairie, and just before her was the new farmhouse Uncle Henry built after the cyclone had carried away the old one. Uncle Henry was milking the cows in the barn, and Toto had jumped out of her arms and was running toward the barn, barking joyously.

. . . Aunt Em had just come out of the house to water the cabbages when she looked up and saw Dorothy running toward her.

"My darling child!" she cried, folding the little girl in her arms and covering her face with kisses. "Where in the world did you come from?"

"From the Land of Oz," said Dorothy gravely. "And here is Toto, too. And oh, Aunt Em! I'm so glad to be at home again!"

The process of creating and accelerating a *Culture of Accountability* is not an ambiguous or magical process that defies explanation. It is the result of taking the steps that engage everyone in the organization in asking, "What else can I do?" to live the beliefs, create the experiences, and perform the actions that will produce results. Creating this level of ownership and participation will certainly speed you on your way to a destination abundant with the results you now seek. So, with that, let the journey begin!

Consulting Services Offered by Partners In Leadership, LLC

Partners In Leadership offers the following consulting services to assist your organization in creating a *Culture of Accountability.*[SM]

The *Partners In Leadership*[SM] Cultural Transition Process

The Cultural Transition Process is a proven approach to accelerating the transition in the way people think and act at all levels in the organization. *Partners In Leadership* offers a variety of consulting services and training workshops that assist leaders and managers in rapidly bringing about this transition in their organization.

The *Oz Principle*[SM] Accountability Training

Partners In Leadership offers a broad array of consulting and training services ranging from high-impact, results-oriented, one-day Accountability Training to presentations for national sales meetings and speeches.

The *Partners In Leadership* Executive Teambuilding Process

Partners In Leadership's services also include a well-recognized, international expertise in facilitating greater alignment, trust, and effectiveness within senior executive teams.

Partners In
Leadership[SM]

27555 Ynez Road, Suite 201
Temecula, CA 92591

800-504-6070

E-Mail Address: pil@ozprinciple.com

INDEX